Engaging Humor

Engaging Humor

ELLIOTT ORING

University of Illinois Press
URBANA AND CHICAGO

Manufactured in the United States of America
c 5 4 3 2 1

∞ This book is printed on acid-free paper.

Library of Congress Cataloging-in-Publication Data
Oring, Elliott, 1945–
Engaging humor / Elliott Oring.
p. cm.
Includes bibliographical references and index.
ISBN 0-252-02786-8 (alk. paper)
1. Wit and humor—History and criticism. 2. Comic, The. I. Title.
PN6147.074 2003
809.7—dc21 2002004453

For Kat
and hard thinkers everywhere

Contents

Preface

DISCUSSIONS AND DEBATES about humor and laughter have been going on for at least twenty-five hundred years.[1] While the chapters in this volume are unlikely to bring any particular lines of this discussion to a definite close, I would like to believe that they can provide some alternate and, I hope, interesting ways of thinking about humor and about specific instances of humorous expression. My goal is simple. It is to keep a conversation initiated by the ancients going.

When one speaks or writes about humor, there is often an expectation that the speech or essay should itself be humorous. I know of no other subject matter that engenders parallel expectations. No one expects a discourse on tragedy to be tragic, a treatise on schizophrenia to be dissociative, or a declamation on music to be melodious. With humor, it is otherwise. This may have something to do with the feeling that what is formulated humorously in social interaction is discountable. Discountable in the sense that something humorous need not be considered as part of the history of the exchange. A promise made in jest is not a promise; a humorous illustration is not evidence. As a result, humor is often considered to be trivial, and it seems that serious talk about humor is regarded as participating in that triviality.[2] A presumption seems to exist that the consequential cannot emerge from a contemplation of the trivial.

I do not believe humor to be trivial. I consider jokes and other forms of humorous expression to be meaningful and sometimes significant communications. I also believe humorous expressions to be art. Some jokes are truly beautiful, and those who create them, reshape them, and orally purvey them are often genuine artists. There are no peoples that we know of on earth who do not laugh and who do not engage in speech and behavior designed to excite laughter. Humor and laughter are cultural universals. They are a condition of our humanity. Humor could be considered trivial only from a perspective that holds humanity itself to be trivial.

This volume is not meant to amuse or evidence my sense of humor. Although some excellent jokes appear in its pages, these jokes were not chosen because they were good ones. They were chosen because they illustrated some point. Quite a few jokes that I would reckon to be of lesser quality are also included in the volume, because they also serve as useful illustrations of principles. In any event, the task of analyzing and explaining humor is ultimately about analyzing and explaining humor in all its variety—not merely that subset of expression that we happen to prize at some particular moment in time.

This book proceeds as a series of questions, analyses, and meditations on what constitutes humor, what motives engender humor, and what messages are conveyed through humor. Chapter 1, "Appropriate Incongruity Redux," restates my position that humor is the perception of an appropriate incongruity and addresses various challenges to this view that have been raised in recent years. Chapter 2, "The Senses of Absurd Humor," reflects on "absurd" or "nonsensical" humor and attempts to explore its relationship to more ordinary varieties. Absurdity, of one type or another, is resident in all humor so that the delineation of absurd humor as a special category is problematic. Chapter 3, "Joke Thoughts," explores a suggestion made by Sigmund Freud that every joke contains a thought. However, the question of whether his observation is true, or how the analyst should identify the thoughts resident in jokes, has scarcely been addressed. Chapter 4, "The Humor of Hate," examines the humorous expressions of a racist group in order to assess the hypothesis that humor is rooted in repression and that jokes afford people a way of expressing feelings of aggression that otherwise would be prohibited. Chapter 5, "Blond Ambitions and Other Signs of the Times," critically reviews the sense that people made of the blond jokes that raced across the United States in the early 1990s and offers a new perspective on that cycle of jokes. Chapter 6, "Humor and the Suppression of Sentiment," proposes that humor has been employed as a substitute for sentimental expression in the United States. It attempts to show that as sentiment began to be devalued at the end of the Victorian Age, humor came to serve as a surrogate form of expression. Chapter 7, "The Joke as Gloss," focuses on the use of jokes as commentaries on the conversations and interactions in which they are embedded. Chapter 8, "Colonizing Humor," contemplates parallels between the humorous traditions of three nations: the United States, Australia, and Israel. Each of these was founded through colonization in modern times, and each cultivated humor as part of its self-representation in ways that were remarkably similar. Sigmund Freud's Jewish identity is the focus of chapter 9, "Sigmund Freud's Jewish Joke Book." In this chapter, aspects of Freud's Jewish identity are revealed through an analysis of the most Jewish of his psychoanalytic works—*Jokes and Their Relation to the Unconscious.* Chapter 10, "The Context of Internet Humor," describes some of the contexts of humor posted on the World Wide Web. A close examination of sites that posted jokes about President Bill Clinton during the period of the Monica Lewinsky scandal and his subsequent impeachment provides a glimpse of the extent to which jokes on the Web may be considered situated communications.

* * *

There are a number of colleagues and friends to thank for their contributions to this volume. Christie Davies and John Morreall read the entire manuscript, and Frank de Caro, Michael Owen Jones, Victor Raskin, Willibald Ruch, and Kathleen Stocks read individual chapters. All offered encouragement as well as constructive comment and criticism. If I did not always heed their advice, I always appreciated it and weighed it carefully. This book is better for their counsel.

Norman Klein and Natalie Olson carefully proofread the manuscript and caught errors of spelling, irregularities in grammar, and infelicities in style. I sincerely thank them for their efforts. The responsibility for any errors that remain is theirs.

I have greatly profited from my conversations with Goh Abe, Mahadev Apte, Salvatore Attardo, Larry Danielson, Alan Dundes, Henry Glassie, Barbara Kirshenblatt-Gimblett, Jay Mechling, Wolfgang Mieder, Larry Mintz, Barre Toelken, Peter Tokofsky, Donald Ward, Bert Wilson, and Kwesi Yankah. All these scholars have engaged wit and humor at some point in their own writings, and their observations and insights inform my own work.

The engaging humor of friends and relatives has kept me interested in the subject and, on occasion, has provided me with examples for illustration and analysis. My thanks to Ben Benson, Bruce Carpenter, Inta Carpenter, Jerry Cirker, Lillian Cirker, Jon Coleman, Linda Coleman, Kerstin Danielson, Harold Dresser, Norine Dresser, Benjamin Fass, Bob Georges, Mary Georges, Bruce Giuliano, Gen Giuliano, Sin Fong Han, Jess Hordes, Naomi Hordes, Bill Ivey, Jane Jones, Rosan Jordan, Judit Katona-Apte, Hanny Laufer, Alan Levi, Dan-de Levi, Irving Levinson, Tadashi Nakamura, Jon Olson, Natalie Olson, Claire Oring, Katie Oring, Mark Oring, Lisa Pittman, Marjory Power, Nathan Power, Fred Reinman, Gloria Reinman, Pál Rózsa, Dianne Smith, Marge Sorenson, and Hannele Wilson.

A variety of folklore texts were made available to me from the Fife Folklore Archives at Utah State University in Logan, Utah, and the William A. Wilson Folklore Archive at Brigham Young University in Provo, Utah. I am also indebted to the Los Angeles office of the Anti-Defamation League for allowing me to examine its collection of publications.

Readers are encouraged to examine the endnotes in this volume. There a more detailed guide can be found to the thinkers who have challenged and shaped my own views on humor. In the notes, readers will also find observations and asides that would have distracted them from the flow of the argument had they been placed in the body of the text.

Most of the chapters in this volume are published here for the first time, but two have been printed before. "Humor and the Suppression of Sentiment" first appeared in *Humor: International Journal for Humor Research* 7 (1994): 7–26, and "Joke Thoughts" was published in *Symbole: Zu Bedeutung der Zeichen in der Kultur*, ed. Rolf Wilhelm Brednich and Heinz Schmitt (Berlin: Waxmann Verlag, 1997), pp. 163–74. A greatly abbreviated version of "Colonizing Humor" was printed in both Japanese and English in *Western Humor and Eastern Laughter*, ed. Hiroshi Inoue (Osaka: Kansai University, 2000), pp. 13–17, 55–63.

Engaging Humor

1. Appropriate Incongruity Redux

Humor, I have argued, depends upon the perception of an *appropriate incongruity;* that is, the perception of an appropriate relationship between categories that would ordinarily be regarded as incongruous.[1] A brief example should suffice to illustrate the notion: "A man goes to see a psychiatrist. The doctor asks him, 'What seems to be the problem?' The patient says, 'Doc, no one believes anything I say.' The doctor replies, 'You're kidding!'" To understand this joke, one must apprehend both the appropriateness and the incongruity of the doctor's response. The phrase "you're kidding" is an expression of surprise and appropriately registers the doctor's skepticism that the situation could be as severe as the patient describes. In some sense, it may even be regarded as a reflexive expression of reassurance. At the same time, "you're kidding" registers the physician's disbelief in the patient's report and seems to affirm the very proposition that the physician seems to be denying—that no one believes anything the patient says. In other words, the doctor's denial is incongruous in that it confirms the very problem about which the patient complains. Even the physician to whom the patient turns for help seems to doubt his veracity from the first moment of their encounter.

It is worthwhile to note that while the linguistic formulation of the doctor's response in this joke is critical, the joke is a conceptual and not a linguistic one.[2] It does not depend upon a precise and unalterable linguistic formula. Had the doctor responded, "That's impossible," or "Aren't you exaggerating?" or "No way!" a joke would still be discernible that traded on the very same idea. Granted, the phrase "you're kidding" is particularly felicitous in that it is familiar, colloquial, and has a certain semantic density that requires some work to unpack. It is not, however, essential to the creation of the joke. Had the psychiatrist responded, "Well, we'd best get to the root of this problem," there would have been no joke, and if he had responded, "Well, in that case you'd best pay me in advance," the joke would have been different in that the reported untrustworthiness of the man would have been extended to the implied promise to pay for his treatment.[3]

While the phrase *appropriate incongruity*[4] is recent and my own, the concept is not. In the late eighteenth century James Beattie proposed that "Laughter arises from the view of two or more inconsistent, unsuitable, or incongruous parts or circumstances, considered as united in one complex object or assemblage."[5] This notion, that humor depends upon the perception of an incongruity that is resolved or made sense of, has come to be known as the *incongruity-resolution* theory of humor.[6] While the notion of appropriate incongruity certainly resembles incongruity-resolution theory, there are two points on which they may be distinguished. The first is that the term *appropriate incongruity* does not suggest that an incongruity is *resolved.* The incongruity remains, even though points of connection between the incongruous categories are discovered. A measure of appropriateness is recognized between the juxtaposed domains, but incongruity and appropriateness characterize a psychologically valid rather than a logically valid relation. In the joke about the psychiatrist and his patient, nothing is resolved; the doctor's expression of reassurance at the same time exacerbates the patient's problem. Both effects of the phrase remain in force. While one sense of the phrase may be secondary to the other in a temporal sense, it is not secondary in a psychological sense. The incongruity and the appropriateness are parallel constructions.

The second distinction between appropriate incongruity and incongruity-resolution theory is that incongruity-resolution theory implies a temporal order such that an incongruity is first recognized and its resolution (or the appropriateness of that incongruity) follows.[7] Appropriate incongruity does not presume the order of recognition. An incongruity may first be registered and then followed by the sense of its appropriateness, or a seemingly appropriate relationship may be supplanted by a sense of its incongruity. I would argue that in the joke about the psychiatrist and his patient that the appropriate sense of "you're kidding" is registered before the incongruous sense. That is, the audience of the joke first perceives the phrase as an appropriate expression of the doctor's surprise and concern before recognizing that the phrase identifies the psychiatrist as yet another disbeliever.

A German joke illustrates a similar order in the perception of appropriateness and incongruity: "If one enquires from a youthful patient whether he has ever had anything to do with masturbation, the answer is sure to be, 'O na, nie!'"[8] This joke ends in an expression that means "Oh no, never." But the words in the expression when linked together make "Onanie," which is the German word for onanism (masturbation). In this case as well, the meanings of the individual words are likely to be apprehended before the meaning of the expression constructed from their concatenation. So the incongruous sense of the expression is only apprehended after a common and appropriate one.

It is necessary to point out that neither appropriate incongruity nor incongruity-resolution theory should be confused with straightforward incongruity theory. There are theorists who hold that incongruities can in themselves be humorous.[9] This seems a difficult position to maintain in that there are numerous instances of incongruities that generate no humor. Were incongruities in themselves funny, incongruous pairings like "snake/veil" or "tomato/carburetor" might be expected to excite laughter, and formulations like "Why did the chicken cross the road?—Because the geese were eating corn" or "What is black and white and red all over?—A palm tree" might prove hysterical.

There are occasions when such riddles may prove humorous, for they may excite laughter in children.[10] First- and second-graders tend to make up riddles that have either realistic or nonsensical answers. That is to say, the riddles of children either describe some object (e.g., "Q: What is brown and has bumps in it? A: A fence"—because a nearby fence is painted brown and its vertical planks are rounded so that the top of the fence could be said to be bumpy), or they appear as puzzling questions that have seemingly nonsensical answers (like the two examples in the previous paragraph). Of course, most traditional riddles are not nonsensical, since there is an aspect of appropriateness to the riddle answer. But this appropriateness may not be grasped by the younger child or may not be highly valued. Thus the riddle "Q: Why should you always wear a watch in the desert? A: Because camels live in the desert" may prove as acceptable and funny to a six-year-old as "Q: Why should you always wear a watch in the desert? A: Because a watch has springs [water sources] in it."[11] As they get older, children abandon interest in riddles with nonsensical, arbitrary answers and come to demand answers that trade upon some relation of appropriateness such as the utility of a watch in a desert environment because of its "springs."[12] By the age of ten or eleven, children are bored with riddles altogether and prefer jokes that escape the question-and-answer format and that depend upon appropriate incongruities.[13]

The fact that children laugh at riddles whose questions and answers seem arbitrarily related does not necessarily undermine the characterization of humor as being rooted in the perception of an appropriate incongruity. When the relations between the questions and answers are characterized as arbitrary and nonsensical, they are arbitrary and nonsensical according to adult standards. When children laugh at the riddle "Q: Why should you always wear a watch in the desert? A: Because there are camels in the desert" are they laughing merely at the incongruity? Is it possible that they are perceiving some appropriate relation that is unperceived by adults or which is otherwise insufficient to generate humor in adults?[14] Or have they simply learned to laugh at seemingly nonsensical question-answer sequences because that is what older people do—or so it seems to them? In children's humor it is often difficult to ascertain precisely what it is that children are laughing at. Consequently, children's humor is a very uncertain critique of humor as the perception of an appropriate incongruity.

Even if it is granted that children do laugh at sheer incongruity—without discerning appropriateness—children's humor appears to be a preliminary *stage* in the development of the adult sense of humor.[15] It is difficult to characterize something from a stage of its development. Crawling is a stage in human locomotion, but it is not clear that crawling contributes significantly to the characterization of human bipedalism. Bipedalism is a different affair entirely and must be characterized on its own terms. This is not to suggest that developmental stages do not inform the nature of the final result. Crawling undoubtedly bears some relation to bipedal locomotion—if only by indicating the kinds of motor and proprioceptive abilities that are prerequisite for upright motion, the absence of which make crawling necessary. Undoubtedly, children's humor has much to contribute to the understanding of humor more generally, but it is unlikely to be able to serve as the basis for its characterization.

There are constructions that do raise questions about the characterization of humor as appropriate incongruity. These are *definition* and *metaphor*. Definitions and metaphors are rooted in appropriate incongruities, yet neither definitions nor metaphors are in themselves funny. If the perception of appropriate incongruity is at the root of humor, the perception of appropriate incongruity in definition and metaphor should prove humorous as well. Yet it does not.

Aristotle holds that a definition is a formula that binds a *genus* to a *differentia*.[16] Thus, in the definition of man as the "rational animal," "animal" is the genus and "rational" the differentia. In this way the genus is divided between those members that possess the differentia and those that do not. Humans, for example, are animals that are differentiated from all other animals by their ability to reason. The characteristic of reason is so prized that the category of human comes to be viewed as opposed to that of animal, despite the fact that the definition of "human" remains rooted in the genus "animal."

In a real sense, the definition of human (or the distinction of any segregates included within the same taxonomic category) creates an appropriate incongruity. "Man" and "animal" are incongruously yet appropriately related. Man and animal are incongruous categories because humans are rational while animals are not. Yet human and animal are appropriately related because a human being is an animal in all remaining characteristics.

If the Aristotelian definition of man is rooted in an appropriate incongruity, why is it not funny? Why does the definition of humans as "rational animals" engender nary a smile?[17] Certainly there is much humor that plays upon the opposition between human and animal. For example, "Man is the only animal that chews its ice cubes." In one Gary Larson cartoon, while a pack of wolves devours its prey, one wolf stands up holding a camera to photograph the event. The caption reads: "For crying out loud Doris . . . You gotta drag that thing out every time we all get together?" From classic jokes and Gary Larson cartoons to Shakespeare's *Midsummer Night's Dream,* a large corpus of humor trades upon humans behaving like animals and animals behaving like humans. Nevertheless, it is one thing to say that jokes, cartoons, and comedy often trade on this category relation. It is quite another to claim that a *definition* that differentiates humans from and links humans to the other animals is funny in itself. Why isn't the appropriate incongruity resident in the Aristotelian definition of man funny?

A similar question may be asked of metaphor. A metaphor is also rooted in appropriate incongruity. A metaphor involves a comparison between two categories; indeed, between two clashing conceptual categories. Metaphors proclaim that one thing is like another; indeed that something *is* something other than itself—a logically absurd proposition. To overcome the seeming absurdity of the metaphor, one must discover appropriate connections between the categories. Thus, in the line "Oh blackbird, what a boy you are" or "Thou art the grave where buried love doth lie," one is provoked to discover the ways that blackbirds are like boys or a person could be imagined as being a grave. Metaphors are appropriate incongruities—juxtaposed incongruous categories whose appropriate connections need be discovered if a sense of the metaphor is to be apprehended. It is no wonder that metaphors have often been compared to jokes.[18] The curious thing about metaphors is that despite the fact that they, like jokes, depend upon the perception of an appropriate incongruity, they are only rarely laughed at. Why are metaphors not—or only rarely—funny?

It seems to me that the reason riddles and jokes are humorous while definitions and metaphors are not is that in jokes the engagement of the incongruity and the search for its appropriateness is *spurious* rather than *genuine.*

That is to say that jokes emerge when some aspect of either the incongruity or its appropriateness (more often the latter) is recognized as illegitimate. It violates logic, the sense of what we know to be true, or the sense of what traditional behaviors or expressions are supposed to do and mean. Thus, in the riddle "Q: Why should you always wear a watch in the desert? A: Because a watch has springs in it," the appropriate relation established between deserts and watches by the word "springs" is not recognized as a legitimate relation. The appropriateness is linguistic only and this linguistic relation does not affect relations between the objects named in the real world. Watch springs do not provide water. If they did, there would be no joke. Consequently, the connection of watches to the desert environment is appropriate but not legitimate.[19]

"Man is the only animal that chews its ice cubes" in some sense parodies the Aristotelian definition of man. The appropriate incongruity upon which it is based also would be regarded as spurious. The definition is incongruous because it chooses a small, very particular, and insignificant characteristic (of only some people)—and one that is often regarded as an annoying habit as well—and proposes it as *the* fundamental distinction between humans and other animals. The incongruity is appropriate because man would seem to be the only animal species to chew ice cubes. But the distinction is spurious because it is trite, is not species-wide, and to chew ice cubes one has to be able to make them, which requires refrigeration and advanced technology more generally. One also has to have drinking vessels to hold them and a cultural preference for chilled drinks. There is so much that is presupposed by "chewing ice cubes" that is more fundamental to the distinction between animal and human that the proposition, though perhaps accurate, is spurious. But were one to formulate the distinction in terms of these presupposed capacities—e.g., "man is the technological animal" or "man is the cultural animal"—one would be left with definitions that have been seriously proposed and entertained and which lack any humorous dimension whatsoever.[20]

The Gary Larson cartoon about the wolf with the camera depends upon the incongruous comparison of wolves communally feeding to a human dinner party. The incongruity is in some measure appropriate because both species are social and feed in groups. Undoubtedly, there are many serious analogies to be observed between wolf and human behaviors. But the cartoon does not focus upon any genuinely appropriate relationship between them. If wolves are of the same genus (Aristotelian, not Linnaean) as humans, it is hardly because they both compulsively photograph their friends and relations at social gatherings.[21] The cartoon highlights one highly peculiar and sometimes irritating human behavior (in that sense it is similar to chewing ice cubes) and spuriously transposes it to the wolf pack.

In the joke about the psychiatrist and the patient, the psychiatrist's comment "you're kidding" was not meant to register the psychiatrist's disbelief in all that the patient says. In denying the patient's report with "you're kidding," the psychiatrist was suggesting that "surely someone believes something you say," since the logical negation of *no one believes anything you say* is *someone believes something you say.* Since the patient's report of his problem also belongs to the class of *things that the patient says,* and since the psychiatrist denies the truth of this report, the doctor's seeming reassurance that the patient must sometimes be believed results in yet another instance in which the patient is disbelieved. In other words, the logical and legitimate sense of the psychiatrist's response is to deny the magnitude of the patient's complaint. The practical result is to evidence the complaint once again.

The seeming corroboration that the psychiatrist gives to the patient's complaint is spurious. "You're kidding" does not validate the patient's report that *everything* he says is disbelieved even if it does provide another instance in which the patient's statements are discounted. Nor does it require a logician to register these points. A colloquial understanding of the patient's claim and the doctor's denial is enough to apprehend that the psychiatrist has not affirmed the patient's description of his problem in actuality or by intention. He intends just the opposite—to reassure the patient. The doctor's affirmation of his patient's claim is fortuitous and seems accomplished by some quirk of language.[22]

It is not necessary for the auditor of a joke to be able to articulate precisely wherein the spuriousness of the appropriate incongruity lies. It is only necessary to have a sense of its presence. In fact, when the spuriousness of an appropriate incongruity is too obvious and transparent, the humor is engaged in a different register. The phonic resemblances at the root of punning humor, for example, are particularly transparent. This is why puns often elicit groans rather than laughter. Groans register the recognition of humor while devaluing it socially and intellectually.[23] When the spuriousness of a humorous technique is too obvious, it is noticed, and the response to the humor may be altered. I suspect that much humor that is labeled "corny"[24] is so characterized because it flagrantly displays its spurious devices. It is not surprising that so much humor is analyzed and explicated only with difficulty. The techniques employed are generally covert and are, for the most part, intuitively discerned rather than formally apprehended.

Unlike jokes, the appropriate incongruities of metaphor and Aristotelian definition are predicated on the engagement of genuine connections between categories. The similarities and differences between humans and animals, for example, are to be sought in substantive rather than spurious terms. In what real sense is a human being distinct from other animals and in what sense is a human being like them? To be serious questions, the answers must be framed substantively; framed in terms of what we know to be true about the world, using modes of argument that are regarded as legitimate, and employing expressions in their recognized and conventional senses in their given contexts.

When substantive relations between categories can be established, humor is not registered even though the attempt at humor may have been recognized. For example, many people would not think a pun funny that traded on the similarity between "Negro" and "Nigeria" since both words derive from the Latin *niger,* meaning "black" or "dark." The terms would be recognized as genuinely related. In his book *Reisebilder,* Heinrich Heine puts the following witticism in the mouth of his character who has been pretending to be an Indian prince but who finally reveals himself: "Madame, I have deceived you. . . . I have no more been in Kalkutta [Calcutta] than the *Kalkuttenbraten* [roast Calcutta fowl] that I ate for luncheon yesterday." Although Heine was Sigmund Freud's literary idol, Freud could not refrain from criticizing this attempt at humor. "The mistake in this joke clearly lies in the fact that the two similar words in it are not merely similar but actually identical. The bird which he had eaten roast is so called, because it comes, or is supposed to come, from the same Calcutta."[25] Freud, of course, is right. To be humorous, jokes must make "use of a method of linking up things which is rejected and studiously avoided by serious thought."[26] Knowledge of the relationship between roast Calcutta fowl and the city of Calcutta would have to be suppressed, forgotten, or unknown for humor to be recognized. When the knowledge of a substantive connection is present and active, a failed attempt at humor is the likely result.

It might be worthwhile for cognitive psychologists and philosophers to take some note of humor, because repertoires of humor provide a catalog of spurious modes of thought: types of thinking that are not recognized as legitimate within a culture. As rationality can be defined only in terms of what is not rational, humor may prove essential to conceptualizing the rational.[27]

Gabriella Eichinger Ferro-Luzzi has challenged the notion that incongruity is essential to humor. Humor, she argues, cannot be defined in terms of a set of necessary and sufficient conditions and thus cannot be conceived in Aristotelian terms. She holds that Ludwig Wittgenstein's notion of *family resemblances* is more suitable to conceptualizing humor, for concepts "need not have any necessary features possessed by all their members."[28] That is to say, the concept of humor may be held together in the absence of any essential or constant feature that defines it. Just as the members of a family may be recognized on the basis of a number of resemblances rather than a single feature, humor likewise is recognized because of a number of overlapping concepts, any one of which may be sufficient to characterize a stimulus as humorous. Eichinger Ferro-Luzzi spends some time reviewing various humor theories in an effort to show that each is inadequate in accounting for humor. This review includes incongruity theory although not specifically the concepts of incongruity-resolution or appropriate incongruity.[29] Despite her rejection of a single categorization of humor, she believes, nevertheless, that there are prototypical elements of humor that "occur frequently without being essential" to it and that incongruity is one of these.[30]

Eichinger Ferro-Luzzi's claims may be challenged on both general and specific grounds. Specifically, her analyses of jokes seem incomplete or off the mark. She cites a Tamil[31] cartoon that depicts a teenager with a bedroll under his arm who tells his mother, "I am going to sleep in the rice queue. Send my morning coffee there and later my breakfast to the sugar queue." She identifies the humor in this cartoon as "the clever way some people have devised to cope with an unpleasant situation."[32] The cartoon is, in fact, rooted in an appropriate incongruity. It is incongruous that one's breakfast should be divided up and shipped all over, coffee going to one place and the rest of the meal to some other. It shatters the integrity of the notion of a meal. But clearly the restricted availability of basic food items and the necessity to wait in various queues to get them make this incongruity appropriate. The need to queue for food takes precedence over having a complete morning meal at home. Even so, the strategy of the teenage son is spurious, for it is unrealistic to suppose that one could assess the time spent in queues accurately enough to determine what portions of a meal should be shipped where, or that one would simply not have the whole meal delivered to a single one of the locations.[33]

Eichinger Ferro-Luzzi believes that linguistic humor is a particularly rich source of nonincongruous humor. She gives the example, "Q: How is your sleeping pill business doing? A: It sleeps."[34] She sees this joke as an example of "heightened congruity" and not as incongruity at all. She does not seem to realize that this heightened congruity is merely the appropriateness that exists within the frame of an incongruity. When someone asks about the general state of a business, there is an expectation that the answer will be unrelated to the actual activities of that business. A business may be described as doing well or poorly in various ways, but that description is *independent* of the description of what the business actually does. If a person asked about the state of someone's laundry business, he would find it incongruous if they answered that "it washes," for though it is recognized that laundries do washing, the activities of the laundry have no relevance in commenting upon the success or failure of the enterprise itself. Business activity and the welfare of a business are conceptually distinct domains that should require different terminologies for their description. In the case of the sleeping pill business, however, the incongruity of the answer is appropriate because "sleeps" can serve as a metaphorical description for the state of a business in a way that "it washes" cannot. So the "heightened congruity" that Eichinger Ferro-Luzzi perceives is merely the appropriateness of an incongruity and not a distinct principle of humor. It is not difficult to generate any number of jokes of this type: "Q: How is your agricultural business doing? A: It's growing"; Q: "How is your plumbing business doing? A: We're flush"; "Q: How is your shipping business doing? A: It's staying afloat." Even "Q: How is your laundry business doing?" can be made to fit the model: "A: We're cleaning up." In each case the answer employs a metaphor that can describe the state of business that at the same time derives from the business activity itself.[35]

Before incongruity can be reduced from a necessary to a merely prototypical element of humor, the examples employed to evidence the argument must be very carefully analyzed. This has not been done. The supposed counterexamples to appropriate incongruity theory presented by Eichinger Ferro-Luzzi are, at best, questionable. Consequently, the claim that incongruity—and consequently appropriate incongruity—is not an essential element of humor cannot be accepted on the basis of the evidence provided.

Apart from the analysis of particular examples, there are other questions to be raised about Eichinger Ferro-Luzzi's claims for a concept of humor based on family resemblances. She argues against the "essentialist concepts and theories"[36] of the Aristotelian approach. Today, the charge of *essentialism* is often sufficient to dismiss concepts and theories without serious or close consideration. But the question should not be "how long will we have to wait until Wittgenstein's anti-essential idea [is] . . . accepted by students of humor?"[37] The question should be, How is humor best characterized?

In fact, the notion of family resemblances may create its own set of problems. Family resemblance assumes that two objects may be classified together because they both resemble some third object. A brother may not resemble his sister, but they may both in some way resemble their father in that the son has his father's eyes and the daughter her father's nose. A cousin who shares the sister's chin in no way resembles the brother or father, and so on. But it is well to remember that family resemblance is not the basis of family *membership.* Someone who bears no resemblance to anyone else will still be considered a member of the family, and someone who bears a striking resemblance to the father may not be. Family membership depends upon descent from common ancestors, not resemblance. (And in those instances when families are characterized in terms of some physical resemblance, the instances are often predicated upon a single pronounced trait, such as the Hapsburg lip, rather than delineated in terms of a series of overlapping similarities.) In other words, who is considered to be a member of the class called "the family" is not based upon ideas of resemblance at all but on some single criterion—descent. It is curious that the very conception that is put forth as an alternative to the Aristotelian notion of class does not itself exhibit the properties it is supposed to illustrate.[38]

Even if the notion of family resemblance were appropriate for the characterization of the category of humor, more is required. We must be able to characterize the linkages: the chain of resemblances that informs the category. What are the relations between the various notions of humor—superiority (Thomas Hobbes), aggression (Sigmund Freud), mechanical rigidity (Henri Bergson), and appropriate incongruity (James Beattie) such that they can be grasped in terms of family resemblance? One can see an overlap between superiority and aggression, and one could regard the reduction of a living thing to something mechanical as a kind of incongruity, but it seems difficult to find the connection between aggression and incongruity. What is the chain of resemblances that binds incongruity and aggression in a concept of humor? Arguing for a concept of humor based on family resemblance involves more than the claim that that's the way things are. There is some obligation to delineate the resemblances involved.

And what of all those phenomena that resemble members of the category but are not considered humor? Certainly there are many phenomena that bear more relations to feelings of superiority and aggression than incongruity does but are not considered humorous and only occasionally excite laughter. Sporting contests, for example, are certainly aggressive and are deeply implicated in feelings of superiority, but they are not considered humorous (even though, like humor, they are framed as something apart from real life with outcomes of little or no consequence).[39] How and why is a chain of resemblances broken? What is the principle that serves to stem the possibility of an infinite chain of resemblances and prevents a category from including everything under the sun? Furthermore, resemblances are not all equal. Why do some count and others not? And what is the status of the prototypical elements of a concept? Why are they prototypical? And why in the case of humor is the prototypical element incongruity (actually, appropriate incongruity)? Finally, if humor should prove to be many things, as a family resemblance concept of humor would suggest, several theories of humor and laughter are going to be needed, not just one. This will serve to complicate and not simplify the problem of humor. Simply arguing that Aristotelian notions of necessary and sufficient conditions are unacceptable in no way advances the understanding of humor. All the difficult questions remain.

I am not convinced that there is no single factor that underlies humor. After all, we are not speaking of some arbitrarily defined cultural category, but something that is cross-cultural, likely universal, that seems to be associated with the very particular and often involuntary physiological response of laughter.[40] It seems that we have not explored the concept of appropriate incongruity closely enough. Even if this characterization should eventually fail, there is something to be learned in seeing how far it can be extended before it does. Its dismissal seems premature.

In any event, things are defined for particular purposes in keeping with particular interests. My interest is to explore humor in our culture in an effort to understand what it might mean to the individuals who employ and apprehend it. I am interested in the interpretation of humor and not its definition per se. In our culture, the overwhelming majority of humor—the word "prototypical" hardly captures the scope—is structured as appropriate incongruity. Analytic and interpretive approaches to humor demand attention to this structure. It is essential to understanding what humor communicates, and how it differs from other forms of communication.

2. The Senses of Absurd Humor

Cold baths are more enjoyable when made with hot water.

He's so perverse, that he likes meat better than any other vegetable, except ice cream.

My father and mother are first cousins, that's why I look so much alike.

It's a lucky thing that water is liquid; if it were a solid like coal or marble, how could we get it to run through faucets?[1]

What is the difference between a duck with one of its legs both the same?[2]

Q: Why is there only one Eiffel Tower?
A: It eats its young.

THERE IS A PORTION of humorous expression that has been termed by various commentators "nonsensical" or "absurd."[3] But what defines this subset of humor and how does it relate to some "standard" humor that lacks nonsensical or absurd characteristics?[4] Does it employ different mechanisms or depend on different principles than other forms of humor?

Mary K. Rothbart and Diana Pien, adhering to the notion that humor depends upon incongruity resolution, hold that jokes are nonsensical when they fail to completely resolve incongruities.[5] To illustrate the notion of complete incongruity resolution, they cite the following riddle: "How far can a dog run in the forest? Only halfway. After that he'll be running out of the forest." Rothbart and Pien claim that the initial incongruity of the question and the punch line is "entirely meaningful" because the riddle answer is "definitionally correct." In contrast, the riddle "Why did the elephant sit on the marshmallow? Because he didn't want to fall into the cup of hot chocolate"[6] is not completely meaningful because it adds an incongruous element—an elephant sitting in a cup of hot chocolate. Similarly, the joke "Why did the cookie cry? Because it's mother was a wafer [away for] so long," while phonologically resolving the incongruity of why the cookie was crying, creates the incongruity of a cookie having a mother.[7]

Rather than refer to the resolution of incongruity, I prefer to characterize humor as the perception of *appropriate incongruity.* If resolution means finding the correct solution to a problem,[8] incongruity is never completely resolved.[9] To perceive humor is to perceive an oxymoron. A tension between the incongruous domains always remains because the "resolution" is always spurious—never legitimate. Consequently, the relations between the incongruous domains can at best be characterized as having a measure of "appropriateness." But there can be no resolution of the kind one expects in a problem of algebra, geometry, or even physical science.

I am skeptical that the difference between completely and incompletely resolved jokes can be maintained. Incongruities are never completely resolved in jokes. There is no structural difference between ordinary humor and what has been called "absurd" or nonsensical humor. Every joke is in some sense absurd in that it rests upon a violation of logic, sense, reality, or practicable action. Conversely, those jokes that have frequently been characterized as absurd or nonsensical conform to the structure of other kinds of jokes—that is, they are rooted in the perception of appropriate incongruities. What remains is demonstration.

> A guy in the garment industry has a son who asks him, "Daddy, what kind of flower is that?"
>
> He says, "What am I, a milliner?"[10]

The incongruity in this joke lies in the father's claim that he cannot recognize flowers because he is not a milliner, as if a milliner, rather than a gardener or florist, were an expert on flowers. The incongruity is appropriate, however. Milliners make women's hats, and women's hats are often decorated with flowers. The listener must deduce that since the father works in the garment industry, his view of the world does not extend beyond women's apparel. Within that narrow world, the only person he can imagine as knowing something about flowers is a milliner. Hence the initial incongruity can be perceived as appropriate.

Nevertheless, the father's parochial view is at the same time preposterous. No one would accept the idea that someone in the clothing industry could imagine the world in terms of that industry alone. No one should first think of a milliner, rather than a gardener or florist, as an expert on flowers.

If humor is rooted in appropriate incongruities, these appropriate incongruities are spurious constructions. They are based upon unacceptable modes of thought and practice. Immanuel Kant was right when he suggested that something absurd must be present in order to stimulate laughter.[11] Jokes "operate outside the assumption of ordinary, serious discourse."[12] Rather they work by what has been called "cartoon semantics."[13] "We are required to accept the impossible in order to allow the joke to proceed to its denouement."[14]

A zero order of absurdity would necessarily be nonhumorous,[15] as in the following exchange:

> A guy in the garment industry has a son who asks him, "Daddy, what kind of flower is that?"
> "I don't know."

This question-and-answer sequence seems totally realistic and represents a straightforward admission of ignorance on the father's part. This exchange is not humorous. It would be tempting to think of the "What am I, a milliner?" joke as one order of absurdity above this nonhumorous exchange. After all, everything within the joke—the characters, the setting (although there is no explicit setting), the language, and the interaction—seems ordinary except for the way in which the father acknowledges his ignorance—by denying that he is a milliner.

What would be the case of the father who answered his son's question with "What am I, a gardener?" Does this also have a zero order of absurdity? I think not. In this case, the father does not straightforwardly answer the question. In fact he does not *answer* the question at all. He responds with his own question. His answer violates H. Paul Grice's cooperative principle for bona-fide communication, specifically a maxim of Quantity—that a speaker should give exactly as much information as is necessary and no more—and a maxim of Manner—a speaker should be brief.[16] Buried within the father's question, however, is an answer in the form of a spurious syllogism: a gardener is an expert on flowers, therefore a gardener would know what flower it is, I am not a gardener, therefore I cannot and should not be able to identify this flower.

Such a response is an exceedingly convoluted—and hence, incongruous—way for the father to convey to his son that he does not know the flower's identity. Yet the incongruity is appropriate. Though a highly inefficient form of communication, stating that he is "not a gardener" allows the listener to infer that the father cannot identify the flower in question. This response also can be perceived as serving to protect the ego of the father. The father maintains his status because he implies that the child's question is properly directed at someone with special expertise. So the father's response is appropriate, because one may deduce from it that the father does not know the answer to his son's question, *and* the convoluted form of the expression is appropriate because we recognize within it mechanisms of ego defense—that the father does not wish to straightforwardly acknowledge that he does not know the answer. In other words, even the formulation "What am I, a gardener?" is something of a joke—even though it is not as trenchant as "What am I, a milliner?"[17] As a joke, rooted in the structure of appropriate incongruity, it cannot be of a zero order of absurdity. The "What am I, a gardener?" or "What am I, a florist?" response can be recognized as a joke in itself.

What if the father had answered, "What am I, a carpenter?" This would seem to be a non sequitur with no measure of appropriateness, since carpenters are not recognized as having floral expertise. Nevertheless, under certain circumstances, even this might produce humor rather than puzzlement. It would depend upon extra-textual factors. For example, two people who know each other and know the "What am I, a milliner" joke might employ it. The reference to a carpenter would be a clear incongruity, but it would be appropriate because they both recognize the joke form in which the naming of an unsuitable occupation, in fact, produces appropriateness. Thus, the reference to a carpenter would have some measure of appropriateness, if only for them. This joke would function as a joke parody. In other words, there are formulations that might seem utterly absurd as texts but that are perceived as appropriate when social context is taken into account.

The following joke text was discussed by Sigmund Freud:

> A man at the dinner table who was being handed fish dipped his two hands twice in the mayonnaise and then ran them through his hair. When his neighbour looked at him in astonishment, he seemed to notice his mistake and apologized: "I'm so sorry. I thought it was spinach."[18]

This particular joke seems entirely absurd. The narrative has the style of a joke, and when the character dips his hands in mayonnaise and runs them through his hair, we encounter an incongruity. Why did he do so? We expect his explanation at the end of the narrative to make this behavior appropriate. It does not. Rather it substitutes one absurdity with another. Applying spinach to one's hair at a dinner party seems no more reasonable than applying mayonnaise. The punch line would not seem to bring any closure to the joke. At the conclusion of the joke, a listener should be as perplexed as he was at the beginning about the appropriateness of the behavior of the dinner guest.

If this joke produced no laughter and resulted merely in the puzzlement or irritation of the hearer, no explanation would be necessary beyond the fact that the joke failed to meet the requirements of encapsulating a discernible appropriate incongruity. Yet this seeming non-joke often engenders laughter; an effect that must be explained.[19]

Freud characterized this text as a piece of "idiocy masquerading as a joke."[20] Freud saw this joke as a trick or "catch" that succeeds in misleading and annoying the hearer. In other words, it is more in the nature of a practical joke. Its humor depends upon the sudden awakening of the hearer to the fact that he has been duped, and that no appropriateness is to be discovered in the punch line regardless of how much the conventions of the genre conditioned such an expectation. The hearer, according to Freud, suppresses his annoyance at the deceit because he anticipates telling the joke to someone else and thus passing the annoyance on.[21]

Freud also suggested that the humor of the mayonnaise-qua-spinach joke depends upon liberating the pleasure in nonsense, a pleasure suppressed in childhood.[22] Even if Freud were right, much nonsense is not regarded as humorous and does not excite laughter. It is regarded merely as nonsense.

Freud's explanations, although they have much to recommend them, are not sufficient. For if the punch line were only a catch, any non sequitur would work, and this does not seem to be the case. If, for example, the diner had reacted to his host's astonishment with "Whales are mammals," I suspect the potential for bafflement would be greater and for humor and laughter much less. If *any* disruption of an expectation of appropriateness would be sufficient to produce laughter, almost anything might succeed as a joke.

In fact, there is a sense to the dinner guest's response "I thought it was spinach." It is not a complete non sequitur. Given the horrified response of the other guest, it is offered as an excuse, and in the situation, some excuse for the behavior would seem to be warranted. Furthermore, it is an excuse not only pragmatically but semantically. The guest maintains that his actions were engendered by an error—a misapprehension. He rubbed the mayonnaise in his hair because he did not realize it was mayonnaise. Misapprehensions are often accepted as grounds for excusing both inappropriate speech and inappropriate behavior.

Yet the dinner guest's excuse that he thought the mayonnaise to be spinach remains absurd. Spinach, a green leafy vegetable, in no way resembles mayonnaise (although, like mayonnaise, one could presumably rub spinach in one's hair). Even if it did resemble mayonnaise,[23] no occasion readily presents itself as appropriate for rubbing it in one's hair at table. Yet, if one were to entertain that it might be appropriate to rub spinach in one's hair during dinner, and if one could entertain the notion that one might mistake mayonnaise for spinach, then the behavior of the guest rubbing mayonnaise in his hair should be apprehended as appropriate. If the listener to the joke can somehow be made—however briefly—to entertain the spinach-is-to-be-applied-to-the-hair-at-table premise, the rubbing of mayonnaise in one's hair becomes understandable. The initial incongruity is made appropriate. This joke trades upon the acceptance of one absurdity to justify another.

Of course, there do not seem to be readily available scenarios in which rubbing spinach in one's hair and mistaking it for mayonnaise might be realistically entertained. Yet if one perceives this joke to be a joke about jokes—that it is a *metajoke*[24]—even the second incongruity of rubbing spinach in one's hair can have a measure of appropriateness. For this joke points to the absurdity underlying all jokes. It trades upon the recognition that all jokes are grounded in absurdity, and that one must accept some measure of absurdity to apprehend the sense of any joke. Although the "I thought it was spinach" joke might be used as a catch, as Freud suggests, the humor of this joke would seem to trade upon an absurdity—but one that is only quantitatively, rather than qualitatively, different from those generally entertained in joking and joke telling. If the "I thought it was spinach" joke is perceived as funny, I suspect it is because the listener grasps that it trades upon the exaggeration of a principle underlying all jokes—the acceptance of one absurdity to justify another. It makes the conventions of the joke visible.

It is curious that Freud considered the following joke in the same class as the mayonnaise-qua-spinach joke.

> "Life is like a suspension bridge," said one man.
> "Why is that?" asked the other.
> "How should *I* know?" was the reply.[25]

Although Freud also sees this as a piece of idiocy masquerading as a joke, there is in fact a rather easy interpretation that does not depend upon the assumption of an absurd premise. Certainly it is incongruous that the first man should propound a simile that he is forced to admit is meaningless. Yet people often philosophize and pontificate without having the slightest idea of what they are talking about. The man in the joke speaks as though he possesses some deep insight into the meaning of life. When questioned, he readily admits that no such insight is at hand. It is easier, after all, to assume the pose of a philosopher than to offer genuine insight into the human condition.[26]

The set of jokes that was presented at the very beginning of this chapter can all be described in terms of appropriate incongruities. In regard to the first joke, since cold baths are usually thought unpleasant, one made with hot water would be regarded as more enjoyable. But the incongruity of the joke hinges on the fact that a bath made with hot water should not be called a "cold bath." The temperature of a bath depends upon the temperature of the water. Yet the incongruity is appropriate because a bath and the water that makes it up are under certain conditions conceptually distinct, and what applies to one does not necessarily apply to the other. (For example, if you reduce a tub of water by one half, it is not clear that you have only half a bath. Also, a bath can be conceived as an experience, rather than merely a relation between water, a person, and a container. One would be correct to state that "I enjoyed my bath" rather than "I enjoyed the water of my bath.")

In the second joke about food preferences, the words "other" and "except" incongruously subsume meat and ice cream in the category of vegetables. Yet there is a certain appropriateness to the statement, since it is grammatical and communicates a clear hierarchy of preferences: ice cream is preferred to meat, which is preferred to vegetables, a hierarchy of preferences that might find considerable support, given the attitudes toward food in American society at large.

In the third joke about parents who are first cousins, the incongruity revolves around the word "alike" which can only be used to define a relation between two objects, events, or ideas. It is not used to describe an entity's relation to itself (although nothing more resembles an entity than itself). What one might expect to follow from the antecedent that one's parents are cousins is some consequent concerning the parents or concerning their child. The statement would hold no incongruity if the cousin relationship were employed to explain some relationship between the parents ("that's why *they* look so much alike"; "that's why they have known each another their entire lives") or if the narrator utilized a first person pronoun to explain some personal consequence of the parents' relationship ("that's why I suffer from hemophilia"; or "that's why my mother is also my second cousin once removed"). It is the concatenation of what the child might legitimately say about the relationship between the parents with what the child might legitimately say about himself that produces the appropriateness in this otherwise incongruous formulation.

The fourth joke depends upon a reversal of cause and effect. Because water is a liquid that is necessary for life and industry, elaborate plumbing works have been built to bring it to homes and businesses. In that plumbing is to accommodate water rather than the reverse, the statement emerges as absurd.

Nevertheless, the statement has its measure of appropriateness. If water were other than a liquid, other means of transport would be necessary. It is true—hence appropriate—that coal or marble would not flow through pipes, but it is based upon the spurious presumption that if water were solid, plumbing, as we know it, would exist in the first place.[27]

The fifth joke frames an incongruous, indeed senseless, question. The incongruity is twofold: first, difference can only be reckoned between two objects, and second, one leg cannot be represented by the plural pronoun "both." Nevertheless, the formulation does not violate either grammar or sense until the word "both." Independently, the first part and the second part of the riddle question might form segments of perfectly appropriate questions (e.g., "*What is the difference between a duck with one of its legs* made out of wood and a blind raven?" or "Aren't the arrangements of muscles in the right and left *legs both the same?*") There is some ambiguity in the use of the word "both." In the joke, "both" follows the plural "legs" and gains a measure of appropriateness from its connection to that plural noun even though the phrase as a whole specifies only a single object.[28] Because the word "both" diverts attention from the question of the difference between a duck and some other object to a relationship between legs, the resulting nonsense emerges from what at first seems an appropriate conjunction between the beginning of the riddle question and its conclusion.[29]

In the riddle about the Eiffel Tower, the incongruity is clear. There is only one because the name refers to the tower built by Alexandre-Gustave Eiffel for the 1889 Centennial Exposition in Paris (although there are replicas of it). Since the Eiffel Tower is not a living organism, it does not eat or reproduce anything, and it seems absurd to explain its singularity in such terms. However, various species, from guppies and hamsters to pigs and polar bears, do eat their young under certain conditions. The behavior is both shocking and fascinating, and the phrase "eat their young" has become salient in American culture to the point of cliché.[30] The application of this phrase to the Eiffel Tower would explain why there was only one of them. The explanation is appropriate, although completely spurious.

Even the most seemingly "absurd" jokes are jokes, and they work according to the same principles as all other jokes. Absurd humor involves the same admixture of incongruity and appropriateness that ordinary forms of humor do. Incongruity is not sufficient to generate humor. There is a difference between humor and nonsense. With utter nonsense, no conceptual frame is grasped that lends the necessary appropriateness to the absurdity.[31] The result is not amusement but puzzlement.[32]

I do not think that the distinction made by Rothbart and Pien between completely resolved and incompletely resolved humor holds. Consider the example of the joke they feel to be completely resolved: "How far can a dog run in a forest? Only halfway. After that he is running out of the forest." "How far can a dog run into a forest?" contains its own absurdities. It is presumed to be a question to be answered in absolute terms—that is, in quantifiable distances. At one level, the riddle question is incongruous because one might assume that the answer to such a question would depend upon a delineation of particulars: the speed at which a particular dog can run, the time allotted to its incursion, the depth of the forest. The answer, "halfway" (with or without the explanatory coda) substitutes a relational measure for the presumed absolute one. This measure is "definitionally correct" as Rothbart and Pien assert. Indeed, that is why it is appropriate and engenders humor. However, it creates its own incongruity precisely *because* it substitutes definition for information.[33] The riddle answer is a tautology. The answer could be appropriately employed to respond to any question about the incursion of any object into a finite space. Consequently, there is much unnecessary information in the riddle question. The query about dogs and forests is revealed as a subterfuge. The question violates Grice's maxims of Quantity and Manner—"do not make your contribution more informative than required" and "avoid ambiguity."[34]

The joke about the elephant sitting on a marshmallow is regarded by Rothbart and Pien as incompletely resolved because elephants don't fit in, let alone sit in, cups of hot chocolate. While the riddle answer would explain why the elephant chose to sit on the marshmallow, no explanation is forthcoming of how an elephant could fit in a cup of hot chocolate in the first place, or how a marshmallow could support his weight even if he could. The joke is incompletely resolved in their opinion because the situation is incompatible with the world as we know it. Certainly, elephants *do not* sit in cups of hot chocolate. But do fantasy scenarios prohibit the recognition of the appropriateness of incongruities in jokes?

> A horsefly kept biting a female elephant near her tail and was driving her crazy, but she couldn't do anything about it. Suddenly a sparrow flew down and ate the horsefly in one gulp. The elephant thanked the sparrow and asked whether there was anything that she could do for the sparrow.
>
> The sparrow said, "Well, I've always wanted to know what it would be like to screw an elephant."
>
> "Go right ahead," said the elephant. "Be my guest!"
>
> The sparrow flew behind the elephant and began to go at it. Just then a coconut fell out of the tree under which they were standing and hit the elephant hard on the head. The elephant cried out in pain.

> The sparrow looked up from behind the elephant and said, "Am I hurting you, honey?"[35]

This joke employs a fantastic setting in which a bird and an elephant engage in intercourse on both verbal and sexual levels. Although absurd when measured against the standards of ordinary reality, this absurdity is not at issue in the joke. As in traditional folk tales,[36] it is a given that animals can speak and behave like humans. The structural absurdity in the joke centers on the disparity in size between the two animals. The sparrow incongruously believes that the elephant not only feels his sexual thrusts but is pained by them. The sparrow's query is incongruous. Yet his belief is understandable and appropriate, if it is recognized that males tend to think their sexual organs larger and their sexual performances more vigorous than they may in fact be. Although the world of this animal joke is more fantastic—more absurd—than the world depicted in the joke about the garment worker and his son, the sparrow's comment "Am I hurting you, honey?" is no more absurd than the garment industry worker's comment "What am I, a milliner?" Once the parochial views that inform both punch lines are grasped, the incongruity in each case becomes appropriate. The differences between them are mainly the differences in their joke worlds and the degree of reality or unreality that is likely to be accorded them.[37]

While the joke world in the joke about the sparrow and the elephant is not in any way distinguishable from the world depicted in folktales and fables, many elephant jokes ask for something beyond the mere acceptance of scenarios in which animals speak and cavort like humans.[38]

> Q: Why are elephants gray?
> A: To distinguish them from blueberries.
>
> Q: What is gray and comes in a red and white can?
> A: Campbell's cream of elephant soup.
>
> Q: What's gray, black, and white?
> A: Sister Mary Elephant.
>
> Q: How do you know an elephant has been in your refrigerator?
> A: Footprints in the cream cheese.
>
> Q: How do you know if an elephant is in the bathtub with you?
> A: By the smell of peanuts on his breath.
>
> Q: Why do elephants paint their toenails red?
> A: To hide in cherry trees.

The first of the riddle questions is a straightforward one that might even be framed by an evolutionary biologist. The second and third have the character of riddle questions of the "What is black and white and re[a]d all over?" type. The last three contain patent absurdities in the questions. The answers in each case are absurd with respect to normal presumptions of knowledge about elephants, the world, and the canons of reasoning: namely, thinking of the grayness of elephants as their only significant distinguishing characteristic such that they might otherwise be confused with blueberries—or that even if this were the case, that it would be the explanation for their color in the first place; that there is such a thing as Campbell's cream of elephant soup, that it would be gray if there were, and that it would be the hypothesis of choice in identifying something that was gray and came in a red and white can; that something that was gray, black, and white would likely be an elephant in a nun's habit; that if an elephant had used one's refrigerator or bathtub, it would only be noticed by very indirect signs such as footprints or the smell of its breath; or that an elephant could paint its toenails, and that if it could, painted toenails would be sufficient to camouflage the beast in a tree that it could not climb.

But these riddles are more than just absurdities; they are jokes. There is a certain sense to each of them. The absurdities figure in the perception of a structure of appropriate incongruity. Thus, the fact that elephants are gray and blueberries are blue *does* serve to distinguish one from the other. Red would blend with the fruit of cherry trees, not orange or lemon trees. You can tell an elephant by the smell of peanuts—not scotch—on its breath. The black, white, and gray would describe an elephant in a nun's habit, not in army fatigues.[39]

Of course, the listener must entertain the notion that the elephant's color was *designed* to distinguish it from blueberries, that an elephant could become a nun, hide in a cherry tree, or could get into your house, let alone your refrigerator. But are these absurdities fundamentally different from those in the joke about the elephant and sparrow? Is an elephant in your refrigerator qualitatively or quantitatively more absurd than an elephant conversing and having sexual relations with a sparrow?

Elephant jokes do work by different rules. Not necessarily by rules different from other kinds of jokes, but rather by rules different from those of children's riddles which they seem to violate and parody.[40] For example, the answers to traditional children's riddles are usually something homey and familiar—a potato, an egg, smoke. The answers to elephant-joke riddles are something outlandish or impossible: Sister Mary Elephant, Campbell's cream of elephant soup, elephants in cherry trees. While such characters, objects, and actions seem bizarre or unreal, they do satisfy the conditions posed in the riddle questions. Each of the answers make a certain amount of semiotic sense, even if this sense bears no relation to the world as we know it.[41]

Elephant jokes were told in series, in part, I suspect, to acclimate listeners to their principles of operation. It might be difficult to apprehend the humor of elephant jokes through exposure to a single example. The rules by which such jokes operate need to be learned. It must be recognized that an engagement with reality in establishing appropriateness is not only not required but, for the most part, undesired.

It is not clear, however, that jokes that ask us to entertain the impossible are structurally different from other kinds of jokes. Compare the "Sister Mary Elephant" joke with the riddle "What is black and white and red all over? A wounded nun." Like the elephant joke, this joke parodies the old children's riddle "What is black and white and re[a]d all over? A newspaper." The wounded-nun joke employs an unusual and horrific image rather than an impossible one in the establishment of appropriateness.[42] Nuns, after all, can be and have been wounded. One joke is set in an impossible world while the other is set in a possible one. But are the jokes fundamentally different? Do they require different kinds of processing?[43]

The question is not an idle one. Willibald Ruch and Franz-Josef Hehl have approached the question of personality assessment with their 3 WD Humor Test.[44] This test asks subjects to rate the degree of funniness and aversiveness of three categories of humor: *incongruity-resolution* humor, *nonsense* humor, and *sexual* humor. Following Rothbart and Pien, they argue that the first two categories of humor are based upon structural criteria, whereas the last, sexual humor, is based on content. Subsumed in the category of incongruity-resolution humor are those instances of humor in which incongruities can be completely resolved. Nonsense humor either provides no resolution, provides only a partial resolution, or actually creates new absurdities or incongruities even if initial incongruities are resolved.[45]

An illustration of incongruity-resolution humor from the 3 WD Humor Test is a cartoon in which a man crouches inside a doghouse in his backyard. A small, friendly puppy stands outside the doghouse wagging its tail. There is a sign nailed to the tree that reads "Caution! Biting Dog!" Action lines in the drawing suggest that the man is barking. The caption reads, "Like this, you stupid dog!!"

An illustration of nonsense humor is a cartoon of an Olympic-type platform set in a stadium filled with spectators. Marked on the platform are the positions for first-, second-, and third-place finishers. In positions one and two stand small, barely visible insects. Standing in third position is a large bear. The caption reads, "Actually I should be glad—third best in buzzing—but still . . ."[46]

Among the interesting and important findings reported by Ruch and

Hehl, the one most relevant to this discussion is that nonsense humor is consistently rated funnier by subjects independently assessed as "sensation seeking"—that is, by curious people with broad interests who are open to novel experiences. "Conservatives," who tend to fear novel stimuli, are more likely to rate incongruity-resolution humor funnier.[47] Ruch and Hehl believe that incongruity-resolution humor and nonsense humor are structurally different and are processed differently.[48] But if we examine the illustrative cartoons described above, the example of incongruity-resolution humor contains a residual incongruity—that a man could teach a friendly dog to be aggressive and dangerous by crouching in a doghouse and barking. Conversely, the incongruity in the cartoon about the bear is appropriate. The bear comes in third place in a buzzing contest, having been beaten out by two small insects. The bear's rumination that he didn't do badly—"but still . . ."—is appropriate because insects buzz and bears do not.[49] The bear *should* be defeated by insects. But given that the bear is so much bigger and more formidable than the puny insects, one cannot help but wonder why he didn't do better. It is true that bears and insects do not engage in buzzing contests in stadiums filled with human spectators. But given the scenario created in the cartoon, the caption is appropriate.

The difference between these examples is perhaps not one of structure but of the joke worlds that are portrayed. Fantastical or implausible joke scenarios will be considered nonsense de facto. Jokes that begin "A kangaroo went into a bar" or "Two Martians landed in New York" are likely to be categorized as nonsense even before an analysis of the joke structure is undertaken. Jokes with realistic settings are more likely to be considered incongruity-resolution humor.[50] In other words, the distinction between these categories of jokes may not involve differential responses in the processing of joke structures, but differential responses to scenarios of realism and fantasy. Consequently, it would be a mistake to confuse the lack of fit between the joke world and the world as we know it as a difference in joke structure and the cognitive processing of that structure. The distinction may only be one of joke content.[51]

This suggestion is congruent with the findings that those who appreciate nonsense humor more also seem to find complex and fantastic art more pleasing, while those who favor incongruity-resolution humor prefer simple, realistic, and representational forms of art.[52] The unfamiliar and implausible may appeal to certain individuals regardless of the particular form they take. A preference for implausible joke scenarios may be indistinguishable from a preference for fantastic art, science fiction literature, or atonal music. The processing of joke structures may not figure in the equation at all.[53]

The quantification of degrees of joke resolution seems a highly questionable enterprise. Differences between resolvable, partially resolvable, and unresolvable joke incongruities are fuzzy rather than clear. Consequently, the distinctions that have been drawn between nonsense and incongruity-resolution humor seem highly problematic. Cartoons and jokes that have been assigned to the incongruity-resolution category contain unresolved incongruities. Cartoons and jokes that have been assigned to the nonsense category depend upon an apprehension of appropriateness or "resolution" for their humor. Nonsense humor remains an intuitive rather than an analytic category. What constitutes nonsense needs to be pinned down. What sensation seekers and conservatives respond to in jokes needs to be precisely identified. For when it comes to meditating on the absurd, one cannot dispense with sense.

3. Joke Thoughts

No figure looms larger in the modern history of symbolism than Sigmund Freud. It was Freud who made symbolism a primary concern of the human sciences in the twentieth century and utterly transformed the conceptualization of human behaviors. After Freud, dreams, nervous diseases, slips of the tongue, rituals, superstitions, myths, folktales, and customs were not the same phenomena they had been before. Even those who have attempted to revise or have opposed Freud's symbolic approach are to a great extent defined by his project.[1]

It should be, therefore, of some interest to note that Freud's most sustained analysis of a literary genre, *Jokes and Their Relation to the Unconscious,* is decidedly unsymbolic. This monograph, which profoundly affected the understanding of jokes in the twentieth century among scholars and laymen alike, thoroughly abstains from using symbolism in deciphering the meanings of jokes. In jokes, rings remain rings, knives remain knives, umbrellas remain umbrellas, and ghosts remain ghosts.[2] This literalism seems doubly perplexing given that Freud's central argument is that there is a deep analogy between jokes and dreams. Yet for Freud, dreams were the royal road to the unconscious and the most symbolic form of imaginative expression.

There are two reasons for the absence of a symbolic approach in Freud's analysis of jokes. First, *Jokes and Their Relation to the Unconscious* was published in 1905, which was some years before Freud fully articulated his notion of symbolism. Freud's notion of those fixed and widely shared representations of the human body, sexual activity, family, birth, death, and nakedness[3]—what have come to be known as "Freudian symbols"[4]—crystallized only some years after the publication of his work on jokes.[5]

There is a second and deeper reason why Freud's analysis of jokes avoids symbolic interpretation. For Freud, jokes are two-dimensional expressions. On the one hand, there is a joking envelope that constitutes the *form* of expression. This form is a consequence of technique. Undo the technical apparatus of a joke, and a joke is no longer in evidence. But a joke is not merely technique. When the technique is undone, what remains is a *thought.* Technique is what transforms a thought into a joke. Freud devotes a significant part of his monograph to analyzing the techniques of jokes. He felt that the techniques of jokes could be conceptualized in terms of three major mechanisms: condensation, displacement, and indirect representation, the very same mechanisms that he held responsible for the production of dreams.[6]

A dream is a jumble of visual, verbal, and other impressions that make little sense to a dreamer. In *The Interpretation of Dreams,* Freud claims to show that the bizarre and puzzling content of the dream makes sense in relation to thoughts underlying the dream. These latent thoughts, however, are alien to the consciousness of the dreamer. Their expression is so transformed by the "dreamwork"—the mechanisms of condensation, displacement, and indirect representation—that they are unrecognizable.[7]

The thoughts underlying jokes are also given over to the unconscious, where they are reshaped by the very same mechanisms that shape dreams. Unlike dreams, however, the thoughts underlying jokes *are completely accessible to consciousness.* They merely acquire their distinctive form by virtue of their detour through the unconscious.

While dreams and jokes are similar in that they are both shaped by the mechanisms of condensation, displacement, and indirect representation, they differ in fundamental ways. Dreams are completely asocial and have nothing to communicate. They do not even make sense to the dreamer. Jokes, however, are among the most social forms of expression. They demand to be communicated. Consequently, jokes must satisfy a requisite condition of intelligibility. When the thought underlying a joke undergoes transformation in the unconscious, it may be distorted only up to the point that it can be reclaimed by conscious understanding.[8]

Thus jokes, in the psychoanalytic view, do not express unconscious ideas in disguised form; rather, they express perfectly conscious ideas in distorted form.[9] Moreover, the distortion is reversible and the original thought completely recoverable.[10] In the broad psychoanalytic sense, a symbol is any word, action, or image that represents an unconscious thought.[11] In this sense, jokes are not symbolic, and consequently, Freud makes no use of symbolic interpretation in their analysis.

Jokes and Their Relation to the Unconscious contains any number of interesting and insightful hypotheses. If one hypothesis among them is basic, it is that underlying every joke is a thought. It seems worthwhile to explore how jokes might be related to their underlying thoughts. Freud implies that the thoughts underlying jokes are relatively transparent, yet this notion has never been critically examined.

What is a joke thought and how is it to be conceptualized? Does a thought necessarily underlie every joke? If so, is there only a single thought in each case? What is the relationship of the thought to the surface features of the text? If jokes represent thoughts, how do we arrive at the nature of what is being represented?

Freud suggested that the thought is prior to the joke; that a joke is a transformed or distorted thought. Perhaps so; but in the interpretation of a joke, we have no choice but to start with the joke and search for the thought. So even if the thought is psychologically prior to the joke, it is not logically prior. Unfortunately, Freud does not provide any definition of a joke thought, nor does he articulate any procedure for identifying it. Of the numerous jokes that he discusses in *Jokes and Their Relation to the Unconscious,* he identifies the thoughts of only a few. As a first approximation, however, a joke thought might be characterized as a proposition: a statement with a subject and predicate contained within the joke that is basically sensible and commensurate with our conceptions and experiences of the world.[12] Certainly every joke thought identified by Freud in the book meets this minimal definition.

A joke thought, however, cannot be considered to be any proposition borne by a joke. Jokes may convey all kinds of information that may be expressed in propositional form.[13] If a joke begins "A man walks into a bar and orders a scotch and soda . . ." one might infer that a bar is a place where it is appropriate to order a scotch and soda. While this proposition is commensurate with our conceptions of the world, we could hardly suppose that this constitutes the *joke* thought, since hearing—let alone understanding—an entire joke is not essential to its formulation. A joke thought should in some sense depend upon perceiving and understanding a joke.

To understand a joke, one must apprehend an appropriate incongruity. The structure of a joke is thus a structure of ideas, and not simply a structure of narrative or text. Consider the following joke: Radio originated in the Garden of Eden when God took a rib out of Adam and used it to make the first loudspeaker.[14] The incongruity is highlighted in the notion that radio goes back to the Garden of Eden, a clear anachronism. The incongruity is made appropriate by the suggestion that a loudspeaker was made from Adam's rib. A loudspeaker is part of a radio. At first, the incongruity persists because no radio component can be imagined to have been made from Adam's rib. The incongruity becomes appropriate when it is understood that "loudspeaker" can refer not only to a part of a radio but to Adam's wife, Eve, as well, whom the joke suggests was loud and domineering in conversation.

What is the thought of this joke? At some level, a joke thought must depend on what one must bring to one's apprehension of the appropriate incongruity requisite to "getting" the joke. To understand this joke, one must first accept the notion that radio is not an ancient technology and also recall that in the biblical account God fashioned Eve from Adam's rib. Then one must grasp that "loudspeaker" can refer to a component of radio technology as well as to people who speak loudly. Ultimately, one must synthesize this information to access the script[15] of wives as loud and overbearing talkers.[16]

Jokes are something like puzzles in that their solutions have to be discovered.[17] Puzzles introduce problematic patterns that can be resolved only when an alternate pattern informing the subject matter is discerned. Jokes, then, are *sequential* not merely in a narrative sense but in terms of the conceptual patterns or domains introduced. Jokes either produce a primary pattern of incongruity and a secondary pattern of appropriateness or they create a primary pattern of seeming appropriateness that is superseded by a secondary pattern of incongruity. Radio technology and the Garden of Eden are the primary patterns introduced in the Garden of Eden joke. These patterns create an incongruity. These patterns are then supplanted and made appropriate by a secondary pattern; wives and their perceived speaking habits.

Is the thought of a joke identical with the secondary pattern? Is the thought of the Garden of Eden joke simply that wives are loud and domineering in conversation? Certainly it is a proposition that demands full attention to all the features that must be processed to get the joke. Such propositions as Adam lived in the Garden of Eden, God made Eve from Adam's rib, Eve was Adam's wife—while all necessary to understand the joke—cannot be said to characterize it. One gets the joke only at the point where these other propositions lead to the realization that Eve, Adam's wife born of Adam's rib, like all wives, tends to be loud and domineering. If this secondary pattern and its relation to the previously registered incongruities is not recognized, no joke is likely to be perceived.

Yet it does seem possible to elaborate the proposition about wives still further. While the secondary pattern would seem pivotal to the formulation of a joke thought, it would also seem that a thought can be articulated that depends upon elements of the primary pattern as well. Since the joke is proffered in the form of a claim about the *antiquity* of radio technology, ludicrously suggesting that it dates back to the Garden of Eden, might not this claim serve to modify the proposition about wives to establish a yet more comprehensive proposition: wives are loud and domineering *and have been so since time immemorial?*

Freud never analyzed this joke about radio in the Garden of Eden, but his analysis of the following joke suggests that he would have favored the more comprehensive formulation of a joke thought in terms of both secondary and primary patterns. "A doctor, as he came away from a lady's bedside, said to her husband with a shake of his head: 'I don't like her looks.' 'I've not liked her looks for a long time,' the husband hastened to agree."[18] The appropriate incongruity is that the seeming agreement between the doctor and the husband is based upon a significant disagreement. The doctor is concerned for the woman's poor state of health; the husband by her lack of physical attractiveness. It is incongruous that they should agree in their assessment of the woman, but as the phrase "liking her looks" can appropriately refer to the medical condition of the woman as well as to her physical attractiveness, the agreement is appropriate. What then is the thought behind this joke? Again, we might assume that the thought resides solely in the secondary pattern that the husband finds his wife unattractive, or perhaps the more general formulation that, in time, husbands come to find their wives unattractive. As in the Garden of Eden joke, there is a way to forge a link between the secondary pattern of the husband's concern and the primary pattern of the doctor's. Freud formulated the joke thought this way: "The doctor was of course referring to the lady's condition; but he expressed his anxiety about the patient in words which the husband could interpret as a confirmation of his own marital aversion."[19] In other words, the husband's comment is cast as identical with the doctor's. Thus, the husband does not merely register his antipathy toward his wife but regards his antipathy *as an objective, professional assessment.*

In the jokes about radio in the Garden of Eden and the doctor and husband, the thought of the joke must be *inferred.* It lies "behind" or "beyond" the surface of the joke text. It is, for the most part, something that is not said rather than something that is said. Is this always the case? Is the thought of the joke ever identical with the text of the joke itself? The following joke was also analyzed by Freud: "A young man was introduced into a Paris *salon,* who was a relative of the great Jean-Jacques Rousseau and bore his name. Moreover he was redhaired. But he behaved so awkwardly that the hostess remarked critically to the gentleman who had introduced him, 'Vous m'avez fait connaître un jeune homme *roux* et *sot,* mais non pas un *Rousseau*'"; that is, "You have introduced me to one who is both *roux* (red) and *sot* (stupid), but not a *Rousseau.*"[20] Freud characterizes the technique of this witticism as "the multiple use of the same material."[21] A word or phrase is used as a whole and cut up into its separate parts.[22] It is yet another means by which a double meaning may be constructed. What is the thought of this joke? Exactly what the joke says: you have introduced me to one who is *roux et sot* but not a Rousseau. The thought of the joke in this instance is not a construction. It does not lie behind or beyond the text of the joke. As Freud put it, "Everything that has to be said is said in the joke itself."[23]

This explicitness of a thought in the surface of the joke may be found in other jokes that depend upon the multiple use of the same material, although not necessarily the use of a word as a whole and in its parts. The following witticisms depend upon the repetition of the same material but with an altered arrangement: "Some people love to go to the movies, and others go to the movies to love"; "Many things are expensive because they are fashionable, and fashionable because they are expensive";[24] "I can marry anyone I please, but I don't please anyone";[25] "Put not your trust in money, but your money in trust."[26] If these jokes can be said to convey thoughts, it would seem that the joke texts express them rather completely.

It would seem possible to talk about the *depth* of a joke; the depth of the divide between the surface of the text and the underlying thought. A witticism from Heinrich Heine's *Reisebilder,* which was analyzed extensively by Freud, can provide an instructive example. In one scene, poor Hirsch Hyacinth says of the Baron Rothschild: "I sat beside Salamon Rothschild and he treated me quite as his equal—quite famillionairely."[27] As Freud painstakingly shows in his analysis, this joke depends upon the compression of two distinct words, "familiarly" [*familiär*] and "millionaire" [*Millionär*] into a single expression [*familionär*]. This compression is incongruous because the word does not exist, but it is nevertheless appropriate because the two words share a number of similar sounds in the same arrangement so that the two words can be merged around this phonemic series. This technique Freud calls "condensation with the formation of a substitute."[28]

Although this condensation[29] is rooted in sound, it is not rooted in sound alone. The joke also depends upon the recognition of a conceptual relationship between the words. That is, in the context of the character Hirsch boasting of his relations with the baron, some significant connection between the meanings of "familiarly" and "millionaire" can be established. The thought underlying this witticism, according to Freud, is that Rothschild treated Hirsch quite familiarly, but only as familiarly as a millionaire can, which is *not familiarly at all.*[30] In Freud's view, aspects of the meaning of "millionaire" come to negate the meaning of "familiarly" to suggest the thought that the rich can never treat the poor as equals.

There would have been no joke if Hirsch had merely produced any composite or portmanteau word. For example, Hirsch could not have said—

assuming for the moment that he were made to speak in English rather than German—that the Baron treated him "quite famillinerily," combining the words "familiarly" with "millinery," the selling of women's hats. The result would have been puzzlement, not a joke. What would the selling of women's hats have to do with anything? If Hirsch had been responding to a question about his relations with a milliner and had said, "quite famillinerily," however, he perhaps would have made a substantial witticism. It could be argued, in a manner that resembles Freud's argument, that the thought behind this joke is that he behaved familiarly and like a milliner, even though most people would be hard pressed to characterize milliners and the nature of their interpersonal skills.

Heine's witticism about millionaires would seem to have a depth not found in a parallel witticism about milliners. The thought "He behaved familiarly and like a millionaire" said of a millionaire resonates differently from "He behaved familiarly and like a milliner" said of a milliner. The depth of Heine's witticism does not depend upon any of the surface features of Hirsch's utterance. It depends upon knowledge beyond that requisite for recognizing a joke. The minimum requisite knowledge to understand the joke is that Rothschild is very rich and the word "famillionairely" is composed of two words: one an adverb ("familiarly"), which characterizes the conduct of a social relationship, the other a noun ("millionaire"), which characterizes the man with whom the relationship is said to exist. The thought that Freud derives from Heine's witticism draws upon additional knowledge of the world; that millionaires cannot treat poor people familiarly even when they try.[31]

The jokes that have been considered thus far have been linguistic jokes: the mechanisms by which the appropriate incongruities are created depend upon such peculiarities of language as homophony, double meaning, and the multiple use of the same material. In conceptual jokes, the primary and secondary patterns are conceptually, rather than linguistically, united.[32] The conceptual nature of the linkage between the primary and secondary patterns might lead one to think it would be easier to formulate a joke thought that is anchored in both patterns.

This is hardly the case in the following joke, however. A bald-headed man and his friend are standing outside a restaurant after eating dinner. Just then, a seagull flies overhead and defecates on the bald pate. The friend is very much upset and exclaims, "Oh, that's awful! Can I do something? Let me get some toilet paper." The bald-headed man rumbles, "Hell, no, he's probably a quarter of a mile away by now."[33] It is not too difficult to identify the appropriate incongruity in this joke. The incongruity is that the man thinks of the toilet paper as being used to wipe the bird's bottom, rather than to clean up the droppings from his own head. The incongruity is appropriate, however, because toilet paper is used for wiping bottoms. And since the bald man's own bottom needs no attention in this situation, what other bottom could his friend possibly have in mind than the bird's? This is a perfect example of what Freud would have called a "displacement" joke, as one train of thought is abruptly diverted to another.[34] This displacement is achieved because of a dual conception of the use of toilet paper. While toilet paper occasionally may be used to clean up small amounts of defiling substances, it is something specifically associated with wiping behinds. This is the secondary pattern that emerges in the joke.

But is the thought of the joke merely that toilet paper is used for wiping behinds? Certainly it seems harder to articulate a coherent, meaningful thought for this conceptual joke than for the previous linguistic examples. Perhaps some perfectly good jokes convey no significant thoughts at all. Perhaps a substantial thought can even be articulated in a joke that depends upon a purely linguistic mechanism (men come to dislike their wives and seek to justify their antipathies) and that a rather insubstantial thought may underlie a purely conceptual one (toilet paper is primarily for cleaning bottoms).[35] In *Jokes and Their Relation to the Unconscious,* Freud only sometimes identifies the thoughts underlying the jokes he analyzes. When he does explicitly identify a joke thought, it tends to be a substantial, and somewhat pessimistic, comment on the world and its ways. Some joke analysts have actually claimed jokes to be storehouses of "truths,"[36] but it would seem that many jokes contain no consequential thoughts at all.[37]

Nevertheless, presuming that jokes can be formulated as thoughts, is a single joke restricted to communicating a single thought?

> A student returns to visit his old history professor after an absence of some twenty years. As he is sitting in the office, he sees that on the professor's desk is an examination for a class that he had taken when he was the professor's student. He picks up the exam and looks it over and says to the professor, "It seems to me these are the very same questions that appeared on my exam when I took this course twenty years ago."
>
> The professor replies, "They are."
>
> "But don't the students get wise?"
>
> "They do," said the professor.
>
> "Don't they pass on the questions to the next class?"
>
> "Certainly!"
>
> "But don't all the students gets A's on the exam?"
>
> "Not really. The questions may stay the same but we keep changing the answers."[38]

The incongruity rests on the usefulness of an exam that doesn't change and to which students have prior access. If students receive the questions ahead of time, how can it measure what they have learned? How can it not be the case that all students will get A's? The incongruity is appropriate once it is realized that if the answers change, not all students will get A's. So the incongruity is made appropriate with the realization that changing answers will be sufficient to ensure that the test continues to discriminate between students. "An exam whose answers keep changing is as good at discriminating between students as one whose questions keep changing," might be one formulation of the thought of this joke.

There are at least three ways in which one might *evaluate* the reason that the professor keeps changing the answers. The first depends upon an image of professors as lazy. Professors do not care about assessing learning; they care only about having an instrument that will allow them to differentiate between students. Capriciously changing the answers to an old exam gives them a viable instrument to achieve this goal. Little effort is required on their part. They do not have to make up an entirely new exam. The thought behind this joke would then be transformed. It is not so much an observation on the ability of an exam to discriminate between students as it is a statement about professors who take the easiest path in fulfilling their pedagogical responsibilities.

That professors are compulsively tricky might be another possible evaluation. Professors try to deceive students whenever and wherever they can. They are even willing to change the correct answers of an exam in order to be able to mark students wrong.

A third evaluation ignores the motives of personnel altogether. The professors have nothing to do with it. Rather, it is change within the discipline itself that causes the answers to change. The field is in flux and new understandings are continually being produced. Under this evaluation, old exam questions are really as good as new ones. The old exam remains viable for assessing learning, since students must demonstrate their awareness of the new solutions being proffered to old problems.

It would seem, therefore, that some jokes may communicate ancillary thoughts that also depend upon getting the joke, but which are more rooted in the evaluation of actions and events than in the secondary pattern itself. In recognizing that an effective exam can be one whose answers change even when the questions don't, a joke listener may be naturally led to evaluate why someone would construct such an exam. Some of the ancillary thoughts that may be formulated from this joke are that professors are tricky, that professors are lazy, or that knowledge is tentative and not definitive.[39]

The surface features of a joke text may come to promote or inhibit particular ancillary possibilities. For example, if the punch line of the joke about the professor had read, "*In history,* the questions may stay the same, but we keep changing the answers," the effect would probably be to promote the third evaluation that the field does not produce absolute knowledge and new answers to old questions are continually emerging. If we look back at the joke about the bald-headed man and the seagull, we can see that slight textual changes might also produce different evaluations and different ancillary thoughts (even though the basic thought was unclear and difficult to formulate). While the text of that joke offers no particular direction for evaluating the man's concern with the bird's bottom instead of his own head, if the joke had characterized the two men as Poles, thus putting it into the class of American Polish jokes, the evaluation of the man's comment would be stupidity. If the joke were about two people who had just come out of a bar rather than a restaurant,[40] the comment might be evaluated as indicative of intoxication. Perhaps if the two men were proctologists, the man's statement might be evaluated as resulting from an overcommitment to his profession and too narrow a worldview

The following joke also offers several interpretive possibilities.

> The hostess at a large party, rather proud of her voice, rendered "Carry Me Back to Old Virginee" in a rich and throaty tremolo. She was touched to notice a distinguished white haired man bow his head and weep quietly as the last notes floated over the room. As soon as she could, she went over to him and said, "Pardon me, but are you a Virginian?"
>
> "No madam," said the elderly man, brushing away a tear, "I am a musician."[41]

The incongruity arises when the man identifies himself as a musician and the listener must wonder why a musician might be moved to tears by the song "Carry Me Back to Old Virginee." The appropriateness of this incongruity is immediately apparent. The man was not moved by the song's sentiment but pained by its performance. There are a number of thoughts that might be accessed in the course of understanding this joke: a performance may be of very different quality than the score or script upon which it is based; art is something other than mere sentiment; tears may signal an emotional reaction, but they do not precisely identify which emotion has been activated; or artistic performers tend to be egoistic and interpret the world from their egoistic perspective. In fact, all these thoughts are compatible with the understanding of this joke. The question is, where should the emphasis be placed? On the characteristics of art and nostalgia, the expressions of emotion, or the foibles of human character?[42]

That jokes may communicate different thoughts to different people is not merely a theoretical possibility. A student submitted the following joke to her professor: A pain machine was supposed to transfer "the pains from a woman in labor to the father of the child. The night the baby was due, the doctor hooked husband and wife up to the machine and, as the labor intensified, gradually turned the machine up to its limit. The wife's pains disappeared, but for some reason the husband felt no discomfort himself. The baby safely delivered, the husband returned home, opened the door, and found the milkman dead on the kitchen floor."[43]

The incongruity, indeed, the seeming non sequitur of the milkman lying dead on the floor, must be understood as appropriate. The pain machine, in fact, worked as designed. It is the milkman who must be recognized as the biological father of the child. His death was caused by the pain transmitted by the machine.[44] The teacher regarded the joke as funny because of the cuckolding of the husband by the milkman. For him the thought of the joke might be something like, "A man cannot presume that he is the father of his wife's child." However, the female student who submitted the joke was pregnant with her second child and feeling some discomfort. She thought the joke was funny because the real father had died from the pain. In her view, "men cannot stand as much pain as women even though they think they can."[45] Both the male folklore professor and the female student who submitted this joke equally grasped the basic structure of the joke. The teacher, however, regarded the death of the milkman merely as revelatory of his status as father. The female, who undoubtedly was influenced by her condition, did not merely register the death of the milkman as a revelation of his paternal status. She went on to evaluate his death in terms of her expectations and assessments of the pain women endure in childbirth. While her reading of the joke may have been in some respects idiosyncratic, it accords with scripts about male responses to both pain and childbirth. For example, in numerous comic depictions, husbands pace, worry, and faint in reaction to the birth of their children. The message the student derived from the joke parallels that of the folk epigram "If a husband bears the first child, and the wife the second, there will never be a third."[46]

If jokes convey thoughts, these thoughts seem rooted in a system of relations and in the evaluation of characters, actions, and events. The specific elements employed in the text are, in themselves, of little significance. In this respect it seems that the problem that we have been facing in articulating the thoughts of jokes is much like articulating the thoughts of proverbs. Metaphorical proverbs are invariably formulated in terms of specific persons, objects, and actions. "Don't count your chickens before they hatch." The thought that underlies this proverb does not concern chickens and hatching per se. Rather, the thought must be abstracted from the relations between these elements. "Don't account anything in the future as certain until it comes to be" might be one formulation. Proverb users who could not abstract such a thought from the proverb would be unable to apply it meaningfully to situations beyond that in which they first heard it.[47]

Jokes tend to be more complex than proverbs.[48] There are a number of relations that might be plotted and the various forms of linguistic and conceptual play in jokes may not make those relations immediately apparent.[49] In addition, proverbs are rarely recited for their own sake but are applied to particular social situations. The situations in which they are applied evidence hypotheses about their underlying thoughts.[50] Jokes, however, are usually told for their own sake. Only occasionally are they employed to characterize a situation. Consequently, the opportunities to confirm or invalidate hypotheses about underlying joke thoughts are considerably fewer.

Actually, a number of observations about proverbs corroborate some of our observations about jokes. Like jokes, some proverbs—"A rolling stone gathers no moss," for example—lend themselves to more than one interpretation depending, in part, upon how one evaluates "rolling stones" and "moss."[51] Some proverbs, the nonmetaphorical ones in particular, like some jokes, also contain their thoughts in their surface expressions. There is nothing to be inferred from "Waste not, want not"; "Honesty is the best policy"; or "A constant guest wears out his welcome."[52] Their thoughts are completely conveyed without any need for additional inference.

Attempts to interpret jokes assume that they communicate thoughts, although there has been very little explicit discussion of joke thoughts and how they might be formulated. A general "impression" of the joke often leads commentators to leap to a statement of the motivation of the teller without pausing for the more demanding effort of analysis. The motivation of the teller, however, is most often a hypothesis that is proposed by the analyst and that hypothesis should depend on a number of factors. Chief among these factors is the thought conveyed by the joke. As I have tried to indicate, the thoughts conveyed by jokes may be very difficult to formulate. They may be tied to different parts of the joke, may or may not be identical with the surface features of the joke text, or may be formulated as very different propositions. Contrary to Freud's suggestion, joke thoughts are anything but transparent.

Of course, even when an analyst can extrapolate a coherent proposition from a particular joke text, it in no way ensures that the thought is communicated in the course of joke telling. There are a number of methods and techniques, however, that can assist in the identification of the operative joke thought and facilitate the assessment of whether that thought is likely to have been communicated. Repertoire analysis, for example, can evidence a hypothesis that certain thoughts are being communicated. A single thought abstracted from a number of different jokes would seem more likely to have actually been transmitted than a thought abstracted from only a single text. Of course, it is not uncommon for people to tell a series of jokes on the same topic. A joke thought, however, is not the same as a joke topic. When jokes on various topics seem to iterate similar thoughts, it is unlikely to be a purely fortuitous occurrence.

There are also individuals who use jokes as glosses, as commentaries on particular situations and circumstances. Used as glosses, jokes are like proverbs, and they may provide a clear insight into the teller's conception of the joke's thought. Although there are any number of individuals who regularly employ jokes in this manner, there have been few descriptions or analyses of this usage of jokes.[53] Individuals who use jokes as glosses are likely to be particularly sensitive to their underlying thoughts. Perhaps we should not be surprised that Sigmund Freud used jokes in precisely this fashion.[54]

Psychology has a long experimental tradition in measuring humor appreciation. Subjects are asked to rate specific jokes in terms of how funny they seem in order to test some hypothesis about humor motivation.[55] An equivalent testing effort has not been directed at questions of what ideas jokes access or what jokes mean. Yet it would seem perfectly possible to conduct tests on precisely this point and begin to assess the degree to which individuals can identify certain thoughts as intrinsic, related, or unrelated to particular joke texts.

Another method available in the attempt to discern the thoughts underlying jokes is the elicitation of oral literary criticism; that is, the elicitation of exegetical commentary from informants about the jokes they tell and hear.[56] Very little commentary by joke tellers and their audiences has been collected and published,[57] yet oral literary criticism is one of the most direct and natural methods through which the investigation of the thoughts that underlie jokes might proceed, and it is surprising that researchers have made so little use of it.

Jokes are probably one of the most commonly performed oral genres in modern times. They are introduced into intimate conversations and broadcast by media organizations. They are exchanged and appreciated by almost everyone. All the same, jokes are not simple. Despite the rather enormous literature devoted to their analysis, the question of how and what jokes communicate remains unresolved. Freud believed that jokes are ordinary thoughts expressed in a somewhat extraordinary form. Cultural researchers have a substantial investment in this hypothesis. After all, if jokes do not convey thoughts, what possible value can there be in the endless collection, classification, and analysis of such expressions? What can they possibly tell us about the groups and individuals that tell them? A serious analysis of the communicative potential of jokes demands some serious reflection on joke thoughts. If the question of what thoughts jokes convey is an old one, it nevertheless deserves the formulation of some new answers.

4. The Humor of Hate

AT THE CLOSE of the mystery novel *A Fine Red Rain,* the prostitute Mathilde accuses Emil Karpo, a detective in the Office of the Procurator General in Moscow, of being a romantic. Karpo utterly denies the charge, asserting there is nothing he has ever done or said to substantiate such a claim. When Mathilde says that she was being sarcastic, Karpo replies, "As you well know, I have no sense of humor. . . . I have no repressions and, therefore, no need for humor."[1]

Karpo's comment mirrors a popular view of the motivations and functions of humor. Humor is born of inhibition; the repression or the suppression of unwelcome impulses or thoughts. There is a measure of unintended irony in Karpo's statement. While it is true that the character Karpo is utterly devoid of humor, he is hardly without repressions. Karpo is a man of extreme personal discipline. He is a virtual ascetic. Except for his passion for work and his commitment to the Soviet state, he has repressed almost everything. If the correlation between humor and repression held true, Karpo should have had an expansive sense of humor.

Sigmund Freud first posited the association of humor and repression. Jokes, in Freud's view, consist of both techniques and thoughts. The joking techniques divert the attention of the listener so that an aggressive thought—which risks censure if stated directly—might be safely expressed. The techniques of the joke are fundamentally duplicitous: they distract attention from the underlying message that the joke contains. Beguiled by the joke's technique, the auditor, through his laughter, affirms the forbidden thought and becomes complicit in the aggression.[2] Thus jokes make possible the expression of abuse in the face of the obstacles raised by social proprieties and conventions.[3]

A corollary of this view is that the more sophisticated a joke is, the more it will be tolerated. The greater the effort a hearer must expend in order to reconstruct an underlying thought, the more sophisticated a joke is thought to be. Sophistication is a function of technique. The greater the distance between what is actually said in the joke and what the hearer must understand, the more acceptable the joke will become in polite society.[4]

Freud introduced the issue of smut to illustrate his theory. Smut is the explicit verbalization of sexual matters to a particular person by whom one is aroused, and who is expected to be aroused by the smut in turn. Smut is thus directed by men toward women as an act of seduction. Should another man be present, however, this act of seduction cannot be realized. In such circumstances hostility is aroused, and smut is transformed into an act of sexual aggression directed at the woman. The interfering man becomes the person to whom the smut is addressed, an ally before whom the woman is exposed and who confirms that exposure through his coarse laughter.

Smut has none of the characteristics of jokes. It is explicit, "undisguised indecency." In lower classes, according to Freud, smut begins when a woman enters the male domain. In higher social classes, the "presence of a woman brings the smut to an end." Smut can become a joke only if it adopts the allusive techniques of jokes. With the acquisition of these techniques, smut becomes an obscene joke and "may venture to climb into good society."[5]

According to this formulation, it seems clear that men of the "higher social classes" would often joke and might on occasion—in the absence of women of their class—resort to smut. It would seem equally clear, however, that for men of the lower classes, among whom smut was acceptable, there should be no need or occasion for obscene joking. Since smut is directly expressible, nothing would be gained by recasting the sexual hostility in the form of a joke.

A more general proposition can be inferred. If there is a hostile thought that in particular situations is directly expressible, joking formulations of the thought should not appear. For if the function of joke technique is to overcome the resistances—both internal and external—to aggression, jokes should be absent in situations where that aggression is open and direct.

This, of course, is a hypothesis that is easily tested. One need only identify individuals or groups that have no hidden agendas and who express their hostilities openly and see whether they also employ humor. In the United States today, there seems to be no dearth of individuals and groups who readily and openly proclaim their antipathies toward racial, ethnic, and religious minorities; governmental institutions and officials; political parties and their candidates. Do such individuals and groups employ humor to communicate their racial, ethnic, and political resentments?

The White Aryan Resistance is a neo-Nazi, racist group founded by Tom Metzger of Fallbrook, California. It was formerly known as the White Aryan Political Association. Metzger had been a member of the Louisiana-based Knights of the Ku Klux Klan led by David Duke and later became grand dragon of the Knight's branch in California. Metzger and his movement have published a newspaper called *WAR* since 1980. In November 1995 *WAR* established its own home page on the Internet.[6]

The White Aryan Resistance—and its associated youth arm, the Aryan Youth Movement (originally the White Student Union) under the direction of Metzger's son John Metzger—is dedicated to restoring the supremacy of the Aryan race on the North American continent. The white race needs to be "advanced and protected" in the face of "non-white invaders" or "mud people"[7] who destroy both the environment and the gene pool. The White Aryan Resistance sees transnational capitalism, communism, democracy, party politics, and religion as threats to Aryan survival. The organization is anti-immigrant and promotes Holocaust denial.[8]

In *WAR*'s view, the Aryan race is being destroyed by non-Aryan groups, particularly through miscegenation with blacks. The environment is being polluted, resources are being depleted, and jobs expropriated by an influx of Latinos, Asians, and other non-Aryan immigrants. The Jews, who are considered to be neither white nor descendants of the Old Testament Hebrews, have created this state of affairs, since they control both the government of the United States and the broadcast media.[9] They are the "World Enemy," parasites who drain the life and wealth of society and who are "at the bottom of every racially and culturally poisonous drive."[10]

These positions of the White Aryan Resistance, which are published and republished in *WAR,* can only be understood in the context of the numerous expressions of racial and ethnic vilification that accompany them. The White Aryan Resistance's policies of racial separation are motivated by a deep animus toward blacks, Jews, Mexicans, other "nonwhites," and homosexuals, an animus that *WAR* takes no pains to disguise. Epithets are employed with abandon. "Nigger," "Jig," "Spook," "Kike," "bagel snapper," "Jew" (as an adjective or adverb; e.g., "Jew culture," "Jew-financed," "Jew maggot"), "Gook," "Slope," "Jap," "Chink," "Spic," "Greaser," "faggot," and "dyke" punctuate the pages of *WAR* in issue after issue. Characterizations such as "the Vietnamese, the Puerto Ricans and Mexicans, the Japs, Chinks, Africans, and 101 other species of spotted-ass apes" or "Gooks, greasers, geeks, freaks,

AIDS carriers and khazars [Jews] swarming into this once pristine America the beautiful"[11] demonstrate that the White Aryan Resistance is a hate group and has no interest in promoting its racialism merely as some abstract ideological program.[12]

Although *WAR* is primarily a political publication promoting a serious racist ideology and agenda, instances of humor are common—indeed, prominent. Puns such as "Jewspaper," "Jewsmedia," "Jewnited States," "Latrino," and "Turd world" regularly appear and reflect *WAR*'s oft-stated view that Jews control government and the media and that Latinos and other "mud-people" pollute the race, culture, and environment. As in many newspapers, headings often parody well-known expressions in the popular culture. For example, a report on a second visit to the Soviet Union is titled "Back in the USSR,"[13] while another on the Zionism of Colonel Oliver North is called "Another Fine Mess You've Gotten Us in Ollie."[14] The section titled "Kikewatch" is itself a parody of the "Klanwatch" program founded in 1979 by the Southern Poverty Law Center to monitor the activities of racist groups such as the White Aryan Resistance. Very occasionally, *WAR* will reprint verbal jokes: "What is eight miles long and has an I.Q. of 68?—The 'Martin Luther King Day' Parade." "How do you stop five niggers from raping a white woman?—Throw them a basketball."[15]

Far and away the most frequent form of humorous expression in *WAR* is the cartoon. Each issue is laced with cartoons and comic strips. Not all these drawings are meant to be funny, but a good number of them are so intended. They create appropriate incongruities employing those techniques—punning, exaggeration, irony, indirect representation, extended analogy, allusion[16]—that characterize humorous expressions in a wide range of media.

Many of the cartoons employ a minimum of humorous technique. Caricature alone would seem to be the basis of many—primarily the exaggeration of physical features. In figure 1, the excessively thick lips; the enormously wide mouth and nostrils; the extra-large, but half-closed, eyes; the heavy brow ridges and absent forehead constitute the physical aspects of the caricature. The figure is marked by certain actions or behaviors that add to the repugnance of the physiognomical representation. The figure has his finger in his nose, he is drooling, and action lines[17] suggest that he is giving off an odor that is attracting flies.[18] The caption enjoins the reader *not* to laugh at the caricature: "Don't laugh, White man! This smelly, baggy lipped moron will get a choice job, college scholarship or emergency health care long before you will in today's world."[19] The caption employs no humorous techniques other than, perhaps, irony.[20] The humor lies in the incongruity between the

Figure 1

odious image represented and the idea that this figure is privileged in society. The incongruity is appropriate because *WAR*'s readers believe that government policies give precedence to incompetent minority-group members rather than to capable white people.

Figure 2 employs a similar caricature of blacks. In addition, a host of stereotypical appetites and vices are associated with the figure—pornography, dance, alcohol, loud music, gluttony, violence, welfare dependency—and serve to define its moral qualities. The whole becomes a joke in that the partaking in all these vices at a single moment is incongruous. The figure is overdetermined and beyond credibility probably even for the readership of *WAR*.[21] The joke is completed by the caption, which suggests that the enjoyment of all these very worldly vices at one time might appropriately constitute some sort of heaven—a "Nigger Heaven"[22]—because of their immense desirability.

Figure 3 uses punning in its caption and excessive exaggeration in its depiction. The caption "Jew-Jitsu" is a pun on "jujitsu," meaning "gentle art,"

Figure 2

which refers to the Japanese martial art that turns the weight and momentum of one's opponent against them. The picture portrays a Jew in a martial-arts outfit using his excessively large nose to "bonk" an Asian figure who is also clad in martial-arts attire. The accompanying text announces "It's the ancient deadly Hebrew martial art for which there is no defense."[23] The humor depends upon the stereotype of Jews having big noses. In the cartoon, however, it is exaggerated to the point of incredibility. However big one might believe a Jew's nose to be, no one seriously entertains the notion that it is so large or strong that it can be used as a weapon in combat. The caption is entirely ironic.

Figure 4 is a little more oblique. The figure of the black man in a stocking cap holding the sign "Will Make Excuses for Food"[24] can be understood only in the context of the experience of those signs frequently displayed by street people that state "Will Work for Food." The implication seems clear. The

Figure 3

black man does not and will not work. He is, at best, willing to make excuses about why he cannot work but, nevertheless, should be supported.

Some cartoons are simply graphic representations and elaborations of verbal joke formulas. One cartoon asks, "What are the most redundant references one can make?" The answer is "Dumb Nigger, Greedy Jew, and Pregnant Mexican." The picture shows a pregnant woman surrounded by seven young children with a child seemingly in the midst of being born. Water puddles between her legs and the small hand of a child extends below the

Figure 4

hem of her dress. Another cartoon states, "We've got some good news and some bad news. The bad news: the Martians have landed . . . The good news: they eat Niggers." The picture depicts a monstrous alien creature with long sharp teeth holding a black teenager (with turned-around baseball cap) in one hand with another already in its mouth.[25]

There is nothing in these cartoons that *WAR* has been or would be unwilling to state directly. On the themes of black violence and moral degeneracy, Jewish physiognomy, and Mexican reproduction, *WAR* writes: "At least 15% of the common street Niggers, or 1 in 6, are mentally ill. Thus when a cop is patrolling and sees some buck with a paper-wrapped open bottle of Cobra or T-Bird, he knows there is a strong likelihood that this man would rather kill him than respond logically to a 'stop and question.' Why? Well, because city streets are full of crazy Niggers."[26] "70% of [their] births are illegitimate, where men only rant or laugh as our society asks them to take responsibility for their birth droppings, where the very concept of holding a job equal to their skills with commensurate pay is deeply offensive, and where the majority would rather sit around drinking, dancing, and 'singing.'"[27] "A Jew can be spotted by his face. . . . There are blonde and blue eyed Jews who still betray the familiar Jewish countenance and psyche."[28] "The capitalists and communists pick gleefully at our bones while the vile hook-nosed monsters of usury orchestrate our destruction."[29] "Only we suckers of White America actually believe the brotherhood rhetoric and throw our borders open so our taxpayers can feed, clothe and medicate the numberless hordes of swarming mud people."[30] "The Mestizo Latrinos desire to take over the entire urban area of North America through immigration and high birth rates."[31] In fact, one could argue that the explicit statements are more odious and more ominous than the humorous cartoons.

If WAR is up front about its animosity toward Jews, blacks, Mexicans, Asians, and homosexuals,[32] it is less direct about its programs for achieving Aryan racial supremacy. *WAR* does not openly advocate specific acts of violence to achieve its aims. When violence is recommended, it tends to be abstract, generalized, deferred, or indirect.

The reluctance to advocate specific acts of violence would seem to be the result of legal concerns. The abstract advocacy of force is protected speech under the First Amendment. The Supreme Court of the United States has held that "the teaching of the moral propriety or even moral necessity for a resort to violence is constitutionally protected." Inciting imminent lawless action, "preparing a group for violent action and steeling it to such action," however, is not.[33]

There is no doubt that Tom Metzger is aware of this distinction. In 1990 the Metzgers were sued in Portland, Oregon, by the Southern Poverty Law Center and the Anti-Defamation League in connection with the skinhead killing of Ethiopian student Mulugeta Seraw. The plaintiffs claimed that Tom and John Metzger "incited or encouraged" the action of the skinheads who killed Seraw. In his defense, Tom Metzger argued that his literature "had nothing to do with going out and physically killing individual black people on street corners." He claimed that he only promoted violence in the course of self-defense, and the revolution he championed was not necessarily a violent one. Many of the seemingly violent and conspiratorial communications in his newspaper and on his telephone hot lines, he contended, were "disinformation" or "satire." He noted that he had not called for "imminent violence," thereby indicating that he was fully aware of the kinds of speech that were and were not protected.[34]

Assuming that humor serves to express what might otherwise be repressed or suppressed, one might expect to find violence depicted in humor. In fact, it is. Various drawings convey the message that violence against blacks, Jews, or Mexicans is an appropriate response to the threat that they pose to the white race. Figure 5 employs a caricature of a black man molesting a white woman. A bearded white man standing behind him is hitting him on the head with a crowbar. The top of the black man's head is depressed from the blow as though it were made of rubber, and his eyes pop entirely out of his head. The caption employs no humorous technique. It is a straightforward message: "Let's face it! Rampant Black crime is bringing this nation to it's [*sic*] knees . . . If you care about the future of your home, your family, your race . . . It's time to strike back!" What humor is contained in the cartoon, from the point of view of *WAR*, would seem to be limited to the gross exaggeration in the car-

Figure 5

icature of the black man. His lips are so large that they extend across his face, and they obscure any view of his chin. His tongue is likewise abnormally long and protrudes from his mouth. The depression of the head and the popping out of the eyes in response to the blow heighten the exaggeration.

The humor here—and that is probably what we must call it—is very much like that in figure 1. It is limited to a caricature and the exaggeration of bodily reactions to force. The caption employs no humorous techniques. It conveys an entirely serious message concerning striking back against blacks and black crime—which in conjunction with the drawing depicts "striking back" as physical violence.[35]

Figure 6 likewise employs a modicum of humorous technique—notably the caricature of the Jewish facial features, and the rendition of the Jew as a spider who needs to be exterminated. Though akin to humor, metaphor is not, strictly speaking, humor. Metaphors tend to become humorous when they are sufficiently extended so that some peripheral aspect of the metaphor proves surprisingly appropriate to the person or situation being represented—in this instance, the eradication of the Jew-spider using gas, and its identification as "Berg spray"[36] rather than "bug spray."

The poem accompanying the drawing seems, for the most part, a serious one, although it extends the spider metaphor depicted in the drawing and effects a humorous tone in its easy and regular rhymes.

> They sting like a bee, dart like a flea,
> Strip you bare like a locust . . .
> You, too, will make a ready meal
> If you remain unfocused.
> Stand up! Take arms!
> Defend yourself . . .
> Like the heroes of the past . . .
> When the Kikes come crawlin'
> Just send 'em sprawlin'
> With a dose of poison gas!

Of course, the suggestion that Jews are insects that need to be exterminated with gas[37] is likely to be interpreted by many as a deadly serious one. It is not clear that the messages that stand transparently behind such humor are, in fact, suppressed or repressed or that they cannot emerge in more direct forms of discourse.[38]

In fact, a great deal of attention is given in *WAR* to the question of violence. It is a position of the White Aryan Resistance that armed conflict may be necessary for living space, food, and the protection of the gene pool.[39] The

Figure 6

White Student Union in a list of "Do's and Don'ts" states, "Do be violent."[40] "If killing, robbing, deceiving and practicing less than chivalry toward another species or race means the survival of one's own race, then this can only be valued as good. . . . If the race is placed in jeopardy by another species, that species which threatens the race must be neutralized," concludes a *WAR* meditation on the concept of race.[41]

Discussions of terrorism, bomb making, and taking the Fifth Amendment are a regular feature of *WAR*. A description of the "disenchantment and discontent of the potential terrorist" and the "sense of belonging," "spirit of camaraderie," and "self-redemption" that come from joining a terrorist group portray terrorism as attractive.[42] Essays define the political goals of terrorism.[43] *WAR* regularly characterizes and honors racists who are in jail for a variety of crimes, some violent, as "political prisoners" and "martyrs."[44] Historical essays about armed rebellions against the central government often appear,[45] and fictional accounts provide guides to bomb building, silencer making, identifying targets, assassinations, postal fraud, grand theft, and resisting police interrogation. Often these fictional accounts include bibliographical guides to further reading.[46]

Likening the present situation in the United States to the failed Russian Revolution of 1905, *WAR* muses on the possibility of one thousand homeless whites demanding that President Clinton meet them outside the White House. The description of the scene is followed by "Have you ever heard M-16s clipping along on full auto?" Concluding with the observation that since every successful revolution requires at least one failed revolution, the essay ends, "Let 'er rip."[47]

In what is possibly the most explicit statement about racial and ethnic violence on a grand scale, the author, in an essay recalling the actions of Joseph Stalin, muses: "What a pity to have shot 15,000 Polish officers . . . instead of 15,000 Jews." The author continues to dwell on the possibilities: "If we had taken fifty million Africans and drowned them . . . if we took 80,000 Mexican wetbacks and burned them alive in the California desert . . . if we took 300,000 Jewish anthropologists, bankers, financial consultants, investment advisors, lawyers, psychoanalysts, psychiatrists, and psychologists and burned them alive in Beverly Hills . . . we would be doing the world a favor."[48]

For all their concern with violence and extermination, however, *WAR* essays do not encourage specific violent acts. Violence is promoted as an abstract ideological principle, or it is characterized as "self-defense." Murder and mayhem are embedded within the frame of fiction, or are otherwise implied. Even the recommendations about the mass murder of Jews, Africans, and "wetbacks" quoted above is framed within the conditional construction "What if?" If the White Aryan Resistance is reluctant to advocate specific acts of violence, this reluctance extends to all forms of expression, humorous and non-humorous alike.

Humor affords no more possibilities for the indirect expression of aggression and programs of violence than any other mode of expression. Neither the humorous forms nor the more expository forms advocate going out and hunting down a "nigger" or "kike" tomorrow. Thus, nothing is communicated through humor that is not communicated otherwise. Whatever insulation and protection might be afforded a serious message by the guise of humor, insulation and protection would not seem to be qualities that recommend humor to the White Aryan Resistance and make it a favored form of expression.

It is only necessary to look at figures 7 and 8 to recognize that racial animus and murderous violence may be even more insidious when they are communicated without the benefit of a humorous frame. Figure 7 vividly portrays skinheads clubbing, slashing, and strangling blacks in what, from the suggestion of flames in the background, would seem to be an all-out race war. Figure 8 suggests that the solution to the problem of illegal immigration is to put the military on the border with orders to kill illegal immigrants on sight. It seems to me that these graphic depictions of violence are darker and more disturbing than cartoons that employ the grossest caricatures or crudest humorous techniques. This is probably because even ardent racists recognize the exaggeration in caricature and the speciousness underlying every

Figure 7

Figure 8

humorous technique. Consequently, the messages conveyed by humorous cartoons are to some extent delegitimized by their humorous techniques.[49] The seriousness of the message is diminished rather than enhanced by the humorous frame in which it is embedded.

If humor is not employed as mask and disguise by the White Aryan Resistance, what other functions might it serve in their publications? Tom Metzger stated that the purpose of the cartoons was to lead readers to the more substantive articles in *WAR*.[50] It seems unlikely that the gross and repetitive caricatures in the cartoons would lead people to dense and turgid articles on labor history, armed resistance, or the roots of Aryan religion. The fact that the cartoons have no thematic connections to the essays with which they appear suggests that the cartoons and the essays are intended as different and unrelated types of communication.

The humorous cartoons in *WAR* supply highly condensed and simplified communications of its racial attitudes and programs. The proverb about the quantitative relationship of pictures to words holds true. A single cartoon communicates White Aryan Resistance attitudes toward blacks or Jews, and about what the White Aryan Resistance feels might best be done with the members of such groups, succinctly. There is no necessity for lengthy exposition. Anyone perusing the newspaper or the Web site would need only a few seconds to gauge the temper of the publication.

The cartoons are deliberately "in-your-face" communications. *WAR* prides itself on the "racist" and "offensive" nature of its artwork.[51] Because they expose rather than disguise, the cartoons communicate to the readership that racism can be and should be open and explicit. They show that there is nothing to fear from liberals, the politically correct, or the law. They demonstrate that explicit racist expression is a right protected under the Constitution. Thus, the cartoons seek to establish racist caricature and epithet as a part of public rather than surreptitious discourse. They encourage others to be more open and feel less shame about their racism. They attempt to create a climate—perhaps even a culture—of racism.[52] By means of this brazen and public defiance of convention, the leaders of the racist movements lay claim to their leadership roles.[53]

While the above might help to explain *WAR*'s heavy reliance on graphic art, it does not necessarily explain the predilection for humor. After all, nonhumorous cartoons may be as succinct and sensational as humorous ones. I would suggest that humorous communications do more than communicate the messages they contain. Humor implies a community; a fellowship of laughers with whom the humor is shared. Although humor may educate, it is not a formal means of instruction. It is not the means by which people are *persuaded* to adopt particular views. Humor, rather, calls upon individuals to invoke an extant body of tacit, everyday knowledge in order to recognize and make sense of an incongruity. Humor succeeds only if individuals are made to access concepts, associations, and values with which they are already familiar. An essay may try to persuade, but there is no assurance that anyone other than the author is as yet persuaded. The fact that an effort at persuasion is undertaken suggests that consensus does not yet exist. Humor, however, implies the presence of those with similar ideas and kindred values.[54] To laugh at the cartoons is to imagine—rightly or wrongly—other laughers like oneself.[55] Since the readers of *WAR* constitute no organized group—indeed the readership seems largely composed of marginal, lonely, and isolated individuals[56]—it is likely that such a sense of community is desperately needed.[57]

The fact that hate groups make abundant use of humor should not be misunderstood. It does not establish some inherent connection between humor and aggression. Indeed, the notion that the function of humor is to disguise aggression is belied by the humor of the White Aryan Resistance. White Aryan Resistance humor disguises nothing. The hatred and fantasies of violence are visible to all. They are reiterated in essay after essay and drawing after drawing, both serious and nonserious. This does not mean that humor never serves to mask aggression, to "evade restrictions and open sources of pleasure that have become inaccessible," as Freud suggested.[58] At the same time, it would be dangerous to assume that the presence of humor always betrays some hidden or unrecognized hostility. When humor is hostile, the motive is more than likely to be conscious and the effects deliberate. Conversely, when a purveyor of humor claims no hostile intention, the claim might be seriously entertained in the absence of compelling evidence to the contrary. Humor is like a sharp knife. It can be turned to dozens of practical uses, but only some of them aim at injury and destruction.

5. Blond Ambitions and Other Signs of the Times

In the last few decades a new attitude has emerged in the United States toward humor. Once thought a crucial aspect of the well-rounded personality, humor has increasingly become problematic as jokes and other forms of humorous expression have been tied to the meanest of motives and implicated in the creation of all sorts of baleful effects. This shift in attitude has had very concrete consequences. In rules and regulations governing conduct in the workplace, jokes have been identified as forms of intimidation—as expressions that often demand a spirited response, whether informal and personal or formal and judicial. Jokes are regularly cited in complaints and suits charging harassment and are frequently accepted as evidence of such harassment.[1] At one institution, 70 percent of women who reported being harassed identified sexual jokes as a common form of that harassment.[2]

A recent book on sexual harassment includes a section on jokes. While acknowledging "the fine line between delighting and offending," and realizing that perceptions are "intensely personal," the authors nevertheless declare that jokes can be forms of harassment. "Whether a joke told in the workplace crosses the line from good-humored to mean-spirited depends first on its contents," for many jokes, they assert, are built around "racist, homophobic, and sexist punchlines."[3]

Such attitudes about jokes have crystallized in the absence of any close analysis of the communicative properties of jokes. There is a presumption that the interpretation of jokes is a rather straightforward affair. Our easy familiarity with jokes, as both tellers and auditors, undoubtedly instills the belief that their meanings are self-evident and can be apprehended in a fairly direct fashion. In fact, jokes and punch lines are not in themselves "racist, homophobic and sexist." Jokes may invoke explicit and disparaging language and images about race and sex, but these in themselves do not transparently reflect the attitudes or motives of their tellers.

Jokes are highly ambiguous forms of communication. Jokes are grounded in a system of relations that are "appropriately incongruous" and thus to some extent self-contradictory. The techniques of jokes would be rejected were they employed in logical argument.[4] Jokes are a species of play, and messages lodged within the play frame are often obscure.[5] Even when particular ideas raised by a joke can be precisely identified, the position of the joke teller with respect to these ideas may be uncertain. Consequently, jokes are not transparent and their messages may not be simple, clear, or unambiguous.

In 1991 a cycle of jokes swept across the United States. These jokes centered on the figure of the dumb blond and were usually referred to as "dumb-blond jokes." These jokes were, for the most part, riddle-jokes; that is, jokes with the question-answer structure of the riddle. Some of them continue to be told today.

"Weed's Enormous List of Blonde Jokes," a rather extensive collection of jokes posted on the Internet,[6] probably gives a fair representation of the dumb-blond cycle. The jokes trade on a few major scripts that are iterated in a majority of the jokes and a number of minor ones represented much less frequently:

> Q: Why should blondes not be given coffee breaks?
> A: It takes too long to retrain them. (#20)
>
> Q: How can you tell if a blonde's been using the computer?
> A: There's white-out on the screen. (#21)
>
> Q: What did the blonde say when she found out she was pregnant?
> A: "Are you sure it's mine?" (#86)
>
> Q: What did the blonde name her pet zebra?
> A: Spot. (#150)

Each of these jokes asks the listener to imagine stupidities so incongruous as to be absurd: having to relearn one's job after a fifteen-minute coffee break; using correction fluid on the screen of the computer; wondering whether a child you are carrying is yours;[7] calling a striped animal Spot. Nevertheless, each of the stupidities is not entirely incongruous; each has its own measure of appropriateness that creates the joke. A coffee break is a duration of time, and things can be forgotten over time; correction fluid is used to fix typing errors; the question "whose child is it?" is one associated with the discovery of pregnancy; and Spot is a traditional name for a pet.

In the jokes, blonds are not merely stupid, nor is blondness simply a sign of stupidity. Blondness is the physical incarnation of stupidity. To escape blondness is to escape this benighted state, if only in an artificial way:

Q: What do you call it when a blonde dies [*sic*] their [*sic*] hair brunette?
A: Artificial intelligence. (#5)

But blonds in blond jokes are not merely stupid. They are sexually active. They invite sex. They will engage in sex with single or multiple partners almost anywhere. They relish oral sex, both as givers and receivers:

Q: What's the mating call of the blonde?
A: "I'm *sooo* drunk!" (#42)

Q: What is the mating call of the ugly blonde?
A: (Screaming) "I said: I'm drunk!" (#43)

Q: Why do blondes drive cars with sunroofs?
A: More leg room. (#62)

Q: What did the blonde's mom say to her before the blonde's date?
A: If you're not in bed by 12, come home. (#121)

Q: What's the difference between a blonde and "The Titanic"?
A: They know how many men went down on "The Titanic." (#103)

Q: What do blondes say after sex?
A: Thanks, Guys. (#64)

Q: How can you tell when a blonde is dating?
A: By the buckle print on her forehead. (#197)

A subsidiary sexual script in the blond jokes is that men have no interest in blonds beyond the sex they provide. Men are not jealous or protective of them nor do they develop relationships with them on any other level. They are only good for sex. They are to be used and disposed of.

Q: Why do blondes have vaginas?
A: So men will talk to them at parties. (#352)

Q: What do you call the irritating part around the blonde's vagina?
A: The blonde. (#137)

Q: How is a blonde like a postage stamp?
A: You lick 'em, stick 'em, and send 'em on their way. (#377)

Q: What's the difference between a blonde and a toilet?
A: A toilet won't follow you around after you use it. (#182)

Q: Why do blondes find it difficult to marry?
A: Because you don't have to marry them for sex. (#125)

Q: What's the difference between a blonde and a Porsche?
A: You don't lend the Porsche out to your friend.

A very few of the jokes suggest that blonds engage in sex only as a strategy to attract men. Their easy sexual ways end with marriage.

Q: Why did the blonde smile when she walked [down] the marriage aisle?
A: Because she realized she gave her last blowjob. (#167)

Q: How do you paralyze a blonde from the neck down?
A: Marry her. (#272)

Q: What's the difference between a blonde and your job?
A: Your job still sucks after 6 months. (#185)

A small set of jokes also suggests that the blond is vain and self-centered.

Q: Why do blondes like lightning?
A: They think someone is taking their picture. (#281)

Q: How do you drown a blonde?
A: Put a mirror at the bottom of the pool. (#116)

Q: What did the blonde say when she knocked over the priceless Ming vase?
A: It's OK Daddy, I'm not hurt. (#250)

This last joke is a clear recycling of a Jewish American Princess (JAP) joke. There are several on Weed's dumb-blond joke list. Recycled Polish jokes are prominent in the dumb-blond repertoire because they share the stupidity script.[8] It is harder to explain the appearance of JAP jokes, since JAP scripts emphasize selfishness, frigidity, an aversion to sex (particularly oral sex), and an inclination to dominate or devalue their men. These characteristics are contrary to the dominant portrayal of the blond in the jokes as someone who is sexually giving, engages freely in oral sex, and seems somewhat dependent on men. The JAP jokes that do appear in Weed's list tend to emphasize the JAP's self-centeredness and rarely invoke the sexually frigid script.[9] In addition to Polish and JAP jokes it is easy to recognize other recycled jokes, including "Little Moron jokes," "Conundrums,"[10] "Confucius jokes,"[11] "Medical Terminology for the Layman,"[12] and a variety of other old chestnuts.

Although lists of jokes posted in cyberspace provide a useful means of recording and distributing such ephemeral cycles as dumb-blond jokes, they do not provide any sense of the frequency with which individual jokes on a list are performed. Compilers of joke lists are often "collectors" and tend to include any joke they perceive as relating to the defined topic. A joke that may have been performed only once will hold the same place on the list as a joke told thousands of times. Consequently, no single text can be said to be pivotal in the interpretation of the repertoire. The list must be approached statistically, identifying the dominant scripts. In Weed's list of dumb-blond jokes, 51 percent of the 404 total jokes utilize the stupidity script (justifying the name of the joke cycle) while 28 percent utilize the sexual-promiscuity script. Only 3 percent of the jokes are of the JAP type. Another 3 percent reflect the male attitude toward dumb blonds. Of the remaining categories, each represents less than 2 percent of the repertoire.[13] It is clear that the stupidity and sexuality scripts together inform the great majority of the repertoire and constitute the core of the problem in the interpretation of the joke cycle as a whole.

What do these jokes mean? What are they about? There is no shortage of opinion. Scholars, journalists, and columnists have weighed in on the question, albeit in sound-bite-sized commentaries. For some, dumb-blond jokes constitute an attack on blond women. Miss Manners felt that blond jokes were insults, plain and simple, that should not be tolerated. One need not pretend to take such jokes in good humor. They should be rejected outright. Blond jokes are told "under the assumption that people who are blonde are so busy being happy about it that they do not notice attacks."[14] Others also saw in these jokes an attack—an unfair attack—on blonds. One eighth-grader in the state of Washington actually conducted an experiment to prove that blonds were not stupid. She surveyed 270 male and female eighth-graders about their hair color and their grade-point averages. She discovered that blonds had the highest combined grade-point average, followed by brunets and redheads. The editorial, in which this experiment was reported, concluded: "We now know that blondes aren't dumb. Dumb-blonde jokes are."[15]

Still others have suggested that blonds are one of the few safe targets for joking in a politically correct society. It is not objectively clear that blonds have suffered because of their hair color. "Blondes are not included in the protected groups covered by civil-rights laws. . . . Blondes are Caucasians . . . and fair game."[16] In fact, a few have suggested that blond jokes are a retaliation for the special status blonds have enjoyed in our culture, particularly for the attention they have received from men. The jokes, according to this view, constitute something of a brunet backlash.[17]

Perhaps the most persistent opinion has been that dumb-blond jokes are really about women in general. "They reinforce all the sexist stereotypes. . . . They aren't Dumb Blonde Jokes. They are Dumb Woman jokes and there is nothing new about them," said an editor at the *Washington Post.*[18] Betty Friedan, who characterized herself as a feminist who insisted on her right to be frivolous and humorous, found nothing funny about them: "In the face of the erosion of women's rights—by the Bush administration, by the Supreme Court, by the state judges, by the mass media—I don't think the new spate of jokes about women is very funny.[19] A Boston University humor scholar, Joseph Boskin, saw the jokes as a continuation of an earlier reaction against feminism. "Every time a group moves up in American culture—blacks, women, or Polish people—there is a corresponding intense joke cycle against them."[20] Given this point of view, it is not surprising that blond jokes have been used in workshops to heighten the awareness of women to abuse and have served as the basis for sexual harassment complaints.[21]

But as the old song goes, "Is that all there is?" Are we left to decide among these possibilities for the meaning of the dumb-blond joke repertoire? A few problems should be noted with some of the interpretations that have been summarized above. It is very difficult to accommodate the view that blond jokes are an assault on blonds that accurately reflects American male or female attitudes of blond intelligence or sexuality. In the first place, I doubt many people sincerely adhere to such views. The dumb blond is a literary conceit and not a sociological category. It is ironic that an eighth-grader, in her effort to prove that blonds were not really dumb, succeeded in demonstrating that hair color *can* be used as an indicator of intelligence. In approaching the blond conceit sociologically rather than semiotically, she produced *data* that have now to be explained. Where the dumb blond had only been a sign, the dumb redhead became a sociological fact. The eighth-grader did not demolish the theory of the dumb blond. In a sense, she made it real, only changing hair color in the process.[22]

If the dumb and promiscuous blond is merely a conceit generally not held to be a credible representation of real blonds, what is the source of the image? Certainly it predates Clairol's advertising slogan, "Is it true blondes have more fun?" or Marilyn Monroe's, Jane Mansfield's, and Goldie Hawn's film careers. Hair color has long been a marker of intellectual and emotional qualities. Blond hair probably gained its current semiotic status from disparate yet convergent chains of signification. One is the ancient association in Western civilizations of light, golden, and fair with purity and innocence.[23] As purity is connected with innocence, and innocence with naivete, the step to stupidity more generally is not a great one.[24] The Western emphasis on the dichotomy of body and soul also probably contributed to the association of blondness with stupidity. Physical beauty comes to be regarded as independent of and even incompatible with mind. To the extent that blonds are held to be more beautiful, they are concomitantly viewed as less intelligent. This is true not only of women. The cycle of Dan Quayle jokes—which also emphasized a stupidity script—was due in part to his being blond, but even more to those suggestions in the press that he was chosen as a vice presidential candidate simply because of his good looks.[25]

The association of blondness with promiscuous sexuality is likewise ancient. In the fourth century B.C., the playwright Menander suggested that "A chaste woman ought not to dye her hair yellow."[26] In ancient Rome, women were dyeing their hair or purchasing blond wigs in the German fashion. The Latin poet Martial commented about Messalina, the unfaithful wife of Emperor Claudius: "Her toilet table contained a hundred lies; and while she was in Rome, her hair was blushing by the Rhine." In a quip about another woman, Martial versified: "The golden hair that Galla wears / Is hers—who would have thought it? / She swears 'tis hers, and true she swears / For I know where she bought it."[27]

Thus two thousand years ago, blond hair was associated with innocence and beauty *and* with artifice and deception. Notions of deception lead naturally to ideas of sexual deception and to promiscuity. The image is certainly fixed in a sixteenth-century English epigram: "Fair and sluttish (or foolish), black and proud, long and lazy, little and loud."[28] Blondness in contemporary society is also regularly connected with artificiality and duplicity. A dictionary of definitions gives only three for "blond," each a comic observation on its artificiality: "A brunette with a top secret"; "An abbreviation for peroxide of hydrogen"; and "The cross between a brunette and a drugstore."[29] Jokes in the dumb-blond repertoire also regularly allude to the fact that blondness is often a question of culture rather than nature.[30]

Blond jokes are not an attack on blond people. They do not reflect genuine opinions about people with blond hair. Nor do the blond jokes constitute some sort of brunet conspiracy. There is no indication that brunets tell them more frequently than other groups. In fact, blonds themselves seem to relish telling them. Blonds also hear them from their nonblond friends.[31] It is not difficult to understand why. It is not a matter of blond self-hatred.[32] The dumb-blond script, like most joke scripts, is not seriously entertained. It is regarded as hyperbole. As the entertainer Dolly Parton commented, "I am not offended at all by the jokes because I know I'm not dumb. I think they're funny."[33] Blonds and their friends know blonds for what they are. Blonds are neither remarkably stupid nor particularly promiscuous. The jokes are funny and fun to share precisely because they are dealing with a literary conceit and not a sociological truth.

I am somewhat skeptical of the notion that dumb blonds appeared in this cycle of jokes just because they were considered "safe" targets in this era of political correctness. In the first place, it is not clear that most joke tellers concern themselves with such niceties. When joke tellers sense that their jokes are likely to offend and cause social disruption, they don't tell them. They save them for those they know will enjoy them and not be offended. Second, blond jokes hardly passed without criticism. "No injustice stung more than the dumb-blonde jokes," was the opinion of one female comedian, of all people.[34] Feminists denounced the jokes as "a manifestation of a new misogyny."[35] One Arizona twelve-year-old saw the jokes as "prejudice against all blondes" and set out to eliminate the jokes at her school. Referring to one blond joke (#190), the blond sixth-grader noted that she was on the honor roll and did not need to climb over a glass wall to see what was on the other side.[36]

So what are we left with? the idea that dumb-blond jokes are an assault against women? a violent reaction against their empowerment and their encroachment into male preserves? a continuation of the attack against feminism? This feminist perspective is based on the fact that blond attributes are evaluated negatively and that the jokes erupted during a period of radical expansion in the political and economic roles of women in the United States. There are, however, two aspects of the blond jokes that this perspective does not address. One is that in the joke texts, brunets are distinguished from blonds. Blonds do not seem to stand for all women, only some women. Brunets do not share their attributes. Why is this distinction made in the jokes, and what significance should it be accorded in their interpretation? The second aspect of the jokes that is never addressed is why the blond is chosen as the vehicle for this assault. Why would an attack against women emphasize stupidity and sexuality almost exclusively? The list of negative human traits is potentially long, but stupidity and sexuality are emphasized almost to the exclusion of all others. (Recall that other traits constitute 4 percent or less of the analyzed corpus of blond jokes, whereas stupidity and sexuality are 51 percent and 28 percent, respectively.) An adequate interpretation of the blond-joke cycle needs to address these questions.

Joke cycles are not really about particular groups who are ostensibly their targets. These groups serve merely as signifiers that hold together a discourse on certain ideas and values that are of current concern. Polish jokes, Italian jokes, and JAP jokes are less comments about real Poles, Italians, or Jewish women then they are about a particular set of values attributed to these groups.[37] The attributions, while not entirely arbitrary, are, for the most part, not seriously entertained. Poles were probably accorded the stupidity script because they were perceived as overrepresented in economically inferior occupations and lacking in social and geographical mobility.[38] The jokes did not appear and spread because Poles were perceived as pushing into and threatening an established middle class.[39] (In fact, Poles, perceived as holding to blue-collar occupations and bounded ethnic neighborhoods, posed no threat to the middle class at all.) Italians were characterized as cowards because of the disastrous record of their armies in African campaigns before and during World War II. As individuals, Italians were not and are not regarded as cowards. Rather, Italian armies were seen as ineffectual, largely, it would seem, because Italians were reluctant to sacrifice their lives in the service of a state to which they felt no particular allegiance.[40] Jews were undoubtedly the target for the JAP jokes because of the perceived material and social success of the Jewish community since their emigration from Eastern Europe[41] and the impression that Jews are overconcerned with and overprotective of their children.

In sum, blond jokes are not really about blonds. The blond is merely a "placeholder" for joking about a particular set of values for which the blond is regarded as a symbolically appropriate—though not a sociologically accurate—representation. The values the jokes focus upon are an extreme lack of intelligence and indiscriminate sexual activity. Why this combination? Because these are precisely the values that are antithetical to the values of the workaday world. As women have moved into the workplace and into positions of power in the public sphere, they must be dissociated from images of ineptitude and sexuality. The workplace is theoretically and semiotically a world of rationality, calculation, organization, and cool efficiency. It is not a world that can accommodate stupidity or the disruptive forces of sexuality.[42] In other words, women in the workplace should not in any way suggest that they are reminiscent of the dumb blond. They must be the stereotypical brunet: competent, intelligent, and asexual.[43] The dumb-blond jokes are not about blonds, nor are they about women per se. Rather they exaggerate and make foolish values associated with traditional images of women. The jokes play with a set of values no longer in tune with a much-changed world.

This interpretation has several features to recommend it over those others previously considered. First, it does not simply categorize the jokes as disparaging and proceed from that point to search for some obvious target. It asks why the jokes invoke the particular scripts that they do and what those scripts might signify. Second, it does not overlook the opposition between blonds and brunets in the jokes. It makes sense of the distinction. Third, it helps to understand why blonds and brunets, both men and women, would tell the jokes. All who share the jokes regard the jokes as playful manipulations of moral values rather than as attacks on a real social group. Last, and perhaps most important, there is evidence to support this interpretation.

The evidence is of two types. One is admittedly anecdotal. The writer Liesl Schillinger noted her feelings and experiences after changing her hair color from blond back to brunet. It seems the blond jokes themselves motivated Schillinger to consider the meaning of her blondness in the context of the workplace. An offhanded comment by a female reporter who thought Schillinger's hair would be darker, and Schillinger's sense that some of her darker-haired colleagues lunched on occasion with the bosses, precipitated her transformation. Schillinger describes her transformation as instantaneous. "I worked harder, felt tougher, and enjoyed the new sensation of frightening strangers. Within a month, I got a raise. I sensed not only that I was being perceived as a more serious and daunting person, but that I had become one. I realized that when I was blonde, I hadn't quite taken myself seriously. I was someone who was looking for easy approbation, and I had known it."[44] Schillinger also noted that as a brunet, fewer men paid attention to her, although she claimed that those who did seemed of higher quality.[45]

Liesl Schillinger's little memoir reveals her own sense of the blond as a sign of the easy, the inept, and the sexual. It is difficult to say whether Schillinger would have been taken more seriously at the office and gotten her raise had she worked harder and taken herself more seriously *as a blond*. Nevertheless, the point is clear. The values signified by blondness are incompatible with the world of work. Although Schillinger neither gives a description nor attempts any analysis of blond jokes, I think she might read them very much as I am suggesting.

The other evidence that I would adduce for this interpretation of the blond jokes is sociological. It depends upon looking at other types that are assigned similar joke scripts. One such type is the "BYU coed," a female student attending Brigham Young University.[46] One major characterization of the BYU coed in jokes is that she is overweight, ugly, and consequently undesirable.

> How does a BYU coed put on a bra?
> She finds her belly button, then counts up three folds.
>
> What do you call a three-hundred-pound coed?
> Anorexic.
>
> Why were the coeds' swimming suits at BYU changed from blue to red?
> Because too many coeds were being harpooned.
>
> Why does the BYU coed wear platform shoes?
> So her knuckles won't drag on the ground
>
> What's the difference between BYU's homecoming queen and a pig?
> The pig doesn't have acne.
>
> Why doesn't the devil bother possessing BYU coeds?
> He's evil, but not desperate.

Despite this characterization, the BYU coed is on the prowl. She has come to the university in search of a man and not a degree.

Trying to get married at BYU is liking trying to get a drink out of a fire hydrant.

The diamond is one of the hardest minerals known. It can even make an impression on a BYU coed.

Q: What's the definition of a BYU coed?
A: A finger looking for a ring.

These scripts have attached themselves to BYU coeds because they attend a Mormon university. The Mormon church promotes early marriage for its members and the prompt establishment of families. Motherhood and homemaking are held by the church to be more important than a woman's profession or career. Thus, the idea that a BYU coed is in search of a husband, rather than a degree, makes sense in the context of a Mormon university in a way that it would not elsewhere. For if a BYU coed's ultimate end is to become a homemaker and mother, what else could her tenure at the university serve to achieve?

The desire of the BYU coed to find a husband and her purported repulsiveness are compatible, rather than contradictory, joke scripts. It is the very desire of the coed to acquire a man in the jokes that makes her unattractive. After all, were she were truly attractive, she would not need to pursue a man. Men would pursue her.[47]

Because the coed is in pursuit of a man, other scripts become applicable as well. The BYU coed is also stupid and promiscuous.

Q: What's the difference between a BYU toilet and a coed?
A: When you're done using a toilet, it doesn't follow you around.

Q: What does a BYU coed put behind her ears to make herself more attractive?
A: Her ankles.

Q: Why don't BYU coeds vote?
A: They don't care who gets in.

Q: What are the best two years of a coed's life?
A: The first grade.

Q: What do you call it when a fly lands in the ear of a BYU coed?
A: Space invader.

Q: What did the BYU coed say after her boyfriend blew in her ear?
A: Thanks for the refill.

These last jokes are identical or similar to blond jokes, but they antedate the blond-joke cycle by at least six or seven years.

The sexual and stupidity scripts that are assigned to the BYU coed are also assigned to a more generic "sorority girl." Sororities were often perceived to be organizations that women joined to socialize and meet men of a certain social class. Like the BYU coed, the sorority girl was imagined as focusing more on social and matrimonial than intellectual accomplishment.[48]

BYU coeds and sorority girls are assigned their joke scripts because they are imagined as pursuing traditional, rather than progressive, female agendas. The college environment in which they find themselves is not for education or preparation for the workaday world. They are out to get a man. College is merely the environment in which this pursuit takes place. Consequently, they are assigned the same scripts as blonds, for, like blonds, their success is reckoned as more dependent upon the use of their bodies than upon the use of their minds.

When the blond jokes arrived in England, their scripts were assigned to girls from Essex. The scripts, and many of the joke texts, were the same.

> Q: What's the difference between an Essex girl and directory enquiries [telephone-number information]?
> A: You can sometimes get through to directory enquiries.
>
> Q: What's the difference between an Essex girl and a supermarket trolley?
> A: A supermarket trolley has a mind of its own.
>
> Q: What's the difference between the Queen and an Essex girl?
> A: Only one stranger has been in the Queen's bedroom.[49]
>
> Q: What's the first thing an Essex girl does after waking up?
> A: Introduces herself.[50]

Essex is the heavily populated county to the northeast of London. Essex girls come to be signifiers only by way of Essex men. "Essex Man" was characterized in the *Sunday Telegraph* sometime in 1990. He was of lower-class East End origins and newly affluent, but without any of the cultural refinements or liberal tendencies that might be expected to accompany upward mobility. "Culturally barren and mildly brutish," was one characterization. Essex Man was seen as the bedrock of Thatcher conservatism.[51]

The image of Essex Man was picked up by other papers and advertisers, who tried to define Essex Man characteristics in specific sociological terms. "'Essex Man' has a higher disposable income than the traditionally well-off classes. . . . Middle class values make you poor. . . . Middle-[class] houses, and so mortgages, tend to be large, and middle-class children go on to higher education, whereas Essex Man's children go to work at 16, carry on living at home, and contribute to the household income."[52] "Essex Man is singularly unimpressed with the trappings of old money. He is honest about his wealth and intent on enjoying it."[53]

Essex Man did not spawn a joke cycle. He was regarded not as a sign but as a real sociological category. In fact, he was but one in a line of "affluent workers" described by British sociologists. The income of these workers equaled or surpassed the income of those in the traditional middle class, but they maintained the fertility, kinship, and social patterns of the working classes and thought of themselves as working-class.[54] When the cycle of blond jokes sought an appropriate local signifier in England, the Essex girl was a logical choice.

Coming from a home that had middle-class income but lacked middle-class values, the Essex girl had no interest in education or culture. She lived at home, had money from her job to spend on clothes and entertainment, and had no career aspirations beyond marriage (which was likely to be with a member of her class).[55] In other words, the Essex girl—imagined as yet another type that pursued a traditional rather than a progressive social agenda—could easily service the stupidity and sexuality scripts of the blond-joke cycle.

There is good reason to reconsider some of the knee-jerk interpretations of blond jokes that were published and republished in newspapers and magazines across the country in the early 1990s. Blond jokes were not some broad-scale attack on women. They were not a response to the threat that women, as women, posed in the workplace. They were about a set of values associated with traditional images of women that were inimical to workplace culture. If anything, it might be argued that the jokes showed that women could and would be accepted as long as they were willing to embrace the coolness, rationality, and efficiency of the modern workaday world.

Blonds, BYU coeds, sorority girls, and Essex girls are not real sociological categories. They are signs—signs of the times. They serve as loci for the crystallization of values in a world where the roles of women have significantly changed. These values are manipulated in jokes to define the boundaries of this world and register new expectations for the role of female intellect and sexuality in contemporary society.[56]

6. Humor and the Suppression of Sentiment

"UNDER THE MASK of humor, our society allows infinite aggressions, by everyone against everyone." "At the root of a great many jokes . . . lies a deep-seated hostility and a desire to degrade." "American humor is violent—and often sexist, racist, brutal and disgusting as well."[1] These contemporary characterizations of humor as aggression are, of course, typical, and the catalog could be easily extended. The perspective they embody derives directly from Sigmund Freud's observation on the tendentious joke in *Jokes and Their Relation to the Unconscious* that "there are only two purposes that it may serve. . . . It is either a *hostile* joke (serving the purpose of aggressiveness, satire, or defence) or an *obscene* joke (serving the purpose of exposure)."[2] That humor would seem to be at the command of less than seemly motives was hardly original with Freud. Freud's particular accomplishments on the topic were the close analysis of particular jokes and their techniques; the delineation of the deep analogy between jokes and dreams; and the integration of humor into a comprehensive theory of the mind. That theory asserted that the rational, conscious mind was directed by powerful, unconscious, sexual, and aggressive impulses,[3] impulses that must be repressed or suppressed for the creation and maintenance of civilization. By distracting the forces of repression and suppression, the techniques of humor permit the expression of sexual interests and hostile intentions in another guise. The individual is thus reallied with forbidden sources of infantile pleasure, but in a way that does not threaten the structure of social relations.[4] These are the ideas that underlie much of the scholarly as well as current popular understandings of the nature and function of humor.

Within a grand psychological theory such as Freud's, it is difficult to imagine what human impulses, other than sex and aggression, could warrant severe suppression or repression. What other emotions, after all, threaten society so fundamentally and necessitate such strict control? What, besides sex and aggression, would need to seek expression under a guise of humor? These questions are difficult to answer. Still, instead of broaching the problem on the level of a universal psychology, the questions might be reformulated with parameters of time and place. That is, instead of asking "What human impulses need to be suppressed in the interests of society?" one might be led to ask "Other than sex and aggression, what is repressed or prohibited in contemporary American society that might find its expression in humor?" In this form, the question demands the consideration of solutions that are necessarily local and historical.

In this form, the question can also be readily answered, and the answer that most immediately springs to mind is "sentiment." By sentiment, I mean feelings of goodness, affection, tenderness, admiration, sympathy, and compassion. I employ the term "sentimentality" to refer to the constellation of these sentiments as well as the larger psychological and philosophical context in which they were expressed, appreciated, and understood. I contend that as sentiments and sentimentality have been criticized and suppressed in modern society, they have had to develop special channels for their expression. Humor is one of those channels.

The primary definition of "sentimentality" in American dictionaries is pejorative. This was not always the case. Sentimentality has a history; and something of this history must be grasped to appreciate the place of sentiment in contemporary American society. Through the eighteenth and much of the nineteenth centuries, the word "sentimental" denoted something positive and good.[5] Sentimentality was an idea that was rooted in the moral philosophy of the eighteenth century. The third earl of Shaftesbury (1671–1713), Adam Smith (1723–90), and David Hume (1711–76) all contributed to the development of an "ethic of feeling." Despite the differences between them, they agreed that reason was an insufficient basis for morality. Morality was less a matter of judgment and calculation than of sensitive and refined feeling. It was the heart rather than the head that discerned and fostered virtue. People were moral not because they obeyed a moral law but because they were motivated by inbred feelings of sympathy, affection, and benevolence. A moral person was simply one who followed the dictates of inner natural passions. Those who did not cut themselves off from their feelings—who trusted their impulses—were inevitably moral.[6]

These eighteenth-century philosophers were to some extent anticipated by the Cambridge Platonists, those seventeenth-century Anglicans who opposed the Calvinist doctrine of man's utter depravity and who championed the view that human beings were made in the image of God and thus shared in his goodness. In their view, virtue was the natural state of the human soul, and virtue—and consequently, human happiness—would proceed from a cultivation of one's inner nature.[7] The emphasis on humanity's inherent goodness promoted by the Cambridge Platonists, coupled with the notion, later championed by the moral philosophers, that this goodness was rooted in sentiments rather than rational judgments, established a new worldview. On the one hand, this worldview disavowed the dour theology of John Calvin and the desperate sociology of Thomas Hobbes. On the other, it tempered the exaltation of human reason,[8] although it still shared the Enlightenment's unbounded optimism. By the middle of the eighteenth century, it could be said that Descartes' "*cogito ergo sum*" had been replaced by Rousseau's "*je sens, donc je suis.*"[9]

This ethic of feeling developed along two distinct paths: one was *sensibility*, the other *sentimentality.*[10] Sensibility was a state of extreme psychological responsiveness both to the world and to the self. The soaring imagination of the sensible soul was scarcely able to tolerate the structures, strictures, and objects of ordinary life. A sensible individual was in retreat from society, inhabiting a wild, desolate, even pagan, nature. Romanticism glorified sensibility. Sentimentality, in contrast, emphasized feeling as the source of goodness, morality, and happiness. These feelings were excited only in the presence of others. The sentimental person was domesticated and thrived in a Christian home and a Christian community.[11] Furthermore, the sentimental person did not displace reason with feeling. The sentiments still were subject to critical review. Even with the noblest of feelings, one could still be guilty of misjudgment and be led astray in the objects of one's sympathies and affections.[12]

Sensibility and sentimentality shared a number of concerns, although the import was different for each. For example, both the sensible and the sentimental soul prized melancholy. Melancholy stirred the sensible soul to soar above the tedium of everyday existence, to escape the bounds of law and convention in the pursuit of a higher wisdom. While sentimentalists shared the romanticist's predilection for the more melancholic aspects of nature and for graveyard poetry, they regarded the contemplation of death, decay, and change as particularly favorable to the moral elevation of the soul. For them, mourning was virtuous and a sign of respectability. They believed the good died young, for they saw death as an escape from suffering and the path to heavenly reward.[13] Furthermore, the dead and dying had the power to save. The sentiments aroused by the death of an innocent could redeem the unregenerate.[14] The heroines in sentimental novels were often to be found attending the dying, sewing shrouds, or otherwise contemplating the paraphernalia of death. Even their beauty was often described as pale, delicate, and, at root, unhealthy.[15]

It was literature, rather than philosophy, that was the great purveyor of the sentimental worldview. Samuel Richardson's novels *Pamela* (1740) and *Clarissa* (1747–48) dwelt upon the virtues of piety, filial duty, humility, and charity and moved women, as well as men, to tears.[16] Persecuted innocence, the heroine's challenge to reform the villain by means of her superior virtue, poetic justice in which rewards and punishments are meted out, protracted scenes of death and dying, and copious tears all found their way into innumerable novels of the subsequent century. Formularization was inevitable. Susanna Rowson (ca. 1762–1824) advised would-be novelists: "Remember to mix a sufficient quantity of sighs, tears, swooning hysterics, and all the moving expressions of heart-rending woe. . . . Be sure you contrive a duel; and if convenient, a suicide might not be amiss."[17] At the same time, she wondered why "novel readers are not tired of reading one story so many times."[18] Victorian sentimental fiction remained true to the eighteenth-century formulas while adding its own peculiar stock characters, sensational situations, and embellishments.[19] Victorians fixated on families and family relations and were positively obsessed with dying children, orphans, and long-suffering women. The point, however, was still to demonstrate the triumph of the good heart and sound judgment over evil and misfortune while arousing in readers an awareness of their own tender sentiments.

The sentimental worldview always had its critics. Samuel Johnson (1709–84) considered human nature to be inherently flawed,[20] and Joseph Butler (1692–1752) argued that morality could not be rooted in the passions but required ascendancy over the passions if it was to control man's coarser tendencies.[21] Sentimental literature came to be criticized as well. By the beginning of the nineteenth century, the word "sentimental" had acquired a pejorative sense. One critic in 1802 felt bound to distinguish Richardson's works from the "froth and sentiment" in the novels of his day.[22] Anthony Trollope (1815–82) dismissed Charles Dickens as "Mr. Sentiment."[23] Indeed, sentimentality came to be parodied. One magazine printed a bogus prospectus for a "History of Weeping" in ten volumes, with an entire volume devoted to novel writing and the classification of literary tears—salt tears, bitter tears, sweet tears, sweet bitter tears, salt delicious tears, and so on.[24] These criticisms and parodies only indicated how firmly the sentimental worldview was rooted in the popular mind. Throughout the nineteenth century, sentimental prose and poetry reigned supreme, and "Mr. Sentiment" was perhaps the single most popular novelist of his century.

Thomas Carlyle (1795–1881) offered one of the most sustained critiques of Victorian sentimentality. Although he also believed feelings to be a source of virtue, he did not hold human nature to be innately good. Rather it was a battleground in which good and evil forces struggled for supremacy. The ability to sincerely respond through feeling was only one aspect of that nature—one that needed to be encouraged—but still only one. Furthermore, Carlyle regarded the emotional expenditures of sentimentality as largely misplaced, devoid of moral purpose, and cut off from moral action. In his view, the preoccupation with "feeling about feeling" necessarily remained one step removed from feeling itself. Sentimentality depended upon an extreme self-consciousness and reflected an unbridled egoism. It was insincere. Even benevolence he regarded as merely a means for evading social responsibility. Carlyle demanded that the gap be closed between feeling and action.[25]

Carlyle had little impact upon the sentimentality of his day.[26] The continual sniping at sentimentality throughout the nineteenth century actually did little to undermine it. The discrediting of sentimentality had to await the twentieth century. And perhaps no single philosopher contributed more to the destruction of Victorian sentimentality than Sigmund Freud.

Freud's psychology of the unconscious undermined some of the most cherished icons and values of Victorian culture. First and foremost was Freud's vivisection of the Victorian family. Held together in a harmonious and mutually beneficial fashion by bonds of affection and moral principle, the Victorian family had offered sanctuary from the sphere of work and the capitalistic competition that defined nineteenth-century Economic Man.[27] But in place of the idealized image of rational, pedagogic father; protective, self-sacrificing mother; and sweet, innocent child entwined in a web of sentimental relations, Freud substituted a family romance impelled by desire and the will to murder.

The child was no innocent but a sexual being. Indeed, in Freud's view the child was a sexually *perverse* being—orally, anally, and genitally eroticized for the fulfillment of its own narcissistic pleasures. The child's love for its parent was not virtuous but incestuous. The respect it paid to its parent masked a deep and potentially homicidal rivalry. The parents were no less guilty—their attachments to the child and to one another were composed of equally wild and ambivalent emotions that they could scarcely recognize or understand.

It was not just the icon of the family that psychoanalysis destroyed. Freud's psychology delegitimized the sentiments themselves. Love, the sentiment underpinning the whole of the Victorian worldview, was reduced to base sexuality. The line between the virtues and the vices, upon which Victorian morality depended, was obliterated. The instincts would prove the common origin of both bravery and cowardice, of kindness and cruelty.[28] After all, affection, admiration, and respect were merely repressed sexual impulses.[29] Compassion originated in narcissism,[30] while melancholy and mourning offered satisfactions that were largely sadistic.[31] Religious piety was precariously close to obsessional neurosis.[32] Morality itself, in Freud's view, was nothing more than society's bulwark against its own destructive instincts.[33]

Freud was no lover of humanity, nor was he particularly optimistic about its future. His psychoanalytic therapy promised no salvation. It might allow a person to develop some distance from the world—even from the most beloved objects in it—and become "a student of . . . guilt and innocence";[34] but it could not make a person happy. At best, it might succeed in converting personal miseries into "common unhappiness."[35] Freud's legacy to the twentieth century was the notion of Psychological Man—a person who might be understood only in terms of some hidden, inner life. The most refined thoughts were not what they seemed. The noblest sentiments were not to be trusted. Everything he or she did was to some extent neurotic, deeply implicated in the pathological and the perverse.[36] After Freud, a person would never quite look or feel the same. "In a unique and subtle way," Freud taught us "how to grow unsentimental about ourselves."[37]

The portrait of human nature and society painted by Freud was no less dark than that painted by Thomas Hobbes some two and a half centuries before. It is no wonder that Freud's conception of humor as aggression was anticipated in Hobbes's notion of humor as "sudden glory"—that is, as the "apprehension of some deformed thing in another" that, through comparison, suddenly reveals some eminence in the self.[38] This kinship between Freud and Hobbes can be reckoned through the era of sentimentality that separated them. Sentimentality rebelled against the philosophy of Hobbes in emphasizing the goodness and morality of man's inner nature.[39] Freud deprived sentimentality of the very concepts and beliefs in which it was grounded. Intellectually, Hobbes and Freud were grandparent and grandchild, bound together by a common enmity.

Freud's psychology had an enormous impact on the popular imagination, particularly in the United States. Freud's name and something of his ideas were known to almost all.[40] Already in the first decades of the twentieth century, his views on sexuality were being widely discussed in the United States. They were publicized in the popular press, often by those who sought to oppose them. Psychoanalytic terminology—libido, Oedipus complex, castration anxiety, slip of the tongue, rationalization, defense mechanism—was adopted into the popular vocabulary. Serious novelists and playwrights were quick to absorb his ideas. While Freud's writings were not always carefully read (if they were read at all) or well understood, his ideas were employed in a general, and increasingly successful, rebellion against Victorianism.[41] Freud's psychology was not altogether a psychology of liberation. In the process of challenging the conventions of Victorian society, he contributed to the creation of a new inhibition—the inhibition of sentiment.

Freud was only one contributor to the creation of this inhibition, however. The discrediting of sentimentality was a larger modernist undertaking in which his psychology played only one—though very important—part.[42] Modernity can in some sense be defined in terms of its rejection and hatred of the past; particularly in terms of its rejection and hatred of bourgeois culture and middle-class values. Modernity repudiated the bourgeois optimism, rationalism, and humanism in which sentimentality was rooted.[43] As sentimentality depended upon the establishment of sympathies, modernity would create distances.[44] Victorian love as a validating emotion would be supplanted by modern angst, while Christian fellowship and community would be abandoned in favor of alienation and existential loneliness. Reason would be suspected as a form of mystification, and Victorian moral certainties would collapse into profound and inexorable doubt.[45]

The modernist attack on sentimentality invoked all Carlyle's earlier criticisms. The best that could be said in favor of sentimentality was that it was innocent and naive.[46] The worst that could be said was that it was hypocritical and brutal.[47] By all accounts, it was inauthentic, self-indulgent, and all too easy. If sentimentality could be tolerated at all, it was only in quotation marks, as a kind of self-conscious, ironical expression—that is, as "camp" or "kitsch."[48]

The modernist perspective in the United States developed in the first decades of the twentieth century among a small and select group of artists and writers. By the end of World War II, modernism, with its profound sense of alienation and its utter repudiation of certainty and virtue, was in complete control. W. H. Auden was shocked by the transformation: "Coming from Europe, my first, my strongest, my most abiding impression is that no body of literature, written at any time or any place, is so uniformly depressing. It is a source of continual astonishment to me that the nation which has the world-wide reputation for being the most optimistic, gregarious, and the freest on earth should see itself through the eyes of its most sensitive members as a society of helpless victims, shady characters, and displaced persons. . . . In novel after novel one encounters heroes without honor or history; heroes who succumb so monotonously to temptation that they cannot truly be said to be tempted at all; heroes who, even if they are successful in a worldly sense, remain nevertheless but the passive recipients of good fortune; heroes whose sole moral virtue is a stoic endurance of pain and disaster."[49] Thus, by 1948, when Auden penned this description, modernism's victory was complete. This victory was not restricted merely to the world of arts and letters. Cynicism, anguish, loneliness, and an overall sense of depression had infected large segments of the general population as well.

To the extent that modernity succeeded in creating an extreme self-consciousness of and uneasiness about sentimentality, modern humans have been left in something of a quandary. They continue to experience feelings of tenderness, affection, admiration, and sympathy. They continue to be moved by the display of these qualities in others. But as modern people, they have also learned to discount these sentiments as "mawkish," "maudlin," "corny," "cornball," "hokey," "schmaltzy," "sloppy," or just plain "sentimental."[50] Those who would claim for themselves any measure of urbanity, education, and sophistication have had to suppress the least trace of their sentimentality.[51]

The situation of a modern, urbane person, however, is not entirely hopeless. Every suppressed impulse discovers its means of expression, and sentiment is no exception. Perhaps the most apt vehicle for the expression of sentiment in the modern world is humor. Humor is singularly suited to circumvent modernist inhibitions of sentiment. First, as a form of intellectual play, humor demands an ability to deal with the things and events of this world—even the most emotionally charged things and events—as ideas to be manipulated within the structure of a joke. Consequently, a level of detachment is a prerequisite for the production and appreciation of humor. Because such detachment is also characteristic of the modernist stance, humor can escape interdictions that would be directed at other forms of sentimental expression.

Second, humor distracts from, diffuses, and deconstructs its underlying thought. Humor, as the perception of an appropriate incongruity, is a self-subverting structure in which ideas are simultaneously presented as incongruous, yet appropriately related.[52] Furthermore, the techniques of humor signal that what is being communicated must to some extent be discounted or ignored.[53] Humor undoes a sentimental, or any sincere, message. It creates ambiguity about whether the intent of an utterance is the communication of an underlying thought or the sharing of its pleasure-producing techniques. That is why the sentimental novels of the previous century were so devoid of humor[54] and why guidelines for the composition of sentimental verse urge the avoidance of even the mildest forms of word play.[55] Because humor and sentiment are at some level antithetical, humor can successfully camouflage the expression of sentiment.

Third, humor has had a long and conspicuous history in the deflation and devaluation of passion and emotion. From William Makepeace Thackeray's poem "Sorrows of Werther"[56] to the bogus advertisement for "History of Weeping" cited earlier to Mark Twain's parody of sentimental verse, "Ode to Stephen Dowling Bots, Dec'd," in *The Adventures of Huckleberry Finn*,[57] to Ambrose Bierce, who in *The Devil's Dictionary* defined "Love" as "a temporary insanity cured by marriage" and "Emotion" as "a prostrating disease . . . sometimes accompanied by a copious discharge of hydrated chloride of sodium from the eyes,"[58] to Morris Bishop's "Ozymandias Revisited"[59] and Ogden Nash's "To a Small Boy Standing on My Shoes While I Am Wearing Them"[60] right up to the cruel jokes and black comedy of the 1950s and 1960s, humor—particularly American humor—had more than established its anti-emotional and anti-sentimental credentials. As a vehicle for the communication of sentiment, humor was very likely to be above suspicion.

A fourth reason that humor could serve to circumvent the inhibitions on the expression of sentiment was the widespread acceptance of Freud's theory of humor. If the essence of humor is popularly regarded to be aggression, humor could scarcely be in the service of the gentler sentiments. Consequently, when humor is employed to mask sentimental expression, its outward form is often framed as hostile, aggressive, or otherwise unpleasant; but the hostility, aggression, and unpleasantness are, in fact, forms of irony. They are not meant to be taken at face value.

The evidence that humor is employed as a vehicle for the communication of the tenderer sentiments surrounds us. I will make reference to only three communicative situations in which humor is regularly employed to convey affection, admiration, and regard. The first is that assemblage of behavioral and linguistic routines that are used by married couples or close friends that I have elsewhere termed "dyadic traditions."[61] For the most part, these consist of a stock of names, phrases, rituals, and routines that are created and perpetuated by a couple. These traditions emerge from their common experiences and serve to symbolize their intimacy and the singularity of their relationship. For example, one Los Angeles couple was given to exclaiming "Cuernavaca!" whenever they encountered dog waste, dead dogs, or heavy diesel fumes because of an experience in that Mexican city, where they found themselves walking along a particular street filled with dog wastes and a dead dog and which opened up onto an avenue filled with buses and their polluting exhausts. The phrase symbolized the couple's intimacy because it was rooted in their shared history and was encoded in a form that was unknown and unintelligible to others. Every repetition of this phrase invoked this sense of intimacy and consequently served to express affection and regard.

Dyadic traditions are typically humorous. The exclamation "Cuernavaca!" was humorous because it was perceived as embodying an "appropriate incongruity." It incongruously reduced a complex urban and cultural scene to a single, atypical, and trivial experience. At the same time, the incongruity was appropriate because the encounter with dogs, dog wastes, and bus exhausts in that city did in fact occur. Dyadic traditions also typically employ some negative image or expression. In its allusion to various forms of urban pollution, the exclamation "Cuernavaca" recalled something negative and invoked something unpleasant.

Another couple would open a bottle of champagne and toast one another on each wedding anniversary. These occasions were not traditional, sentimentalized commemorations of the day they were wed. Rather they were commemorations of their first anniversary, on which a bottle of champagne had slipped from their grasp, rolled across the floor, and emptied its contents under the refrigerator. It had taken them several hours to move the refrigerator and clean up the mess. The image of this awkward and unpleasant experience was what they resurrected in their subsequent celebrations. Had the mishap not occurred, they would probably have not continued to mark their anniversary with champagne.

Again we find a humorous recollection of a shared, unpleasant experience at the core of a dyadic tradition, but it is precisely through such humor that affection and tenderness are expressed. Those who utilize dyadic traditions may resist "regular" terms of endearment.[62] As direct sentimental expressions have come to be regarded as unsophisticated or insincere, humor has become a primary means for the communication of affection. It is within the humorous frame that "a part of the self not otherwise shown"[63]—a sentimental self—may be displayed. That such humor often centers on something annoying or unpleasant only serves to further insulate the expression from the sentiments that underlie it.

Another means by which respect, affection, and regard can be communicated is the roast. By "roast" I mean those occasions—retirement parties are a common example—on which co-workers and friends gather to "roast" the honored guests; that is, humorously belittle their personalities, behaviors, and achievements. "Roast" has had the meaning of "bantering unmercifully" at least since the mid-eighteenth century. It was only in the 1930s and 1940s, however, that American journalists began to use the term to refer to the event in which such banter took place, and then it was employed only in quotation marks. This nominal sense of the word did not find its way into dictionaries of standard or even slang English usage until recently.[64] Although humorous banter flourished in the English dining clubs of the eighteenth century, the roast seems largely to be an American phenomenon. The Clover Club was founded in 1882 by prominent and professional men of Philadelphia, ostensibly to institutionalize "good-fellowship, broad hospitality, love of humor, wit and culture."[65] Mark Twain, who attended one of their annual dinners in 1885, commented that at first he thought the members "a pack of fools . . . [but] then I heard some of the finest speeches I ever listened to, and when they turned from grave to gay I heard witticisms and repartee which would have done credit to a collection of noted wits."[66] The banter at the Clover Club was for the most part spontaneous heckling of those prominent and powerful persons who were invited to address the assembly. The Gridiron Club of Washington, D.C., founded by journalists in 1885, began as a direct copy of the Clover Club. Their roasts, however, were at once more elaborate and less spontaneous. In the course of their annual dinners, skits, songs, stunts, costumes, and props were employed to satirize their political guests.

The type of event that is perhaps most typically regarded as a "roast" was developed by the New York Friars Club. Founded by a group of press agents in 1904, the Friars was and is composed largely of people associated with the entertainment industry. As with the Clover and Gridiron clubs, the roast was associated with a meal, but instead of spontaneous heckling or involved skits, the Friars designated a panel of individuals to humorously abuse the main guest, who was later permitted to respond in kind.[67] As this was the pattern that carried over to television by George Jessel in the late 1960s and on the *Dean Martin Comedy Hour* in the early 1970s,[68] it became the commonplace conception of the roast event.

It is not clear when the roast moved out of elite dining clubs and became a folk form of celebration. Roasts have yet to attract the serious attention of folklorists and anthropologists. Roasts have, however, been noted among a wide variety of occupational groups from firefighters[69] to physicians and academicians. While some of the humor in roasts may be spontaneous, most is elaborately planned, even scripted. One script began with the following tribute to three retirees: "What can we say to Max, Carl, and Phyllis, who are retiring from active service in our department, except those heartfelt words, 'Go ahead, make my day!'" At the same time, a slide of Clint Eastwood in the role of Dirty Harry was projected on a screen visible to the entire audience.[70]

A roast should not be regarded as an effortless way to mark a retirement or other life transition. It is not easy to be funny. The work involved in preparing the script and props is time-consuming. Indeed, the length and the elaborateness of a roast is to some extent a measure of the regard the group has for those being roasted.

Like dyadic traditions, roasts mask the expression of sentiment behind a façade of witty remark and exaggerated insult. As the toleration for protracted pronouncements of commendation and praise have dramatically diminished in modern times, humorous slights and slurs have come to represent the sincerest expressions of appreciation and warm wishes. As Milton Berle described the roast, "It's just a crazy way of telling people you love them."[71]

Greeting cards are yet another example of the use of humorous insult in the communication of sentiment. Although humorous greeting cards have existed since the nineteenth century, the popularity of humorous cards increased after World War I[72] and exploded in the decades after World War II.

A short essay written on greeting cards in *Fortune* in 1947 begins with the following scenario.

> As the middle-aged housewife hurried past a counter display of greeting cards, she remembered that it was her husband's birthday. She paused, thumbed through the cards and picked up a couple at random. One, bearing the legend "Birthday Greetings To My Dear Husband From His Loving Wife," showed two pink hearts entwined amid a mass of flowers. The housewife frowned slightly, put the card aside and glanced at her other selection, which featured a tough bulldog in a red sweater with a cap over one ear. A balloon emerging from the bulldog's mouth read: "It's Yer Boithday . . . So What?" The housewife chuckled and handed the card and some change to the salesgirl.[73]

The article was about Robert J. Bender, president of Gartner and Bender, a leading greeting-card manufacturer. In the article, Bender perspicaciously commented that the woman in the above example "seeks to avoid a declaration of romantic love by taking refuge in humor." Bender would thus seem to support the hypothesis that humor is an expression of suppressed sentiment. However, Bender believed that the woman makes her choice not because sentimental expressions were becoming problematic but because she "is deeply confused about the nature of her relationship with her husband." Yet Bender's own philosophy of greeting cards and greeting-card symbolism make his the less likely hypothesis.

The *Fortune* article went on to describe Bender's use of Freudian psychology to determine the kinds of symbolism and messages that will sell greeting cards. Bender felt that a lot of the guesswork could be taken out of the greeting-card business if the cards were designed to accommodate people's unconscious motivations and taboos. According to Bender, Valentine's and Mother's Day cards should stress a massed central design of smooth circular forms while Father's Day cards should be more angular and feature pipes, newspapers, and the like. A newly designed Gartner and Bender card featured the word "Dad" written in sand on the beach. Bender claimed, "They won't be able to resist it . . . because it panders to the average person's desire to see Father washed away in the waves."[74] What Bender failed to recognize, however, was that this kind of psychologizing is precisely what inhibits the explicit expression of love and affection and elevates humor to a new communicative role. To the extent that companies like Gartner and Bender designed their products with Freudian theories in mind, and to the extent that magazines like *Fortune* reported these machinations to the American public, it was inevitable that humor would increasingly supplant expressions of explicit sentiment as a preferred form of greeting. It was also inevitable that such humor would take ever more aggressive and outlandish forms.

It was not until the late 1950s that there came on the market greeting cards that were aggressively humorous.[75] Alternately known as box cards, studio cards, or contemporary cards (depending on their publishers), most of the messages assaulted the recipient: "Despite your many faults . . . you're still a bum,"[76] declared one card. Another: "I wish I had a nickel for every time I've thought of you . . . I'd buy some gum." And yet a third: "When you leave it will be like a part of us is missing . . . like a WART, maybe." A graduation card congratulated the graduate on overcoming his "first big obstacle in life . . . Being dumb!" A get-well card reassured, "Sick? Don't worry. The death rate is the same as it's been for 100,000,000 years . . . One to a person."[77] All the above cards were published between 1957 and 1962. A birthday card of more recent vintage will serve to demonstrate that the humorous insult remains a popular style of greeting. On the outside of the card is a photograph of an old man with a beard standing next to an empty chair in an otherwise empty field. The caption below the photograph reads: "This is your birthday card." Inside the card is the message, "Now sit down and shut up."

Besides insulting the recipient, such cards often profane the traditional sentiments associated with a holiday or occasion. For example, one Easter card depicts a bunny hippity-hopping down the road pausing only long enough to bite a little boy. A Christmas card advises the recipient to tiptoe quietly to the window and peek out in the yard to see the group of young carolers . . . stealing his hubcaps.[78] A recent Valentine's Day card shows a cartoon figure of Cupid pinned to the wall by a quantity of arrows shot by a woman who does not want to be bothered when she is suffering from P.M.S.

An Easter card declares that "There is no Easter bunny. . . . Santa Claus ate him for Thanksgiving," while a birthday card assures, "I think you'll like this birthday card . . . because it has a lot of flowery shit all over it." Each of these cards perverts the traditional icons, images, and sentiments of the holiday but at the same time serves to communicate a greeting that depends upon those sentiments remaining fully intact.

Although sentimental cards have by no means disappeared, over the years humorous cards and studio-type cards have claimed larger shares of the market. I believe this recourse to humorous and aggressively humorous cards reflects the disrepute into which the open expression of sentiment has fallen in a significant segment of the American population, rather than any quantum leap of emotional ambivalence in interpersonal relationships.[79] The greeting cards themselves would seem to agree. As one birthday card acknowledges: "People just don't send warm, tender, emotional birthday cards anymore. . . . I guess those sentimental little bastards are hard to find."

Certainly, at some level, Freud was right. It would be absurd to argue that humor plays *no* role in the expression of sexual or aggressive impulses. It would be a great mistake all the same to believe that humor communicates only, or even largely, about these impulses. Freud at once expanded and contracted our sense of humor and its purposes, for while he opened our eyes to the potential of humor to contain serious messages, he provided a myopic view of what those messages might be. In his effort to alert us to the forces of repression, he unwittingly contributed to the creation of new repressions. The modern world depends upon much that is new, but it is rooted equally in the denial of the old. The suppression of sentiment is fundamental in the creation of modern consciousness, and this suppression must be seriously entertained as a hypothesis in explaining the pervasiveness and aggressiveness of humor today.[80]

7. The Joke as Gloss

THE SCHOLARLY APPROACH to humor has tended to focus upon the analysis of repertoires of traditional or "canned" texts on the one hand, and spontaneous witticisms embedded in conversational exchange on the other.[1] Although some attention has been given to telling canned jokes in social interaction, the emphasis has been upon the characteristics of performance itself, the movement in and out of performance, and the response to and evaluation of the joke by members of the audience.[2] Little concern has been directed at the relation between the contents of jokes and the interactions in which they are embedded; that is, to the way a joke can serve as a comment or gloss on conversation, interaction, or communication.[3]

There are various degrees to which a joke may be embedded in conversation. A joke may be performed as an independent humor-producing text making no claims of relationship to the interactional situation (other, perhaps, than that the situation is regarded as appropriate for joking).[4] A joke may also be so embedded in the conversational exchange that it loses its identity as a preexisting traditional text.[5] The intermediate position—in which a canned joke is told that is claimed to relate to ongoing social interaction—will be explored here. In other words, the focus is on how people use jokes as communications about their communications.

In joke-telling sessions, in which jokes are exchanged, the telling of one joke is a sufficient justification for the telling of another. The insertion of a canned joke into conversation, however, usually requires some kind of introduction.[6] These introductions not only signal a forthcoming performance of a joke text, they also make some claim of its relevance to the ongoing interaction: "That reminds me of a joke"; "That reminds me of the one about . . ."; "That's like the guy who goes into a bar . . ."; or "Speaking of kangaroos. . . ." The audience expects to be able to ascertain how the conversation "reminds" the teller of the joke; how the joke is "like" what has just been discussed; or whether kangaroos are somehow featured in the joke text. Even when no such introduction is offered, relevance is expected. A joke abruptly performed in medias res is still expected to bear some relation to what has taken place. When context-independent jokes are introduced into conversation, however, they are framed differently: "By the way, I have a joke for you"; "I heard this new joke"; "Before I forget, let me tell you the one about . . ."; "Have you heard the one about. . . ." These kinds of introductions make no claims of semantic relevance for the forthcoming joke to the conversational and interactional flow.

The nature of the semantic relation between a joke and its social contexts varies. In many instances, the connection between the joke and the situation is purely topical. The joke acts as an *association* to the conversational or social context and not a *representation* of it. For example, at a scholarly conference, a group of four male university professors were having a late-night snack in a restaurant. Because one of the professors was a Russian émigré and another had visited Russia, the conversation had turned to the economic and social situation there. Somehow the topic of whether Lenin's body was still on display in the Lenin Mausoleum in Red Square arose along with the question of whether anyone else was on display there. The émigré professor said that the body of Stalin had been removed and buried behind the building and that some people had suggested that Lenin's mummified body be removed as well since it was not "doing well." The other professor, continuing the conversation on the state of Russian society, started to talk about a time when he had attended a conference in Krakow, Poland, and the utterly dismal condition of the conference center there. At that point one of the other professors interrupted with "That reminds me of a joke":

> During the Soviet Regime, the Politburo decided they needed to cement ties more closely with Poland, so they decided to stage a major public event in Warsaw celebrating Lenin's visit to Poland. On that occasion they would present the Polish people with a monumental work of art commemorating Lenin's visit. The date was announced and the festivity was planned. A committee of Politburo members approached the Soviet Academy of Arts and asked them to design a monumental piece of art that they could present to the Polish people on the designated day. The artists in the academy were aghast. They said, "But Lenin never visited Poland! It never happened. We are social realists here. We cannot represent something that didn't happen. There is no way we can do what you ask." The Politburo members were in a real quandary, because the celebration was scheduled to happen within two weeks.

Then one of them remembered the dissident artist Rabinovich. He had been expelled from the academy but he was a talented painter and would not be bound by commitments to realism. He would be able to do something. They approached Rabinovich with their problem, promised him all sorts of rewards for his cooperation, and the painter agreed to do something. He told them to return in one week. At the end of the week, the members of the Politburo returned to Rabinovich's studio, and they could see the outline of a canvas of truly monumental size covered by a drape. They got all excited, knowing that they would have something to present to the Polish people at the celebration the following week. They asked to see the painting, and Rabinovich drew the drapery aside. They stared at the painting in disbelief. There was a scene of a bedroom, and in a large bed lay a naked man with a naked woman who was smoking a cigarette. "What's this?" they asked. "Who is that man?" "That's Trotsky," said Rabinovich. "But who is that woman lying next to him?" they asked. "That's Krupskaya, Lenin's wife," Rabinovich replied. "Trotsky! Krupskaya! Where's Lenin?" "Lenin?" Rabinovich said, "Lenin's in Poland."[7]

This joke claimed relevance to the previous conversation on the basis of three distinct topical links: the figure of Lenin; the mention of Poland; and the notion of absence (from the mausoleum in the conversation; and from Moscow, presumably, in the joke). The joke narrator claimed to have been aware of only two: Lenin and Poland. The parallel idea of absence was overlooked. Since the narrator had come to entitle his joke "Lenin in Poland,"[8] the mention of Poland after the discussion of Lenin was sufficient to bring the joke to mind and to provide an excuse to perform it. The narrator claimed no intent to characterize, represent, or comment upon the ongoing conversation. When asked to think about whether the joke contained any particular message, the best that he could come up with on the spur of the moment was the proverb, "When the cat's away, the mice will play." This message bore no obvious relevance to the discussion of the Lenin mausoleum or the state of post-Soviet society, but interestingly did highlight the previously unstated notion of absence.

The "Lenin in Poland" joke, like all jokes, is structured around the perception of an appropriate incongruity; that is, a set of incongruous semantic domains that are brought into an appropriate, if spurious, relationship. The sexual subject matter of Rabinovich's painting emerges as incongruous with, even opposed to, the kind of artistic work that the Politburo requested and expected. This sexual subject matter is made appropriate, however, when it is connected to the leitmotif of "Lenin in Poland" iterated throughout the joke. To grasp the appropriateness of the painting to the Lenin-in-Poland idea one must access the notion that when husbands are away, wives are especially free to have affairs, or as the narrator termed it, "When the cat's away, the mice will play"; but can this knowledge, whether put literally or metaphorically, be regarded as the message of the joke? It is easy enough to imagine a situation in which a narrator could employ this joke to make exactly that point in a conversation. In such a case, the conversation would probably have fewer direct topical linkages to the joke than the example above. That conversation would not concern the subject matter of Lenin and Poland but the themes of absence and marital infidelity.

The narrator of the "Lenin in Poland" joke had occasion to tell it in another situation. This time the joke served not merely as an association to an ongoing conversation but as a representation of some part of it. The narrator had been telephoned by a friend who was asking for a letter of recommendation for a job that he was applying for. There was some banter back and forth about what the narrator could write, and the narrator wondered aloud what he could write that would truly prove persuasive. The friend then wittily suggested that the narrator had once taken a class in creative writing and therefore should be able to produce a "credible piece of short fiction." Acknowledging that "realism" could often be a problem, the narrator then told the joke of "Lenin in Poland." The narrator stated that the point of telling the joke at that moment was its connection to the idea of the failure of realism (i.e., the inability of the realist artists in the Soviet Academy to do anything to solve the Politburo's problem). But as he finished the joke, the narrator told his friend, "So you see, creative fictions can prove to be problematic as well" (i.e., Rabinovich's creative solution proved totally inappropriate).

There are a number of interesting features about this report of the use of the "Lenin in Poland" joke as a gloss. The first is that the narrator's usage of the joke to gloss the conversation about the letter of recommendation as creative fiction was extemporaneous. Even though the narrator indicated that he employed jokes as glosses with some regularity, he had never consciously considered the joke's potential to comment on issues of realism and creativity.[9] His usage was a spontaneous application of the joke to a specific and unanticipated conversational exchange. Undoubtedly, the joke was meant as a humorous response to his friend's humorous comment about "short fiction." Then, as the narrator began to tell the joke based upon its linkage to the idea of realism, he sensed that the joke could be used to amplify aspects of the exchange and comment on the dangers of *both* realism and creative fiction. The joke as gloss was not a prefigured performance but an emergent one. The gloss was an outgrowth of the moment and the course of conversational exchange. The narrator had performed the "Lenin in Poland" joke on any number of occasions before and after his conversation with his friend about the recommendation, but he had never used the joke as a gloss before that occasion and has not used it as a gloss since.[10]

The second interesting aspect of this joke usage is its distance from the narrator's first approximation of what the message of the "Lenin in Poland" joke might be. The narrator's first approximation focused upon the knowledge requisite to make Rabinovich's salacious painting appropriate to the idea of Lenin in Poland; that is, that when husbands are away their wives may prove unfaithful. "Lenin in Poland" is a joke that employs an explicit sexual script. Sexual scripts are highly salient. A joke that invokes a sexual script is likely to be categorized as "sexual humor."[11] The narrator's usage of the "sexual joke" as gloss, however, involved a dampening—suppression is perhaps too strong a term—of this sexual script. The semantic significance of Rabinovich's painting in the joke gloss is not that it is sexual, but that the subject matter is highly inappropriate to the occasion for which it has been commissioned. If the joke had managed to employ some other inappropriate subject matter that could be linked to the motif of "Lenin in Poland," it might still have served to gloss the conversational exchange in the same way. In the gloss, sex is not sex but merely an instance of gross inappropriateness.[12]

A third interesting aspect of this joke gloss is the element of parallelism between the joke and the conversational situation that was never mentioned or even alluded to by the narrator.[13] The friend requested that the narrator write a letter—a formal letter—that would recommend the qualifications and talents of the applicant to a prospective employer and characterize his suitability for the advertised position. The painting that the Politburo members seek to obtain in the joke is also meant to be part of a formal presentation that is to recommend, in a sense, the Russians to the Polish people and to assure them of the "suitability" of their continued relationship and alliance. Whether this implicit correspondence between joke and context stimulated the narrator to use the joke in his conversation and contributed to the creation of the gloss is difficult to ascertain. Nevertheless, this additional affinity between the circumstances in the joke and the social communication seems more than mere coincidence.

The last interesting feature of the use of this joke is the message employed by the narrator in representing the conversational exchange. The message would seem to be that even though a piece of fiction might be crafted to recommend the applicant for the job, it might nevertheless prove as ill-suited to the situation as Rabinovich's painting proved to be. In crafting a gloss, the narrator makes use of the *whole joke*—that is, elements of both text and punch line—to make his point. Whatever message the gloss attempts to communicate is extracted from the joke as a unit. It would seem possible to construct a gloss that employed elements of the narrative without reference to the appropriate incongruity wrought in the punch line. One might, for example, draw upon the theme of the insincerity of the Soviet state in its relation to its satellite allies to register a point about duplicity and insincerity. Or one might use the idea of the Soviet state's willingness to alter history in the pursuit of its own interests to register a message about manipulation or the unreliability of history. This was not how "Lenin in Poland" was used by the informant, nor was any other gloss formulated in this way. Every single joke gloss I collected made use of the joke as a whole.[14] Not one drew its message solely from aspects of the narrative preceding the creation of the appropriate incongruity in the punch line. In other words, when joke narratives are employed as glosses on conversation and interaction—and not merely as associations to conversation and interaction—it seems that the joke as a whole constitutes the gloss and not merely aspects of its narrative development.

Elements of joke narrative may be employed if the purpose is merely to establish an association to the conversational situation rather than to construct a representation of it. This is what the narrator did when he told the "Lenin in Poland" joke in the restaurant setting. The mere mention of Lenin and Poland in the narrative development was sufficient to permit the proffering of the joke.[15] The reverse, however, is not true. A narrator may, in fact, use a whole joke even if only establishing an association to a conversation or interaction.[16]

While the great majority of the joke glosses that I have observed or that have been reported to me are extemporaneous like the "Lenin in Poland" gloss, this is not always the case. In some instances, the usage of a gloss may be planned long in advance. I had the occasion to tell a friend the following joke. It was unrelated to the substance of our conversation. It was told simply because it was a good joke, and I had been telling it to all my friends.

> Jesus was in Jerusalem and, seeing that he needed a new cloak, he went into the shop of Finkelstein the tailor. He approached the tailor and told him that he needed a new cloak. Finkelstein looked at him and said, "Aren't you Jesus of Nazareth?"
>
> Jesus said, "Yes, I am."
>
> "Well, I'll tell you what," said Finkelstein. "As you go about healing the sick and giving your sermons, if you would mention that your cloak is by Finkelstein the tailor, I will give you a new cloak for free." Jesus agreed, and as he wandered about Judea giving his sermons and performing miracles, he would mention that his cloak was made by Finkelstein the tailor in Jerusalem. And Finkelstein started to get a lot of new business as a result.

> The next time Jesus was in Jerusalem, he stopped in to see Finkelstein to see if he could get another new cloak, and Finkelstein said to him, "Look, let's go into partnership together. I will take care of production, and you handle the marketing." Jesus agreed to the partnership but they couldn't agree on what the name of their new business would be. Jesus wanted "Jesus and Finkelstein," and Finkelstein wanted "Finkelstein and Jesus." It went back and forth between them: "Jesus and Finkelstein, Finkelstein and Jesus. Jesus and Finkelstein, Finkelstein and Jesus." Finally they agreed to call it "Lord and Taylor."

Lord and Taylor is the name of an old and famous department store founded by Samuel Lord and George Washington Taylor in New York City in 1836.[17] Today there are stores in a number of cities doing almost $2 billion worth of business a year. Most Americans would instantly recognize the retailer's name. The joke depends solely on the recognition of Jesus as "Lord" and Finkelstein as "tailor," albeit the occupation and not the proper name. There is no deeper knowledge that one must access to comprehend the joke. I was surprised when my friend told me that she couldn't wait to use the joke. I was surprised, because I didn't perceive the joke to be particularly "usable" and had no idea how it might be applied. She explained that in her university, the administration was merging her department with another—much to the consternation of many faculty members. Furthermore, heated discussion of the merger revolved around what the new department would be called. The departments were fighting with one another about which department name would come first in the merged program. Would it be "Urban Studies and Geography" or would it be "Geography and Urban Studies"? She said the departments were behaving pretty much like Jesus and Finkelstein in the joke. When I asked her whether there was any greater message that emerged from the joke, she said, "Now that you bring it up . . . after all the fighting between Jesus and Finkelstein, you come up with a totally different set of names." In other words, the joke suggested that the departments needed to transcend their old identities and come up with a name that defined a new program with a new outlook.[18]

There are a number of points of interest in this example. First, the use of a joke as gloss is being planned long in advance. My friend is *waiting* for a situation in which the fight over the name of the program resurfaces so that she can make use of it.[19] Second, although my friend was anticipating using the joke, she had not fully realized its critical potential. She had grasped the parallel between the bickering over the order of "Jesus and Finkelstein" and "Urban Studies and Geography." Undoubtedly, the farcical image of Jesus quibbling with some German-Jewish tailor in first-century Jerusalem over the order of names in their partnership conveyed something of the ludicrousness and irrelevance of the bickering over the names that was going on between the two departments. Nevertheless, until I asked my question of whether there was some further message to be derived from the joke, the idea of transcending the names had not been explicitly formulated. I suspect that had I never asked my question, she would still have come upon it. The notion of transcendence would have emerged in the course of the telling, and she would likely have added an epimythium explaining the significance of the joke—centering on the idea of getting past the old names—to her colleagues. Her grasp of the joke was very much like the user of the "Lenin in Poland" gloss who first connected the joke to the conversation around the nexus of "realism" but who recognized a larger message as the narration of the joke developed.

A question arises as to what joke glosses accomplish both conversationally and interactionally. Certainly in using a joke as a gloss, narrators present themselves as witty and entertaining individuals, capable not only of telling an amusing joke, but also of labeling and defining situations or conversations in novel or amusing ways. The joke glosses I have recorded have been used to advocate a course of action; disengage from answering a delicate question; question authority; support a friend; ridicule a behavior; criticize a point of view or policy decision; and illustrate any number of scientific and sociological principles.[20] In most of these cases, the results could have been achieved more directly. For example, the narrator of the "Lenin in Poland" joke could have simply told his friend that fictions could be problematic without having to derive this message from the joke. Unlike proverbs, jokes are not considered repositories of past wisdom,[21] and they cannot claim the authority of tradition to bolster the argument that is being made. For example, I once opened the door to an office of one my university colleagues, who was seated at her desk reading. The lights were off and the room was fairly dark. I asked her whether she wanted me to turn on the lights, since I was standing right by the switch. She replied, "No, that's all right. I just had my eyes checked." I replied, "That's like the guy who went to be fitted for his first pair of glasses and asked the doctor, "Doc! With these glasses will I be able to read music?" "Certainly," the doctor replied. "Wonderful!" said the man. "I was never able to read music before." My colleague laughed.

My colleague's reply to my question seemed, at some level, a non sequitur. What did having one's eyes checked have to do with reading in the dark? Even people with good eyesight must have light to read. There was no disagreement between us about the darkness of the room. Her response to my question in part acknowledged the lack of light. My intention was to convey that just as the man would not be able to read music with his new glasses, she would not be able to read in the dark no matter how positive her eye checkup had proven to be. My point was facetious. There was enough light in the room to make reading possible, although it seemed dark enough to make it an unnecessary strain. That was why I asked if she wanted me to turn on the lights. Had she simply said in response to my question, "There's enough light," I could not have responded with the joke, since the joke was meant to characterize the incongruity in her response. I might have dispensed with the joke altogether and simply said, "Even with good eyes one needs light to read," or I might have said nothing at all. Beyond highlighting the incongruity of her response, providing an occasion for shared amusement, and presenting myself as a witty fellow, little else was accomplished by the gloss. Our talk drifted in other directions (and the light remained off).

Nevertheless, there are instances in which a joke gloss may accomplish what would be difficult or risky if broached more directly. The following joke was reported to me by a student who was born in Guatemala and immigrated to the United States in 1986 when he was ten years old. One evening he was bowling with four friends, and one of them started telling about being robbed the previous week. The robbers took his wallet and leather jacket and tried to steal his car. He was so angry about what happened, he said that were he to see the robbers again, he would kill them with a gun he had recently bought. He claimed he would never forget their faces. When he finished making his threat, my student said that the victim would forever remember the faces of the robbers because "A robbery is a robbery." The whole group—except for the victim—erupted in laughter because the phrase was the punch line of a joke that the student had told to them some time before.[22]

> There were three young women living with their grandmother all alone in a big house. One night, four robbers broke into the house. When the robbers broke in, the three beautiful women were in the living room with their grandmother watching TV. When the robbers saw them, one of them said, "Let's take the TV."
>
> Another one said, "Let's take the couch."
>
> A third robber said, "Let's take their jewelry."
>
> And the fourth one said, "Let's rape the women."
>
> When the three young women heard this, they said, "You can do anything to us, but leave our grandmother alone."
>
> When the grandmother heard this, she said, "Wait a minute. A robbery is a robbery."[23]

By alluding to this joke, my student suggested that this erstwhile victim would remember the faces of the robbers because he was involved in a sexual encounter that, like the grandmother in the joke, he had enjoyed. Of course, there was no sexual encounter, and all the victim's friends knew it, but by identifying him with the grandmother, his friends feminized him and jokingly challenged his macho posturing. Consequently, the joke served to characterize his claim that he would shoot the robbers, should he see them again, as sheer bravado. Directly challenging his assertion—"You would not do it"—or ironically challenging it—"Oh, sure you would"—or even seriously trying to dissuade him from his anticipated revenge—"Don't even think about it"—might have led to conflict. The joke, however, is so divorced from reality that it can assert what his friends cannot: his claim for revenge and violent retribution is intemperate, unseemly, and dangerous. Such things happen. He should forget about it. A robbery is, after all, a robbery. The victim—who did not laugh at the joke allusion—weakly responded to the laughter with, "Oh, come on," but gave up his talk about exacting revenge.

The following example also illustrates the effects a joke gloss can have on social interaction. A situation had developed in which a father had promised to take his children to the movies on several different occasions only to renege each time because he became busy at the office. Finally, one evening at nine o'clock, he tells his children that they can go to the show. It was too late in the evening, however, and no one wanted to go. His children were upset with him and his wife was furious and not talking to him. He turned to his sister, who was visiting during the course of this family episode, and said, "Tell me what is wrong with a father wanting to take his children to the show? What have I done? Have I committed a crime? I want my children to go with me to a show. They all say I have done something wrong. What's wrong?" And she says, "It reminds me of a story my mother used to tell me":

> A man once came to a rabbi to ask a *shayle* "question regarding ritual purity," forgiveness. He [the rabbi] says, "What is it? What did you do?" He [the man] says, "I didn't wash. . . . I didn't say the prayer before the meal." He says, "How come?" He says, "Because I didn't wash my hands." He says, "Well, why didn't you wash your hands?" He says, "Because I wasn't eating Jewish food." He says, "How come you weren't eating Jewish food?" "Because I was eating in a Gentile restaurant." He says, "How come?" "Because it was *Yonkiper*"—Yom Kippur, the day of Atonement, most solemn Jewish holiday and fast day, when every man's fate for the coming year is said to be decided—"and the Jewish restaurants were closed."[24]

Orthodox Jews are supposed to ritually wash their hands before saying the blessing over the bread that commences a meal. In the joke, the man goes to the rabbi and confesses this oversight in ritual performance. Each small confession of sin reveals the commission of a much bigger sin, culminating in the admission of eating on the Day of Atonement, the most solemn fast day in the Jewish ritual year.

The narrator claimed that she found herself in an untenable position in the family conflict. If she had taken her brother's side and tried to convince the family to go to the movies even though it was late, she would have antagonized her sister-in-law. If she had lectured her brother and told him that he worried more about his business than about his children, she would have made him feel badly and alienated him. She could not respond directly to her brother's question, and so she told the joke.

Telling the joke seemed a way to communicate with her brother without confronting him directly. The joke revolves around a man who is willing to openly acknowledge a small sin but not the underlying events that engender it. The father's protestations that even though it was late he could still take his children to the movies likewise belied a history of offenses. In telling the joke the sister suggested to her brother that his conceptualization of the problem was inadequate.

Most important, the brother's response to the joke was laughter. In that laughter, he acknowledged the applicability of the joke to the social situation and an admission of his own guilt. That acceptance permitted his wife to laugh as well. The charged family situation was diffused and the interactional impasse overcome. The "air was cleared." The joke proved a genuine interactional accomplishment.

Despite the above examples, the greatest percentage of joke glosses would seem to have little strategic value in their interactional settings. Humor may fulfill all sorts of functions in conversation.[25] The problem is not simply to specify these functions but to determine why humor is employed in some situations while more direct approaches are utilized in others.[26] While there are contexts in which it is relatively easy to see the advantage of employing a witty comment or joke gloss, in most instances it is not. Perhaps the best one can hope for is a characterization of those conditions under which a humorous option is closed.

Linguists have focused on the fact that jokes, and humor generally, violate one or more of H. Paul Grice's maxims of cooperation that underlie bona fide communication.[27] For them, humor constitutes a non-bona-fide mode of communication. The implication of this view is that jokes should lack communicative import, since no communicative effect should follow from a violation of the cooperative principle.[28] Beyond the presuppositions that a joke text may contain,[29] or the signal that the situation is appropriate for joking, jokes should contain no message at all.[30] Jokes do not, however, lack communicative import. Joke glosses make eminently clear that jokes are deliberately employed to communicate messages. A structural aspect of the text is held to parallel some structural aspect of the communication or interaction.[31] The communication takes place above the surface features of the joke text in a domain of relations from which abstract principles may be induced (e.g., fictions can also create problems; old names and mind sets must be transcended; good eyes do not allow one to read in all circumstances; being robbed has its own benefits; minor sins conceal numerous bigger ones). Jokes are literary genres and, like all forms of literature, they are capable of modeling the world: defining, ordering, and commenting upon it.

This fact might give some pause to those who would see some hostile impulse underlying every joke about religious, racial, or ethnic group members; women; homosexuals; lawyers; or politicians. Those who use jokes to convey deliberate messages rarely focus upon elements of plot or character. As a gloss, "Lenin in Poland" was not used to convey a message about Lenin, Poland, or painting. The anticipated gloss of the joke about Finkelstein and Jesus suggested nothing about Jewish-Christian business relations either in the first century or today. The joke about getting fitted for glasses was not employed to communicate any message about reading music. The joke about the man who confesses to the rabbi was not used to make any kind of statement about the relationship between clergy and laity in Jewish culture or about Jewish ritual observances. When jokes are consciously used to convey a message, they are concerned with more abstract categories of relationship, not with the surface features of the joke text.[32] In the analysis and interpretation of humor, it seems a point worth remembering.

8. Colonizing Humor

Despite the recognition that jokes and anecdotes migrate, the content and style of a people's humor is usually assumed to be peculiar to the people to whom it belongs. This sense of peculiarity extends beyond the recognition that the humor of a nation will be expressed in its own particular language, will employ wordplay meaningful only in that language, and depend upon the idiosyncrasies of the nation's history, belief, and custom. For it is further believed that humor is an index of a people's opinions and character.[1] It is held to express its temper and embody its spirit. Consequently, the humor of different nations will of necessity be different because their people and their temperaments differ. Such views have given rise to the numerous anthologies and studies of American humor, Jewish humor, Irish humor, Chinese humor, and so forth. Such works are invariably efforts to characterize and celebrate difference, but differences in history, language, and custom may mask more fundamental similarities. Furthermore, the presumption of difference in character and temperament may engender a perspective that is sensitive only to distinctions between nations.

When difference is assumed, the contemplation of resemblance can become surprising, interesting, and potentially productive. Here I wish to explore resemblance;[2] the resemblances between the humors of three different nations—the United States, Australia, and Israel.[3] These nations, of course, are distant from one another and are the products of very distinct histories. The environments, periods of development, and circumstances of the founding of these nations differed in many particulars. Australia began as a prison colony, whereas the United States was a place both of refuge and economic venture. Israel's colonization was ideologically motivated, influenced by nineteenth-century romantic nationalism, utopian socialism, and the political circumstances of the Jewish people in Europe and the Near East. North America and Australia were entirely new places to their colonists, while Palestine was a land that was both old and new, for it was—until the twentieth century—the land from which the Jewish people had been exiled since Roman times but with which they felt a spiritual, although not necessarily a religious, connection.[4]

All these societies were a product of colonization. The lands that were settled—while only sometimes vast—were always strange and harsh to the newcomers. Early settlements were often isolated from urban centers situated on seacoasts or along navigable rivers.[5] In moving out onto the land, the settlers of these countries experienced cultural loss. Many had to give up material objects and social practices with which they had been familiar and had valued in their home countries. Women were scarce, since few accompanied men to the frontiers. Survival demanded adaptation, and that adaptation exacted cultural costs.[6] The loss was not permanent, however. It was merely a stage in a larger process of civilization and domestication.[7]

The settlement on the land by these colonists was not unopposed. The colonists encountered native peoples who had successfully adapted to the environment but were regarded in most cases as technologically, socially, or spiritually inferior. These native peoples were often viewed as a physical and moral threat—a physical threat to the settlers and their families and a moral threat to the civilization they represented. Ultimately, these peoples were either eliminated by the settlers or dominated and controlled by institutions that the settlers brought to or created in their new lands.

In sum, all these nations were founded largely under preindustrial conditions, all were initially rooted in agricultural or pastoral production demanding extensive manual labor, and all possessed indigenous populations with cultures radically different from those of the colonizers. To the extent that these societies were born and developed under similar conditions, it would also seem that they produced humor of a similar type. The similarities tended to play out in the humor of language, tall talk, anecdotes about civilization and the native population, and the comedy of character.

Language

The languages developed in the new land were different from those spoken in the countries from which the colonists came. In Palestine, the contrast was most dramatic, since the colonists revived Hebrew, a language that was primarily liturgical and literary and that had not served as a spoken language for thousands of years. Although English was spoken in the United States and Australia, and thus continued the language brought by colonists from Great Britain, the language that developed in the new country invariably differed from that spoken in the old one. Over time, all languages change, but in a new land, language changes more dramatically. The language of the colonists is a skewed sample of the language spoken in the country of origin.[8] Colonists may come from different countries and language communities, and their vocabularies, grammars, and accents may react with one another and combine to produce new forms of expression. The languages of the native peoples also influence the language of the new nation enormously—particularly, although not exclusively, in the naming of places, features of landscape, flora, and fauna.

The creation of these new languages was often a humorous process in itself. Whether intended or not, colonial language eventually came to be regarded as humorous—especially when compared to the cultivated speech of the home country. In Australia in 1844, an anonymous correspondent to the *Colonial Literary Journal* offered a translation of a German sonnet into Australian vernacular. In this rendition of the poem, the words "cottage," "verdant lea," "brook," "tree," "nightingale," and "rising wind" are replaced, respectively, by "bark hut," "patch of maize," "creek," "wattle," "cocky-bird," and "brickfielder." The journal editor commented that the "Colonial manner in which he [the correspondent] has translated the Ode will amuse our country subscribers."[9]

The converse was also true. The landscape of Australia did not lend itself to poetic description. In 1819, Barron Field had written an ode to the kangaroo that begins: "Kangaroo! Kangaroo! Thou spirit of Australia. That redeems from utter failure, from perfect desolation, and warrants the creation of this fifth part of the earth." It is likely that Field's little ode was intended as a joke, and that the application of exalted poetic language and form to the description of the strange and comical animal so characteristic, yet distinctive, of the Australian continent was a deliberate incongruity. Even if Field's Muse had been serious, many Australians saw the poem as ludicrous, and it was thus rendered comical from the point of view of its readers.[10]

Those who lived in the country's interior away from the urban settlements and civilization—in the outback, wayback, rightback, backblocks, back-o'-beyond, beyond the beyond, the other side of the Black Stump, malle, mulga, and never-never[11]—coined a wealth of terms that were deliberately humorous. Indeed, sometimes the very proliferation of terms was humorous. Certain terms were in themselves jokes. A whip was called an ox-persuader or a buffalo navigator; a comb, a flea rake; and a rabbit, underground mutton. God was referred to, for some reason, by the personal and familiar name Hughie, as in "Send her down, Hughie!" when asking for rain.[12]

The situation was similar in the United States.[13] The colonizers of the frontier were likewise prone to create new words.[14] Plenty of nouns in the frontier American vocabulary could not be found in the cities of England or the eastern seaboard. Like the Australians, Americans often had a variety of comic terms for everyday objects. Liquor, for example, was alternately called bottled courage, bug juice, gut warmer, neck-oil, nose paint, wild mare's milk, and anti-fogmatic.[15] But Americans of this period seem to have devoted particular attention to verbs, adjectives, and adverbs: "flumex" (to defeat), "absquatulate" (to disappear suddenly), "discombobbolate" (to frustrate or inconvenience), "explunctify" (to subdue or annihilate), "catawampusly" (fiercely or eagerly), "slantindicular" (slanted), "circledicular" (round), "identicular" (identical), "angeliferous" (angelic), "poundiferous" (heavy), "hugeacious" (huge).[16] Any competent speaker of English would recognize such words as exaggerations of standard vocabulary—particularly those that contain protracted adjectival and adverbial suffixes. The terms deliberately present themselves as "high falutin"—as high class—but at once betray themselves because high-class vocabulary is not simply reckoned by the number of syllables that can be strung together. In other words, such terminology is *mock high class* and expresses a humorous contempt for class, privilege, and inequality—a notion that will be considered later.

The humorous language of the Americans and Australians did not simply reside in the items of their respective vocabularies. American and Australian folklorists and linguists have commented on the propensity of frontier dwellers to employ humorous metaphorical comparisons: "as useless as tits on a boar"; "as awkward as a pig with a serviette"; "as ugly as the south end of a north-bound mule"; "as handy as a cow with a musket"; "looking like a consumptive kangaroo"; "so ignorant he couldn't drive nails in the snow"; "so dumb he couldn't pour piss out of a boot if the instructions were written on the heel."[17]

The situation for the Jewish colonists in Palestine was somewhat different. The first settlers had to master Hebrew, which was not their native language. Their native-born children spoke Hebrew fluently, which their parents never did. The speech of the first settlers, even if it was fluent, often revealed its literary origins and did not always display the free and casual character of a language used in the discussion of mundane affairs. What quickly developed in the rural areas of Palestine was a colloquial Hebrew that was permeated with Arabic words and Yiddish expressions and which came to be seen in itself as comic[18] when compared with the literary and liturgical Hebrew that had been imported from Europe.[19] When a dictionary of colloquial Hebrew was published in Israel, its style of presentation was humorous. Its terms were often defined with comic examples and the pages were illustrated with humorous photographs and drawings.[20] In other words, the very idea of a colloquial Hebrew was treated as a comic affair.

There are some other differences between the three groups in the matter of language. While there is no reason to doubt the presence of profanity in any of these countries, it would seem that strong language was realized somewhat differently in the humor. On the American frontier, invective was often an art form. It was conceived as poetic speech and its phonology and structure were essential characteristics: "You no-souled, shad-bellied, squash-headed old night owl you—you hay-hookin', corn-cribbin', fodder-fudgin', cent-savin', whistlin'-of-nothin', you."[21] Among cowboys, profanity was common, although they tried not to use it in front of "ladies."[22]

In Australia, the art largely depended upon the number of obscene intensifiers employed in the course of a declamation.[23] The central, although by no means the sole, profanity employed was "bloody." In print, the word was often replaced by "blanky" or was not fully spelled out. It has been referred to as the "Great Australian Adjective."[24] A. Majoribanks, in his mid-nineteenth-century account of his travels in inland Australia, wrote of a bullock driver who used the word "bloody" twenty-five times in fifteen minutes. Majoribanks projected that in the course of his fifty-year life—subtracting time out for sleep—the bullocky would use the "disgusting word" no less than 18,200,000 times.[25] Majoribanks seems to have been what the Australians would come to call by the end of the century a "wowser."[26] The following anecdote suggests that Australian attitudes toward "bloody" were more forgiving and affectionate.

> A prospector stumbled into the bar in Kalgoorlie. The barmaid said, "What'll it be, sport?"
>
> "A b—— beer."
>
> The barmaid said curtly, "Hey, you can't talk like that here. I'm getting the manager."
>
> The prospector repeated what he'd said to the manager, who called the cops, who in turn arrested him.
>
> In court the next day the beak said to the prospector, after hearing the charge, "Well, what have you got to say for yourself?"
>
> "I've b—— well got plenty to b—— say!" reported the accused. "All I b—— well done was to come to this flamin' tinpot town and b—— well ask for b—— beer to quench me b—— thirst. And the b—— barmaid wouldn't b—— well serve me. Instead she called the b—— manager, who b—— well had me arrested; and the next b—— thing I know, I'm b—— well confronting b—— you."
>
> A know-all bloke at the back of the court yelled out, "Hey, you can't say 'b——' in this court!"

> The magistrate stood up, slammed his gavel down on the bench, and pointing an accusing finger at Mr. Know-All, shouted, "You shut your b—— trap."[27]

Other anecdotes reveal that the Australian bushman had recourse to a more extended repertoire of obscene expressions even if these expressions are not always recorded in print.[28]

Israel does not seem to have developed a comic obscene language to the same extent. It has been observed that Hebrew, as a sacred language, lacked profanities.[29] Obscenities were borrowed from Arabic and were certainly employed, but beyond the use of certain basic words, they required a deeper familiarity with Arabic to employ poetically. There were those who possessed such knowledge of Arabic, but profanity was a trait never attached to the early generations of settlers. Perhaps because Palestine was being settled to found a Jewish homeland, and the agricultural villages and communes were seen as central in this ideological program, profanity never assumed the significance that it did in the United States and Australia, where people settled the land for economic reasons.[30] There was a definite puritanical strain in the people who grew up in Palestine.[31] Nevertheless, Arabic profanities do show up in the Hebrew texts of printed collections of early Israeli humor: the most frequent exclamation is *Walla!* which is Arabic for "by God!"; some others are *yilan abuk* (may God curse your father), *yikhrib beytak* (may your house be destroyed), *yakhrib dinak* (may your religion be destroyed), *in'al dinhum* (may their religion be cursed). More obscene expressions were also in use.[32] In fact, it is estimated that 30 percent of the Arabic words borrowed into Hebrew slang were curse words.[33]

Another aspect of frontier language has less to do with the language itself than the way in which speech is regarded. In these frontier societies, speech is supposed to be an instrument. When not being deliberately employed for artistic purposes, it should be brief and to the point. It is not for idle speculation, theorizing, or emotional expression. It is a stimulus to action. Consequently, the Australian, the native-born Israeli, and the American are straight talkers. They speak directly, and they speak of practical matters. The extreme example of such speech is taciturnity—no speech at all.

In the 1840s, Richard Howitt described his efforts to draw out an Australian swagman (hobo) about his travels:

> I passingly inquired, "Whence he came?"
> "From the last station," was his ready reply.
> And "Where was he going?"
> "To the next," was his ready reply.[34]

The account purports to report an actual event, but the taciturnity of the swagman was a matter for more traditional folk humor:

> Two swagmen who had been mates for a long time were tramping out west in the wheat country. There were good young crops on either side of them.
>
> Harry took his pipe from his mouth and pointed to one of the paddocks. "Nice crop of wheat," he grunted.
>
> Five hours later, when they were seated by the campfire, Bill broke the silence. "Wasn't wheat. 'Twas oats." Then he rolled up in his blanket and went to sleep. The sun was well up when he woke next morning. Harry and his swag were gone. Bill found a roughly scribbled note under a stone at the foot of the nearest tree. "Too much b—— argyment in this here camp," it said.[35]

An almost identical tale is told about two Americans holed up for the winter in a Rocky Mountain cabin.[36]

Taciturnity could also characterize those living on the kibbutzim in Palestine. Thus when the very strong Kuchu volunteered to participate in a judo demonstration, he was told by Mikhah, the instructor, to tell him if he was being hurt. At one point in the demonstration, Kuchu said to Mikhah, "'Enough, friend, you've broken my arm.' 'Why didn't you say it hurt?' asked Mikhah. 'It's unpleasant,' answered Kuchu."[37]

The squatter on the American frontier could be as unforthcoming as the Australian and Israeli counterparts. In a classic confrontation, a traveler encounters a settler near a house in the backwoods.[38] The traveler asks:

> "Whose house?"
> "Nog's."
> "Of what built?"
> "Logs."
> "Any neighbors?"
> "Frogs."
> "What kind of soil?"
> "Bogs."
> "Your diet?"
> "Hogs."
> "How do you catch them?"
> "Dogs."[39]

Taciturnity is merely one extreme of a speech complex that favored directness, practicality, and a rejection of abstraction, emotion, allusion, and innuendo.[40] In a small agricultural settlement in northern Palestine, a miserly village member, a Mr. Brenner, died. Everyone in the village delivered long eulogies emphasizing his agricultural work and his contributions to the settlement, until one character who liked to talk to the point interrupted: "Mr. Brenner was a very good man. An outstanding man, but pardon me, gentlemen, a bit of a tightwad."[41]

There is also the story of Abraham Shapira, born in Russia, who came to Palestine in 1880 at the age of ten. He served as a guard for the Jewish village of Petah Tikvah against Arab attack. He got along well with the Arabs and spoke better Arabic than he did Hebrew. When he was asked to address a gathering of Jewish youth, "he went up to the stage, scanned the audience, and said, 'You are youth? You're shit!'" and left the stage.[42]

The story about Mr. Brenner is mirrored in the Australian anecdote of the old pioneer couple who had been married more than fifty years when the husband died. Neighbors summoned a parson from a nearby township, who told the widow that God must have wanted her dear husband in heaven. "'Well, 'e's right welcome to 'im,' declared the old girl. ''E was a cantankerous old sausage.'"[43]

Although there are differences in humor concerning the language and speech of frontier Americans, Australians, and Israelis, the fact is that the languages and speech styles of these frontier dwellers are matters of comedy. Moreover, the comic aspect is not something that is merely perceived by those on the outside looking in, but something that is relished by those who dwell within as well.

Tall Talk, Tall Tales, and Practical Jokes

Tall talk and tall tales refer to creative acts of lying and exaggeration. The farmer who told a stranger, "When it *really* gets hot in these parts the farmers start feeding cracked ice to the chickens to keep 'em from laying hard-boiled eggs," is engaging in tall talk. The tall tale has a narrative structure, as in the one about the champion jumper who tried to jump across the Grand Canyon but when he found himself twenty feet short of making it to the other side, turned around and went back.[44] The point is not generally to dissemble and deceive, for in many cases, the lie or exaggeration is so absurd as to be clearly recognized by the audience for whom it is performed. In fact, audiences often expect tall talk and tales and deliberately seek out their star purveyors. The art of the tall tale lies in the genuine knowledge of the raconteur about his subject, the concern with specific circumstances and concrete detail, the use of ludicrous understatement, deadpan delivery, and asseverations of factuality and truth.[45]

Although tales of lying and exaggeration were known in Europe, it seems that they greatly proliferated on American soil.[46] Not only on American soil, however. The tall tale also thrived in Australia. There are the tales of Crooked Mick of the Speewah. The Speewah was a place just beyond the back-o'-beyond, always a little further out than any other known remote place. It was inhabited by the Ker-ker bird, which flies over the plains in the summer calling, "Ker-ker-keripes, it's hot!" Heat had some part to play in how Mick became crooked. It is said, he was plowing on a day so hot that the barbed wire had begun to melt. He put his left leg into a bucket of water to cool it, and when he shifted his weight to cool the other one, it buckled under him and stayed that way.[47] Such tall talk was not confined to Crooked Mick and the Speewah but was spread throughout folk and literary accounts of outback denizens. Almost every collection of Australian humor and folklore contains a section of tall tales.[48]

Palestine also had its tall tale tradition in the oral literature of the Palmach, an underground military that was formed at the beginning of the 1940s. Throughout the 1940s, these men and women lived and worked on the communal settlements that had been central in the establishment of Jewish agriculture in Palestine. At the same time, they conducted secret military training. Initially they were mobilized to prepare for an invasion of Palestine by the German army. After the German field marshal Erwin Rommel was defeated by the British in Egypt, their mission was directed to responding to Arab attacks against the Jewish community. Ultimately the Palmach became the vanguard of the Israeli armed forces during the War of Independence and was absorbed into its military organization. In its earliest years, the Palmach was composed of mostly young, Palestinian-born Jews who had been raised in rural agricultural villages. The members of the Palmach eventually came to hold the same place in the national imagination of Israelis as did the backwoodsmen in the United States and bushmen in Australia.[49]

The humorous repertoire of the Palmach members was called *chizbat,* an Arabic word meaning "lies."[50] It was so called because it was largely composed of tall tales, outright lies, and embroidered accounts of actual occurrences. There is, for example, the story of Dr. Mahmud, who agreed to heal an Arab woman after all the European doctors had given up hope. She had dislocated her legs at the hips, and all the doctors agreed that it was impossible to push the legs out from the inside. Dr. Mahmud assured the woman's husband that he could heal her. He starved a donkey for a week and then put the woman on the donkey with her legs tied together under its stomach. He mixed water and bran and fed them to the donkey. The donkey devoured the mixture and his belly began to expand. With a pop, the woman's legs returned to their place.[51]

In all three societies, the early years of rural settlement and activity are associated with tall talk and tall tales. The tall tale has been characterized as a form that depends upon a tension between outsider and insider, old-timer and greenhorn, country folk and city folk. Its predominant theme is the natural environment. It celebrates the perseverance of the people living off the land under harsh conditions and reinforces their sense of solidarity in relation to outsiders who know less than they do but who might think otherwise.[52] It is a symbol of those who are in the know; those who know the real conditions of life on the land and recognize their distance from and proximity to the events described in the tales and talk. For the conditions of life on the land may often seem as extreme and preposterous as those so artfully fabricated in the talk and tales.[53]

In some sense, the tall tale is a kind of practical joke—a hoax in which everyone knows what is happening except the dupe, who is often a greenhorn or outsider. The point of the joke is the physical or psychological discomfiture of the dupe.[54] Practical jokes are both events and stories, because when a practical joke is well executed, the recounting of the trick and the description of the discomfiture of the dupe is likely to be repeated for some time to come. Although there may be stories of practical jokes that were never executed in fact, the practical joke begins as a staged event. It requires action, and not merely words. It is a genre for doers and not merely talkers. Although it is often at the expense of the greenhorn or outsider, the joke is usually meant as a joke, and if the joke is received in an appropriate spirit, it is critical in transforming the outsider into an insider. It is a rite of passage. Consequently it is not surprising that the practical joke found a home in the American West, on the Australian station, and in the Palmach.[55]

Civilization

As might be expected, those living on the fringes of civilization had a particular attitude toward it. The conditions of the frontier invariably demanded the abandonment of many accoutrements of civilized society. Technologically and socially, life on the frontier involved cultural retrogression. Those on the frontier recognized their comparatively primitive state and told anecdotes about it. For example, there is the Australian anecdote about "Strike Me Die" Johnstone, who described the elegance and modernity of the house of a grazier: "The whole blanky building was carpeted inside an' out an', believe it or not, they had the bloomin' outhouse *inside!*"[56] There is the story of Zemerli, a resident of the northernmost Palestinian settlement of Metulla, who took his first visit to the city of Haifa. Upon returning to his village, he reported to his fellow villagers, "The bank is sealed with a big iron door—a needle couldn't get through it."[57] Given the conditions in his settlement, the idea that a door didn't have cracks in it was truly wondrous. There is also the story of the American youth who is sent to some well-to-do neighbors who have a rug on their parlor floor. As he conducts his business, he is forced to hop around the parlor, because he "knows better" than to step on the rug.[58] Of course, the very ability to laugh at their own primitive and unsophisticated characteristics betrayed their knowledge of civilized society and its ways. Often they made themselves out to be more primitive than they really were.[59]

They also laughed at those who did not know how to adapt to the conditions of the new land and society. In the United States they were called "greenhorns," in Australia "new chums" or "jackaroos," and in Palestine "paratroopers."[60] The parallels between some of the anecdotes is striking. An Englishman is found in the American wilderness with his tongue swollen out of his mouth. After he is given water and revived, he is asked whether he had been aware of a nearby river. "'Oh yes,' he replies, 'I saw the river.' 'Then why didn't you go to it and get water?' 'I didn't have a cup.'"[61] In the Galilee, a Jewish immigrant from Germany working on a small agricultural settlement is packed a lunch and sent out in the morning with the mules to plow the field. At lunchtime, they see the immigrant returning. Did the plow break? What went wrong? When he reaches the house, he is asked what happened. He says, "I forgot a fork."[62] An Australian farmer sent his new English worker off in a horse and cart to dig out rabbits. Before leaving, he gave the worker his dinner of sandwiches and a billy of cold tea. Some hours later the worker returns. "'What's the matter,' asked the cocky [farmer]. 'By goom, guv'nor,' complained the migrant, waving his billy of tea, 'thee forgot t' send coop! [cup].'"[63]

Ultimately, the frontiersman and the squatter, the bushman and the cocky farmer, the kibbutznik and the Palmachnik saw themselves as morally superior to the city dwellers and immigrants. While they recognized the rudeness of their own conditions, they also sensed that the society depended upon the hard and rude work in which they were engaged.

The Native Population

The history of relations between the colonizers of the United States, Australia, and Palestine and their respective native populations was generally not a happy one. Hatred and violence often characterized these interactions. Although the particular circumstances were different in each case, the native populations were eventually displaced from their lands by force. Indians, Aborigines, and Arabs do not seem to have played a major role in the humorous repertoires—at least the published repertoires—of America, Australia, and Israel. Even though humorous texts about these native peoples are few, there is a certain sameness in those that do appear.

The hatred and violence that often characterized relations between colonizers and colonized do not figure significantly in the humor. When natives appear as major characters in jokes and anecdotes, they are not hostile but naive and unsophisticated. Yet they also possess natural wisdom and discernment. Despite, or rather because of, the relative simplicity of their way of life, they often see issues clearly. They are not deceived by the manners and forms of colonial society and culture. Confronting the colonizer in the jokes, they may give as good as they get.

The Aboriginal stockman Jackie Bindi-i is being tried for cattle stealing. He is asked by the judge if he knows what will happen if he tells a lie.

> Jackie says that he thinks he will go to hell. Then the judge asks if he knows what will happen if he tells the truth. Jackie replies that he reckons he will go to gaol.[64]

> In the Oklahoma Osage country an Indian was said to have walked into a bank and asked for a sizeable loan. The banker inquired as to what security the Indian had.
>
> "Me gottum five hundred horses," replied the Indian.
>
> The banker checked on this and found it to be true, so he made the loan. Some time later, the Indian returned to the bank with a huge roll of bills in his hand and paid off his note. The banker, noting how much the Indian had left, suggested that he let the bank take care of it for him. The Indian looked suspiciously at the banker. "How many horses you gottum," he asked.[65]

The Aborigine and the Indian are portrayed as recognizing the political and economic forces they are confronting. Jack Bindi-i knows that he is trapped between the institutions that European settlers have imposed upon his people. He is in trouble no matter what he says. Then, when he naively reveals that if he tells the truth he will go not to heaven but to jail, he admits the crime with which he has been charged. The Indian, in asking the banker how many horses he owns, reveals that he does not fully comprehend the workings of the bank. Still, the question he asks implies a more penetrating one: why should bankers be trusted more than borrowers, and what guarantees the money that people deposit there?

In Palestine, before the partition and the establishment of the Jewish state, the institutions of government were in the hands of the British. Arabs had their own economic and religious institutions. As a result, there are no jokes about Arabs confronting Jewish economic or political institutions.

All the same, the Arab, like the Aborigine and Indian, is also portrayed as naive:

> Once Hayyim the Fat went to visit his friends in a Bedouin tribe, al-Huzayel in the Negev. He sat with the dignitaries on the dung heap and told stories. When his turn came he told them stories about the Garden of Eden.
>
> "In the Garden of Eden there is no swamp and everyone lives there like a king," said Hayyim. "Everyone has a *deluxe* car like the Prime Minister. There is a radio and telephone in every house, and the women wear silk clothing from India, and each man has a knife, sword, rifle, and machine gun. Money rolls in the street and houses are of precious stones."
>
> The Bedouins gaped and listened. One lad whom they had just admitted into the men's group also listened gaping, and finally dared and asked, "Tell me *sheikh,* how's the pasture there."[66]

Despite the bounties of Eden that are described, the Bedouin youth remains concerned about the availability of pasture for his flock. There is no hostility here, only the depiction of a childlike naivete. The youth is incapable, even in fantasy, of imagining a world not rooted in his own immediate circumstances and concerns.[67]

The role of the Arab seems to have played a more significant part in early Israeli humor than the Indian in American humor or the Aborigine in Australian humor. There may be several reasons for this. Before the partition of Palestine, the Jews were a minority. Also, the intermingling of the Arab and Jewish population in Palestine was much greater than the intermingling of colonizing and colonized populations in other societies. Although Arabs and Jews lived in separate villages and urban enclaves, there was considerable economic and social intercourse between them. Except, perhaps, for the Bedouin, Arabs were never confined to some remote geographical frontier. Furthermore, there were many Jewish immigrants to Palestine from Arab countries. These Jews were often viewed by Jews of European origin as culturally more Arab than Jewish. In the humor, it is often difficult to distinguish the characteristics of Arabs from those of Jews from Arab countries. The same naivete characterizes both. The brother of Abu Layish, who was a member of the Palmach, was one such character.

> The cease fires that fell during the struggle with the British depressed the gang, and Beni the Politruk [propaganda officer] was sent from squad to squad to lecture and boost morale. In a two-hour lecture for the squad at En Harod, Beni explained the reasons for the cessation of the conflict and expressed his own private opinions. He reviewed the impression his words made on the fellows, drank a hot cup of tea with sugar, and asked, "Any questions?"

> The brother of Abu Layish . . . raised a finger and said, "O.K. But why don't we blast the English?"[68]

Beni tries to convince the Palmachniks of the soundness of a new order to suspend military operations against the British in Palestine. As a propaganda officer, he offers a long tortuous argument in defense of the change in policy. The Palmachniks themselves are not happy about the new state of affairs but are prepared to follow the directive. When Beni asks whether there are any questions, the brother of Abu Layish—who has not understood a single word of Beni's convoluted rationalization—asks the single question that is really on the minds of all the Palmachniks. Precisely because of his lack of understanding, the brother of Abu Layish goes directly to the heart of the matter.

The portraits of indigenous peoples may be patronizing, but they are not hostile. Even the naivete of the natives in the jokes points to a deeper wisdom. They have the ability to cut through the artifice of institutions, manners, and mores.[69] This is not to say that less sympathetic portraits were not conveyed in other forms of expression. Plenty of serious stories demonized natives.[70] They seem, however, to be absent from the humor. Humor is not a major channel for the expression of hostility.[71] Furthermore, natives were ambivalent figures to the colonists. Even as the settlers replaced the natives on the land, they believed that they were, in some sense, kin. The first natives possessed a wisdom that enabled them to survive in the hostile landscape to which the settlers had come. Settlers and natives were similarly at odds with the civilization represented by governmental regime and urban institution.[72] Like the original inhabitants, the new people of the frontier claimed a deep knowledge of the land and its ways. In some sense, the frontiersmen made claim to the inheritance of this wisdom along with the inheritance of the land from which the wisdom sprang.[73] In this way, the humor might reflect the colonist's kinship with, and perhaps even admiration for, the native while registering the enormous distance between them.

Character and Type

Frontier humor is often tied to places and characters—places and characters specifically identified by name. Even though many of the anecdotes are migratory, having traveled across regional and national boundaries, frontier humor is not anonymous. The humor is often affixed to specific people and places: "'Bob the Dog' was a strange character who knocked about the Victorian Mallee in former times . . ." and "There was this old German up at

Daintree, Borman, or something like that" (Australia).[74] "One day Giora met Sasson in the port of Haifa" and "Once in Yagur, one of the group started to argue seriously with Abd" (Israel).[75] "Charlie Cugar quit punchin' and went into business for himself" and "Rueben Custer was working his corn" (United States).[76] These characters are not celebrities, and the places mentioned will not be familiar to outsiders. The individual and geographical attributions in part stem from the fact that the humor is rooted in communities where people actually do know one another, that tall talk is deliberately grounded in realistic settings, and that an effort is made to keep the outsider feeling like an outsider. Although there are plenty of anecdotes in published collections without such attributions, there are enough to give the humor a local flavor, even if that flavor contributes little or nothing to the point of the humor for an outside audience.

Of course, anecdotal humor is not peculiar to frontier societies. It is likely to be found in any social group—peasant village or factory workshop—rooted in face-to-face relations. What are significant are the character types delineated in these numerous anecdotes.

When frontier humor focuses on frontier characters, it focuses on a particular set of traits. Frontier characters are ludicrously portrayed as strong, slovenly, practical, primitive, direct, improvisatory, impious, egalitarian, playful, unsentimental, and unromantic. Space allows illustration of only two of these traits.

> A station-owner . . . is driving back to his property one hot dusty day. Out in the middle of nowhere he sees a swaggie humping his drum down the road. The station-owner takes pity on the swaggie battling along, pulls up beside him and offers him a lift. The swaggie slowly turns a baleful eye on the station-owner, spits, and replies: "You can open your own bloody gates."[77]

> [A] young man, ordered by his father to fetch some wood, was heard to say, "Go get it yourself you old son of a bitch." The father turned to the witness, his face aglow with satisfaction. "A sturdy republican, sir," he said.[78]

The Australian and the American ludicrously react against the notion of service defined by wealth, class, and position. Such a structure was the legacy of the British in Australia and the United States. Jews, while often occupying a low-caste position in European society, were not so rigidly structured among themselves. As an egalitarian ethos was reflected in European-Jewish jokes,[79] and as so many of the institutions in Palestine were founded on socialist principles, there were few formal hierarchies to react against. Nevertheless, Palmach pranks and thefts[80]—directed against the kibbutzim and against members of the urban population—were common and well represented in humorous narrative. The only true authoritarian structure was the military, and even here a strong antihierarchical ethos was maintained.[81]

> Hayyim Ben-David got orders to catch the first vehicle he could in Haifa to get a course in Hanitah. When he showed up for the course four days late, they called him to the staff tent and wanted to know what happened to him.
>
> "They told me to take the first hitch regardless of what it was. I got a hitch with a steamroller."[82]

In addition to being egalitarian, the people of the frontier were depicted as unromantic and unsentimental, and these characteristics form the basis of the respective Australian, Israeli, and American anecdotes.

> Mabel: "Isn't it a beautiful moon tonight Dave?"
>
> Dave: "Yairs Mabel. Cripes a bloke's a silly coot not to be out after possums on a night like this."[83]

> Ike brings a girl an art book from Europe, and on the flyleaf where one writes beautiful dedications he writes, "I brought this book as you asked. I came to your house and didn't find you. You can find me this evening at 8 in Atarah. . . . If I'm not there call 6745 and leave a message."[84]

> Two city men I knew had come to a cow ranch on business and had an old-time cowboy taking them around. One day they were discussing the beauties of nature, and when each one decided what he thought was the most beautiful thing he ever saw one of them asked the cowboy his idea of beauty. He promptly answered: "The prettiest thing I ever saw was a four-year-old fat steer."[85]

In each of the above anecdotes the possibility of romantic behavior and expression is ludicrously repudiated or ignored.

The characteristics assigned to the frontiersmen and made ludicrous in such jokes are not arbitrary. The traits—strength, primitiveness, the lack of romanticism, matter-of-factness, antiauthoritarianism, and so forth—have been seriously ascribed to, and accepted by, the peoples of these lands.[86] It seems that in such jokes as these, Americans, Australians, and Israelis step back from their own defined characters, highlight their peculiarities, and render them laughable.

Ever since Frederick Jackson Turner delivered his address on "The Significance of the Frontier in American History"[87] in 1893, Americanists have been attentive to the impact of the frontier in shaping American institutions, mores, and character. American humor was also a product of this frontier. In the introduction to his anthology of antebellum southern and southwestern humor, Franklin J. Meine proclaimed that "nothing is more American than the frontier" and he identified the humorous sketches written between 1830 and 1860 as the earliest literary reactions to that frontier. Rooted in oral tradition and local event and experience, they heralded the beginning of an American realism that would have a profound influence on the development of an American literature.[88] As I have tried to show, however, the frontier—at least as it relates to the creation of humor—may be less distinctively American than one might have previously supposed.

Australia and Israel, after all, developed humors of similar style and shape. Like those in the United States, their peoples viewed their newly created languages and dialects as sources and subjects of humor; they emphasized and expressed a particular attachment to tall talk, tall tales, and practical joking; they comically contemplated their manners in relation to those of civilized society; they were bemused by the naivete and wisdom of the native population; and they toyed with a set of nearly identical traits that they nevertheless felt uniquely characterized them.

Undoubtedly, elements of this kind of humor can be found in other than frontier societies. It is, however, this particular *constellation* of traits that seems a product of the type of societies that I have described—societies establishing themselves in landscapes that are wild and exotic; far from the original homelands of the colonizing population; in contact with a "primitive" native population; with economies initially rooted in labor-intensive rural production; lacking many of the amenities of, although not lacking knowledge of, "civilized" life. Despite the many differences between these societies, their frontiers were meeting points between savagery and civilization,[89] and it was in the double vision[90] of how life actually was and how life could and should be that the humor of the frontier was born.

Frontier humor is rooted in the local and oral. It is a folk humor. But it does not remain so. It is promoted in newspaper articles, jest books, short stories, novels, and even scholarly works[91] as being an authentic reflection of the national character. It is purveyed to the citizens of the nation, who accept it as their own. It is held up as a mirror of the whole and is accepted as such.[92]

Of course, humor of and about the frontier does not represent the humor of the society in any statistical sense. The anecdotes about the frontiersman and the cowboy, the swagman and the cocky farmer, the kibbutznik and the Palmachnik do not constitute any sort of representative sample of the humor in these societies. These very localized humors came to be conceptualized as national humors because of the place these characters held in the national imagination. What tends to become national humor is humor by and about the kinds of people who come to stand for the society as a whole—who are believed to embody the identity of the nation. In new countries, these groups are thought to be new kinds of beings, utterly unlike those in the societies from which the colonists have descended. They are imagined as having sprung up from the land as new and original creations.[93]

To create a new society, old identities and memories must be eradicated or suppressed. When the humor of the frontier began to receive national attention in the United States, the country was just beginning to emerge from the centuries-long political and economic domination by England.[94] Two wars had been required to win independence. The hero of the second of these conflicts—a genuine frontiersman—was elected to the presidency at the very moment that the comic figures of the frontier were catapulted into national consciousness. In eastern Australia, some 150,000 convicts had been transported by the British government between 1788 and 1840. The "convict stain" dominated the Australian sense of self until the mid-nineteenth century.[95] The image of the Jew as genetically weak, religious, urban, and mercantile was one that the colonists of Palestine were consciously determined to overthrow. All these societies had an interest in defining themselves in terms of where they were going rather than in terms of where they had been.[96] The frontier and its denizens admirably served this purpose.

Perhaps what is most remarkable about the United States, Australia, and Israel is that the peoples of these nations came to imagine themselves in ludicrous terms. Using the characters, environments, and situations of frontier life, they constructed for themselves a "comic mythology."[97] While it would be misleading to suggest that they entertained only humorous images of themselves, or that these were necessarily the dominant ones, it nevertheless distinguishes these nations from those that have never tied their identities to comic representations.

It has been suggested that there is a difference between old and new societies. In old societies, the culture of the society is shaped by the manners of the upper classes. Style and taste flow from the top to the bottom. In new societies, however, modes and manners flow upward, and the culture of the society as a whole is shaped by its lower classes.[98] New societies are topsy-turvy. In some sense, they are inversions of the societies from which they come. They are fundamentally incongruous. There are grounds, it would seem, for seeing themselves as comic entities. It may not be only a matter of how such societies were born, but when they were born. The United States, Australia, and Israel became nations in the nineteenth and twentieth centuries. Only in the nineteenth century did a transformation occur in the notion of what humor is and how it relates to the notion of self. Only after such a transformation could laughter be viewed primarily as a sympathetic rather than an unsympathetic expression. In addition to a sense of honor, a sense of justice, and a sense of decency, a sense of humor emerged as a core cultural value. The ability to laugh, especially at oneself, became not merely an admirable, but an essential, trait. This was not only true of individuals, but of nations as well. In the early nineteenth century, humor began to be viewed as an utterly "national and original" form of expression.[99] Consequently, new societies could imagine themselves in ways that older societies could not. If new societies could not take pride in noble lineages and ancient traditions,[100] they could take pride in their sense of humor and in a humorous sense of themselves. They could do this because they were born at a time when ideas of humor and self were changing; at a time that humor could be thought of as the expression of self.[101]

This chapter began by questioning the assumption that a nation's humor was unique because it is an expression of its own peculiar character. It concludes that the humor of different nations may prove strikingly similar. The very notion that humor may be intimately linked to the character of an individual or group is one that arose with the development of these very same societies. The association may not be fortuitous. Perhaps the birth and development of such new societies contributed to a transformation in the conceptualization of self and to a transformation in how that self might be represented.

9. Sigmund Freud's Jewish Joke Book

Almost a century ago, Sigmund Freud published a book that continues to shape the understanding of humor by scholars and the general public alike. In *Jokes and Their Relation to the Unconscious,* Freud attempted to corral humor, and aesthetic expression more generally, into the domain of the unconscious and the purview of psychoanalytic insight. While Freud presents important hypotheses and stimulating observations on jokes, he also perpetuates classificatory muddles, displays some remarkable blindness, and rides roughshod over data in his effort to wed jokes, the comic, and humor to his metapsychology. So while *Jokes and Their Relation to the Unconscious* is in many respects a genuine tour de force, it owes something to the sheer force that Freud brought to bear on the materials he was analyzing.

Yet *Jokes and Their Relation to the Unconscious* is interesting for reasons other than its contribution to the analysis and interpretation of humor. For in the course of analyzing jokes in order to discover their techniques and purposes, Freud raises the issue of Jewish jokes; those jokes that Jews tell about themselves. As no other ethnic, religious, or social grouping is so featured in the book, the highlighting of Jews and their jokes in the context of a psychological work on joking is at once striking and perplexing.[1] For Jewish jokes were in no way essential to any of the points in Freud's argument about the techniques or purposes of joking. Any number of jokes might have been employed to evidence his arguments. Given his theoretical orientation, the Jewish jokes seem entirely gratuitous. Furthermore, in Freud's previous psychoanalytic works, Jews are mentioned only in passing, if at all. Only in *Moses and Monotheism,* written in the very last years of Freud's life, do Jews assume a more prominent position than they do in this joke book. All in all, there is something about *Jokes and Their Relation to the Unconscious* that can't help but strike one as just "too Jewish."[2]

In fact, Freud himself suggests that this is the case. In his introduction to the book, Freud acknowledges how he is compelled to use many of the joke examples employed by previous scholars. He adds, however, that it is his "intention to turn to fresh material" and that there is a "personal motive" behind his wanting to understand the workings of jokes; a motive that will only come to light in the course of his investigation. The fresh materials that Freud brought to his study were undoubtedly the Jewish jokes. Freud never again referred to the personal motive that impelled his study, but it undoubtedly had something to do with his being a Jew; a Jew who felt some particular kinship with and appreciation of those seemingly trivial entertainments called "Jewish jokes."[3]

The number of jokes explicitly identified as Jewish by Freud is 20.[4] This is in the context of some 172 jokes and witticisms that he employs in the course of the book, or 12 percent of the total.[5] But the great majority of the 172 examples are joking analogies, allusions, aphorisms, and riddles[6] rather than jokes and anecdotes proper; that is, rather than texts that describe setting, dramatis personae, action, or dialogue.[7] Only some 62 texts meet these latter criteria, and of these, the Jewish jokes constitute a full 33 percent.

The Jewish jokes revolve around relatively few topics and themes. Seven (35 percent) concern the *schadchen,* or Jewish marriage broker, and his efforts to promote a prospective bride to a would-be groom. Five (25 percent) deal with *schnorrers* [beggars] and borrowers and their tendency to treat their benefactors' money as their own. Four (20 percent) concern the dirtiness of the Galician Jew[8] and are mostly set outside the public bathhouse. The remaining 4 (20 percent) are diverse and deal with a disciple who boasts of the telepathic abilities of his rabbi; a Jew who is facetiously encouraged by his officer to take an entrepreneurial approach to army life; a Jew who accuses a fellow traveler of lying when he has in fact told the truth about his journey; and the presumption of a religious Jew who discovers that the gentleman who has entered his train compartment is also Jewish.

In *The Jokes of Sigmund Freud,* I examined the relation of these jokes to Freud's personal situation and circumstances.[9] Here I am more concerned with Freud's *presentation* of these Jewish jokes in the context of his scientific book and in relation to late-nineteenth- and early-twentieth-century discourse about Jews. *Jokes and Their Relation to the Unconscious* may be viewed as an act of identity-based expression. The display of Jewish jokes must relate to how Freud sees Jews and how he sees himself as a Jew, read against the way Jews were perceived in Central Europe at that time.

What has Freud explicitly to say about Jews and their jokes? How does he frame Jewish jokes with respect to other types of jokes? Freud's first Jewish joke in *Jokes and Their Relation to the Unconscious* is one of the Galician "bath jokes," which turn on these Jews' aversion to bathing.[10] Freud acknowledges that the joke under discussion lacks "nobility" but suggests that one need be concerned only with whether his joke examples are capable of provoking laughter and whether they are of theoretical interest. Later still, Freud characterizes two other jokes about Galician Jews and their dirtiness and aversion to baths as "of a coarse type."[11] Nevertheless, according to Freud, such jokes that are told by Jews should be distinguished from the "brutal comic stories"[12] of non-Jews. Finally, Freud highlights the self-critical nature of Jewish jokes, which he sees as one of their unique characteristics. The passage has often been cited but is probably worth quoting again:

> A particularly favourable occasion for tendentious jokes is presented when the intended rebellious criticism is directed against the subject himself, or, to put it more cautiously, against someone in whom the subject has a share—a collective person, that is (the subject's own nation, for instance). The occurrence of self-criticism as a determinant may explain how it is that a number of the most apt jokes (of which we have given plenty of instances) have grown up on the soil of Jewish popular life. They are stories created by Jews and directed against Jewish characteristics. The jokes made about Jews by foreigners are for the most part brutal comic stories in which a joke is made unnecessary by the fact that Jews are regarded by foreigners as comic figures. The Jewish jokes which originate from Jews admit this too; but they know their real faults as well as the connection between them and their good qualities, and the share which the subject has in the person found fault with creates the subjective determinant (usually so hard to arrive at) of the joke-work. Incidentally, I do not know whether there are many other instances of a people making fun to such a degree of its own character.[13]

Jewish jokes may be coarse and uniquely self-critical, but they are rooted, according to Freud, in the Jews' perception of their own good qualities—in a sense of self-worth and self-esteem—that decisively differentiate them from the brutal comic stories told by anti-Semites.[14]

Freud illustrates the linkage between the notion of faults and good qualities with the joke about the Galician Jew in the railway compartment:

> A Galician Jew was travelling in a train. He had made himself really comfortable, had unbuttoned his coat and put his feet up on the seat. Just then a gen-

> tleman in modern dress entered the compartment. The Jew promptly pulled himself together and took up the proper pose. The stranger fingered through the pages of a notebook, made some calculations, reflected for a moment and then suddenly asked the Jew: "Excuse me, when is Yom Kippur (the Day of Atonement)?" "Oho!," said the Jew, and put his feet up on the seat again before answering.[15]

The Galician Jew assumes a polite demeanor when a presumed gentile enters his compartment. He abandons it as soon as he recognizes the stranger as a fellow Jew. According to Freud, this joke reflects the "mode of democratic thinking" of Jews such that they recognize among themselves "no distinction between lords and serfs." This positive quality, in Freud's estimation, is intimately tied to a distinct fault as well. As he remarks, it "also, alas, upsets discipline and co-operation."[16]

The relation between the other self-critical jokes that Freud presents and the positive qualities of the Jews is not so straightforward, however. Nor does Freud seek to definitively establish these connections. In interpreting the *schnorrer* jokes, Freud argues that the *schnorrer* who acts as though his benefactor's money were his own has the "right" to do so "according to the sacred ordinances of the Jews." The *schnorrer* jokes, in Freud's view, serve as criticisms of Jewish law that commands, and not merely invites, acts of charity. A rich man's money is not really his to give. The rich are actually indebted to the poor for providing "the opportunity of beneficence."[17] By invoking the context of Jewish injunctions to charity and interpreting the jokes as a protest against its extreme demands, Freud seems to be suggesting that Jews are committed to a higher and more onerous morality than obtains in the gentile world.[18]

Similarly, Freud interprets the *schadchen* jokes as criticisms of the institution of arranged marriage—loveless and financially motivated—as well as criticisms of those suitors who expect too much from a prospective bride, and who should be ready to take as a "wife a human being with all her inevitable defects."[19] The jokes therefore would seem to promote the values of love, choice, and a forgiving attitude toward human beings and their shortcomings.

There is a difference, however, between the way Freud connects these jokes to the supposed "good qualities" of the Jews. In the joke about the Jew who puts his feet back up on the seat and says "Oho!" when he recognizes the gentleman as a co-religionist, the democratic thinking that Freud finds so attractive is actually called to our attention by the behavior of the joke character himself. It is the Jew who reverts to familiarity when he recognizes a fellow Jew, and one must register this familiarity if one is to apprehend the joke. In contrast, any positive qualities evoked by the *schnorrer* and *schadchen* jokes are secondary elaborations on the jokes themselves. Knowledge of Jewish injunctions to charity or a sense of the fundamentally flawed nature of arranged marriage is not essential to understanding these jokes. The presumption of the *schnorrer* in the joke remains a presumption; the prevarication of the *schadchen,* a prevarication. If there is anything to be admired in these characters, it is perhaps their capacity for presumption and prevarication. It is only Freud's interpretations that manage in a roundabout way to ally these jokes with the positive principles of charity, choice, and love.[20]

The bath jokes add yet another dimension to the problem. The behavior of the joke characters alludes to no positive qualities whatsoever.[21] The Jews in the jokes reveal themselves to be irredeemably dirty and remarkably unaware of and unbothered by their condition. Freud makes no effort to link these jokes with any good qualities of the Jews, but one might suppose that they serve as condemnations of slovenliness and uncleanliness and thereby ally the Jews who tell and appreciate them with that body of civilized humanity who hold to standards of hygiene and tidiness. After all, who but those who believed that they conformed to such standards could find the behavior of the joke characters ludicrous.

It would seem, therefore, that there are at least three distinct types of relation that might be established between Jewish jokes and the positive qualities of Jews. The first relation depends upon the recognition of a positive aspect to the behavior of a joke character (e.g., the democratic mode of thinking). The second relation depends upon the evocation of a context—positive (e.g., injunctions to charity) or negative (e.g., the loveless nature of arranged marriage)—with which the joke is in alignment or in opposition. The third relation depends upon the assumption that a joke about a purely negative trait cannot characterize the tellers of such jokes. To joke about dirtiness, for example, is to distance oneself as joke teller and joke aficionado from that stigmatized category. After all, one can laugh at the blindness of the Galician Jew to his own dirtiness only if one can discern the difference between dirty and clean and the appropriate values assigned to each.

Freud explicitly commits himself to placing Jewish jokes in a positive light. He seems to be trying to frame the negative traits of Jews as they are portrayed in the jokes so that the jokes do not appear to be of a piece with what he calls the "brutal comic stories" told by anti-Semites. But if *Jokes and Their Relation to the Unconscious* constitutes an attempt at the rehabilitation of Jewish jokes, his efforts betray some curious inconsistencies and contradictions.

It should be noted at the outset that even the "Oho" joke with which Freud illustrates the positive aspects of Jewish character is not without its negative side. The behavior of the Galician Jew on the train that Freud characterizes as "democratic" can also be viewed as impertinent and discourteous. After all, even an equal should be entitled to courteous behavior. The joke suggests that Jews are polite and decorous only in the presence of gentiles—when there is a presumed threat. Among themselves, in contrast, where no such threat exists, they revert to slovenliness and ill-mannered behavior. The Jews' claim to civilization is all show. To know how they really are, it is only necessary to see them behave among themselves.

Later in *Jokes and Their Relation to the Unconscious,* Freud makes a comment that would seem to undo his notion that Jewish jokes are rooted in the Jews' sense of their own worth. Freud suggests that Jews tell self-critical jokes because they find "criticism or aggressiveness difficult so long as they are direct, and possible only along circuitous paths."[22] If Jews are directing aggression against themselves because aggression against non-Jews is forbidden to them, it does not seem likely that the self-critical jokes would be anchored in a sense of self-esteem. One would think the self-criticism crueler and more relentless for being born of inhibition and frustration. In any event, it is difficult to reconcile this remark about displaced aggression with Freud's earlier notion of the jokes as emerging from the Jews' sense of their own good qualities.

Otto Weininger, in his book *Sex and Character,* also characterized Jewish jokes as self-critical, but without any of the appreciation that Freud tried to convey. Weininger, who attempted in his book to solve the question of the psychological constitution of males and females, devotes a chapter to Judaism. According to Weininger, no one considers the Jew to be lovable, least of all the Jew himself. Jews are the bitterest anti-Semites. The Jews lack dignity and breeding, are arrogant, deceitful, and materialistic. The Jews, in Weininger's opinion, are unlikely to overcome their Jewish constitution. To do so, Jews would require a self-understanding and self-respect of which they are incapable. They have no belief in themselves or in anything else. Their skepticism is so profound that they doubt their own skepticism. Consequently, Jews joke about everything, particularly about "their own peculiarities" and "sexual things." Because Jews have no transcendental inclinations and lack the creative freedom of the will, they have no true humor; they are addicted rather to mockery, satire, and irony.[23]

Weininger's book was published in 1903, two years before *Jokes and Their Relation to the Unconscious,* and Freud undoubtedly read it.[24] In fact, Freud had met Weininger and had read *Sex and Character* before it was published.[25] Weininger was born Jewish but converted to Christianity in 1901 after completing his dissertation. *Sex and Character* got some attention when it was first published, but it got quite a bit more some six months later, when Weininger killed himself.

Thus Weininger's anti-Semitic claims about Jews find some echo in *Jokes and Their Relation to the Unconscious.* Like Weininger, Freud accepts the idea of self-critical jokes as typically Jewish; and although Freud makes some attempt to root these jokes in the positive qualities of Jews and their own sense of self-worth, this attempt is both problematic and halfhearted.[26] Freud, like Weininger (and others), also considers humor [*Humor*] as a category distinct from jokes [*Witze*]. According to Freud, humor proper depends upon the transcendence of pain and suffering so that a person maintains hold on the customary self in "disregard of what might overthrow that self and drive it to despair."[27] In other words, humor is a triumph of the ego over adversity.[28] In this line of reasoning, humor, for Freud, has some of the transcendental aspects that Weininger also assigns to it. Freud ranks humor as one of the "highest psychical achievements" of mankind,[29] yet he includes no Jewish examples at all in his discussion of humor.

In fact, the Jewish jokes are not equally apportioned throughout *Jokes and Their Relation to the Unconscious.* They are absent in the entire first section of chapter 2 where Freud analyzes the joking techniques of condensation. They make their appearance in abundance later in the chapter when Freud discusses the techniques of displacement, faulty reasoning, sophistry, and absurdity that operate in conceptual jokes. They appear again in chapter 3 in Freud's discussion of the purposes of jokes, where Jewish examples are employed almost exclusively as illustrations of "cynical jokes"—jokes that attack social institutions and values—and "skeptical jokes"—jokes that attack the certainty of knowledge itself.[30]

The significance of this unequal distribution emerges vis-à-vis the perception of Jews in Central Europe at the turn of the century. For Weininger's treatise on the Jews was only a part of a wider discourse about Jews; a discourse most thoroughly documented by Sander Gilman.[31] Jews were viewed as spiritually and morally corrupt. Innumerable signs of this corruption marked the Jew's body—his feet, gait, skin, eyes, nose—and was manifest in a variety of physical and mental diseases. The language of the Jews was equally corrupt, a reflection of their eternally corrupt spirit. In the Middle Ages, that corrupt language was identified as Hebrew. In the seventeenth century, that language was Yiddish—a German pidgin peppered with Hebrew words and spoken with a distinct phraseology and accent. Even when Jews entered the mainstream and mastered the language of the dominant society, it was held that their rhetoric, if not their accents, continued to betray them. Their subtlety, loquacity, impertinence, superficiality, materialism, duplicity, faulty logic, and penchant for irony, wit, and mockery marked their discourse as utterly distinct from the abstract, aesthetic, truth-seeking discourse of German literature and philosophy.[32]

In the context of this view of the language of the Jews—a view widely circulated in literary, philosophical, and scientific works as well as the popular press—Freud's use of Jewish jokes seems self-defeating. Despite his claim of a positive foundation for the Jewish joke, Freud's use of these jokes to exemplify displacement, duplicity, sophistry, and faulty logic, as well as assaults on social values, the notion of truth, and the possibility of knowledge, serves to reaffirm the traditional anti-Semitic image of a corrupt Jewish discourse.

Even the types of jokes that Freud highlights in *Jokes and Their Relation to the Unconscious* seem problematic. The preponderance of the Jewish jokes that Freud presents are *schadchen* jokes. In these jokes, the full range of Jewish deformity—in both language and body—is displayed. The marriage broker's speech betrays the sophistry and duplicity stereotypical of corrupt Jewish discourse, and the would-be bride exhibits that range of physical deformities characteristic of the depraved Jewish body: deafness, humpback, limp, squint, and bleary eye.[33] One of the most important bases for the argument of Jewish difference was that the Jews married young and were endogamous. It was held that this "inbreeding"—an inbreeding which it was the job of the *schadchen* to perpetuate—condemned the Jews to physical and moral decay.[34] Weininger had argued that matchmaking[35] was the quintessential trait of the female. This "pairing instinct" revealed the inescapable tie of women to sexuality.[36] Consequently they could have no regard for individuality, no sense of asceticism, and no part in the higher transcendental life.[37] Jews, according to Weininger, were also habitual matchmakers, and all their negative characteristics stemmed from their matchmaking propensities.[38]

Matchmaking, in other words, was hardly a benign field for humor. In fin-de-siècle Vienna, the *schadchen,* as a symbol of Jewish marriage and its peculiarities, was highly charged. And in highlighting *schadchen* jokes in his book, Freud dredged up for his readers a spectrum of associations concerning the physical and moral corruption of the Jews. It is no wonder that Richard M. Meyer, a professor of language and literature at the University of Berlin—himself a Jew—wrote in his 1905 review of *Jokes and Their Relation to the Unconscious* that "Freud's insistence on 'Jewish' jokes as a separate category easily becomes unpleasant."[39]

How does Freud position himself with respect to the Jewish jokes that he discusses? To what extent has Freud erected barriers between himself and the characters and behaviors depicted in the Jewish jokes? Gilman has pointed out that in many of the Jewish jokes that Freud includes in his work, the characters speak in *Mauscheln,* that stereotypical representation of Jewish-German dialect.[40] The language of the jokes themselves, Gilman adds, though not of the joke characters, is good German, as is Freud's own scientific commentary on the jokes. Gilman argues that in restricting the corrupt language of the Jews to the characters within the joke, Freud has distanced himself from the caricature of the Galician Jew in an effort to frame his own discourse as rational, scientific, and thoroughly German.[41] Others have made similar arguments about the relation of dialect and distance in joking.[42] If Freud's rehabilitation of the Jewish joke was equivocal, however, his distancing himself from the language of the Galician Jew was equally equivocal, for Freud compromises his claim to a neutral scientific discourse in a number of ways.

First, in the introduction to *Jokes and Their Relation to the Unconscious,* Freud registered these Jewish jokes as his favorites, the ones by which he had been most "struck" and which made him "laugh the most." That is, these jokes were not merely those analyzed in the context of a scientific book, but jokes that he himself enjoyed telling to and hearing from his Jewish friends. Actually, Freud states that his scientific interest in these jokes stems from his personal interest in them, and not the other way round.[43] Also, it is Freud who introduces the terms *schadchen* and *schnorrer* into his text. Since he uses German (e.g., *Heiratsvermittler, Bettler*) to gloss these Yiddish terms for his readers,[44] he might have employed the jokes without any use of Yiddish at all. Furthermore, Freud is aware that the use of dialect enhances the humor of some of these jokes.[45] All in all, rather than distancing himself from the language of the joke characters, Freud gives his readers every reason to believe that he himself told these jokes in that peculiar and corrupt language of the Jews.

Second, Freud repeatedly throws in the face of his readers the quips of the quintessential Jewish wit—Heinrich Heine.[46] If any literary figure symbolized for the gentile world Jewish proclivities for mockery, satire, and crass commercialism, it was Heine. More than any other author, Heine's work showcased the *Judenwitz* that was regarded as contrary to true humor and the values of German culture. By embracing Heine, Freud further allied himself with Jewish wit and Jewish modes of discourse.[47]

Freud's third reduction of distance was effected through the jokes themselves. Shortly after recounting bath jokes in which the characters speak in dialect,[48] and immediately after introducing the joke about the Galician Jew on the train who exclaims "Oho!" (which in the original, is actually the Yiddish "*Aesoi!*"), Freud recounts the following joke:

> The doctor, who had been asked to look after the Baroness at her confinement, pronounced that the moment had not yet come, and suggested to the Baron that in the meantime they should have a game of cards in the next room. After a while a cry of pain from the Baroness struck the ears of the two men: "*Ah, mon Dieu, que je souffre!*" Her husband sprang up, but the doctor signed to him to sit down: "It's nothing. Let's go on with the game!" A little later there were again sounds from the pregnant woman: "*Mein Gott, mein Gott, was Für Schmerzen!*"—"Aren't you going in, Professor?" asked the Baron.—"No, no. It is not time yet."—At last there came from next door an unmistakable cry of "*Ai waih, waih geschrien!*" The doctor threw down his cards and exclaimed: "*Now* it's time."[49]

As the pains of the baroness increase, she progressively abandons the refined languages she has acquired in the course of her education. When the moment of delivery is upon her, she cries out in Yiddish.[50] The joke reveals that the Jew may acquire many languages, but in crisis, the original and corrupt language will out. Culture for the Jew is merely a veneer. Underneath, Jewish language and character do not change. A cultivated scientific discourse will not protect the Jew from the charge that his language is corrupt. Freud seems to knows this and proclaims it through this joke.

There is also a perspective by which Freud's scientific language itself might be viewed as corrupt. In *Jokes and Their Relation to the Unconscious* Freud makes constant recourse to an economic model in order to conceptualize the difference between joke, the comic, and humor, and to account for the presence and absence of laughter. This economic perspective goes back to his unpublished manuscript known as *Project for a Scientific Psychology* (1895)[51] in which Freud attempted to reduce mental functioning to a kind of psychophysics. In Freud's view the nervous system is like an electric grid through which energy flows. The health of the organism depends upon keeping levels of stimulation low and discharging any buildup of energy through appropriate activity.

Some believe that Freud abandoned this physical model for a more purely psychological approach, while others believe that ideas developed in the *Project* continued to influence his thinking throughout his career.[52] In any event, the influence of the *Project* is quite visible in Freud's early works—particularly in *Jokes and Their Relation to the Unconscious.* Shortly after exploring the various joke techniques that Freud characterizes as "condensation," Freud asserts, "It all seems to be a question of economy" [*Ökonomie*].[53]

On the last page of the book, he outlines the mechanisms for pleasure in the joke, the comic, and in humor. The pleasure in jokes comes from an economy of expenditure in inhibition; the pleasure in the comic comes from an economy of expenditure in ideation; and the pleasure in humor comes from an economy in the expenditure of affect.[54]

It is not necessary to explicate these ideas here, but it is worthwhile to see how Freud's notion of economy affects the language he uses to explain the workings of jokes. For example, a psychical inhibition demands some "psychical expenditure" [*Aufwand*]. Pleasure and laughter come from a psychical expenditure that is "saved" [*erspart*]. Jokes "bribe" [*bestechen*] their hearers with a "yield" [*Gewinn*] of pleasure. The "value" [*Wert*] of a thought in a joke can easily be "overestimated" [*überschätzen*]. The weight of a joke can be "thrown into one scale [*Waagschale*] or the other."[55] Freud's economic metaphors culminate in an elaborate analogy. It is not necessary to grasp its sense—only its language:

> I may perhaps venture on a comparison between psychical economy and a business enterprise. So long as the turnover in the business is very small, the important thing is that outlay in general should be kept low and administrative costs restricted to the minimum. Economy is concerned with absolute height of expenditure. Later, when the business has expanded, the importance of the administrative cost diminishes; the height reached by the amount of expenditure is no longer of significance provided that the turnover and profits can be sufficiently increased. It would be niggling, indeed, positively detrimental, to be conservative over expenditure on the administration of a business.[56]

While Freud's psychophysical approach derives from the so-called Hemholtz school, the work of Gustav Theodor Fechner, and others,[57] the language that Freud brings to the analysis of jokes, the comic, and humor is that of economics and business. The distance that Freud would establish between his own scientific discourse and the *Mauscheln* of the Galician Jew is obliterated. Freud's scientific discourse on a problem in aesthetics is conducted in the stereotypically Jewish language of the marketplace.[58]

Thus Freud's presentation of Jewish jokes in *Jokes and Their Relation to the Unconscious* recapitulates the charges brought against the Jews by Otto Weininger and others. The language of the Jew is corrupt, it is the language of spurious logic, business, and deceit. Jews cannot pursue truth and beauty, for they have neither the character nor the language for such a pursuit. They are materialists, devoid of all spirituality, and incapable of a true humor that demands the ability to transcend the physical world. Instead of transcendence, the Jew engages in a malign mockery of values he can never appreciate, share, or hope to understand.[59] If Freud fails to counter the charges leveled against the Jews and their corrupt language, he also fails—whether deliberately or inadvertently—to distance himself from that language. Ultimately, Freud remains very much betwixt and between.

Freud may have hoped to create in the language of psychoanalysis a language far removed from the corrupt discourse of the Jews, a new language to describe the human condition.[60] In highlighting Jewish jokes in his study, however, he serves to corrupt his own discourse. When Freud states that the joker is likely to be a "disunited personality, disposed to neurotic disorders,"[61] he succeeds in identifying propensities for joking with what were conceived to be stereotypically Jewish tendencies to neurosis.[62] When he asserts that faulty reasoning in jokes—with Jewish jokes as prime examples of that reasoning—is no more than the usual mode of unconscious thought,[63] he has dashed any hope of establishing a universal language for the unconscious. For the language of the unconscious, as Freud presents it, turns out to be nothing more than a generic Jewish joke. It is no wonder that only three years after the publication of *Jokes and Their Relation to the Unconscious,* Freud expressed his concern that psychoanalysis was in danger of being viewed as a "Jewish national affair."[64] Instead of succeeding in universalizing the Jewish, Freud managed to Judaize the universal. Karl Kraus's observation was all too apt: "Psychoanalysis is the disease for which it claims to be the cure."[65]

In *The Jokes of Sigmund Freud,* I concluded that Freud was deeply ambivalent about his Jewish identity, and although he consciously acknowledged and defended it, he also unconsciously repudiated it. I have no reason to alter that assessment. The sense of conflict and compromise in *Jokes and Their Relation to the Unconscious* is too strong. Of course, one cannot and should not be held accountable for one's unconscious. Besides, Freud was no more than a product of his time, one of a multitude in fin-de-siècle Vienna conflicted over his sense of identity. He, and so many others, were trapped in a double bind by a society that invited Jews to join the civilized mainstream while simultaneously signaling that they would ever remain alien and apart.[66] It was a condition destined to induce self-examination, a profound sense of contradiction, and discontent.

There is, moreover, another double bind with which figures such as Freud must contend. It is the bind imposed by those who would read, interpret, and evaluate their works. As objects of interpretation, their identities are expropriated. Under the guise of acceptance, and even admiration, these figures from the past are distanced from the present as they are made to serve as standards of our identities. They serve as points by which we fix our own positions and plot our own courses. Within historical discourses, these figures are less in control of who they are and how they would be seen than they were in the anti-Semitic discourses of their own time. Images of Freud serve to secure our own sense of identity no less than images of Jews served to secure the sense of an Aryan identity a century ago. While this double bind exacts no psychological toll—the principals, after all, are dead—it reminds us that identity is necessarily reckoned through the imagination of others. We can never control who or what we are.

10. The Context of Internet Humor

IF 1998 AND 1999 were not favorable years for the person of William Jefferson Clinton,[1] they were exceedingly favorable for humor about him. By the end of January 1999, late-night television talk-show hosts had told some 1,712 jokes about President Clinton and 749 jokes about others associated with the scandal.[2] A search for "Bill Clinton jokes" on the World Wide Web identified thousands of sites that contained or referred to such humor.[3] These sites might contain the posting of a single joke; or an archive of jokes, joke lists, and parodies; or graphic illustrations, cartoons, and photos; or original attempts at satire; or some combination of the above. The immensity and anonymity of the World Wide Web lend a superorganic character to the humor that is located on it.[4] Bill Clinton jokes, blond jokes, lawyer jokes, Princess Diana jokes all seem to exist in a realm above and beyond particular individuals. They seem to constitute a single phenomenon to be conceptualized, analyzed, and interpreted as a whole. They appear to be the unified expression of a culture responding to the exigencies of time and circumstance.[5]

Certainly, there is much to be gained from examining the total corpus of a joke cycle for messages about the temper of the times and the character of the culture. Given the anonymity and lack of context of joking in cyberspace,[6] it might be assumed that this is the only approach. In fact, it is not. For cyberspace is not anonymous and Web sites do not lack context. In many respects, communication in cyberspace may be less anonymous than many conventional face-to-face encounters. While the real names and addresses of the inhabitants of cyberspace may be unknown (and even this may only be sometimes true), more may be known and knowable about the creators and purveyors of humor in cyberspace than about many joke tellers encountered face-to-face in everyday social interaction.

I have closely examined twenty sites that have posted Clinton humor on the World Wide Web. These were haphazardly—although not randomly—chosen from a list of sites identified by a popular search engine. Only some of these sites were joke archives or joke lists. In most cases, Clinton jokes were situated within a Web site that contained several kinds of materials. They were not simply, or even primarily, lists of jokes. Five sites contained detailed personal information about the Web masters—their personal philosophies, employment histories, personal experiences, and avocations. Five sites included photographs of the Web master. Almost half provided e-mail addresses at which the Web master might be contacted.[7] All in all, the posting of jokes and other kinds of humor on the Web is only sometimes an anonymous activity. Often a great deal can be learned about the creators and purveyors of the humor, and sometimes something can be learned about the audiences for that humor as well.

Many things should be considered when examining a joke site. For example, what kinds of statements, warnings, disclaimers, and manifestos frame the site? At one site, which contains a substantial collection of Clinton jokes,[8] the viewer is instructed: "Please click on my sponsors that you see throughout the site and then just come back once you've checked them out. You're enjoying the site so please help a poor republican [*sic*] teenager make some money." After some advertising links, the statement "Bill Clinton Sux" appeared below a picture of Bill Clinton with an international prohibition symbol superimposed on it. Further below, the page reads "This site has the best Clinton Jokes on the Internet. Poor Mr. Clinton has a lot on his mind right now. He has the sex scandal, Hillary for a wife, and the possibility of being impeached. So I thought lets [*sic*] make his life a little worse. So hear's [*sic*] this site. Keep up the good work Bill and I'll always worship you, you the PIMP!!!"

It was not difficult to ascertain the attitudes of the Web site master toward Bill Clinton. The antipathy expressed toward Hillary Clinton suggested that this Web master's attitudes predated the sex scandal involving Monica Lewinsky. The advertising that appeared throughout the site was also significant. Most was for gambling, although it also included ads for Icom.com, offering Web hosting, as well as At Hand Network Yellow Pages and "The Best Larissa Webring Sites." The gambling advertisements indicated that this anti-Clinton Republican teenager may not have been aligned with the Moral Majority or other religious groups that would deplore such activity.

At another site, the Web master announced that the fiction he read was exclusively science fiction; that his favorite television shows were *Babylon 5*, *The Highlander*, and *X-Files;* but that he read mostly nonfiction. He stated that he worked as an engineer and was an atheist "terribly concerned about the influence of the religious right." His personal introduction concluded with the statement, "The Moral Majority is neither." It might be suspected, given this Web master's interests and his anti–Religious Right stance, that he might not be particularly interested in bashing Clinton by posting jokes about him. In fact, the jokes posted at his site were limited to a single list of sixteen of "The Top 16 Chelsea Clinton Pet Peeves about College." Only four of these were linked directly to Bill or Hillary Clinton. They were "No room in the dorm for all those boxes of Whitewater papers"; "Daddy won't sign the Cafeteria Food Reform Bill"; "No one wants to waste good pot on a Clinton"; "The man makes 200 grand a year—you'd think he could bring his own weed when he visits." There was nothing about Clinton's sexual escapades, Monica Lewinsky, oral sex, or his impeachment. Other items on the list targeted Al Gore, Tipper Gore, Ted Kennedy, and Janet Reno. When I e-mailed the Web master and asked him about his attitudes toward Bill Clinton, he indicated that his site was a catalog of humor e-mail messages that he had received and was "not a Clinton joke or satire site." In fact, he said he was a Democrat, and he had "edited out all the cruel and stupid Clinton emails" because they "annoyed" him.[9]

In attempting to assess the attitude of a Web master toward the Clinton humor posted, it seems important to register whether Clinton humor is the only kind of humor posted, or whether other kinds appear as well. At one joke site,[10] Clinton jokes were just one of many choices, which included tech-related, college/school, miscellaneous, naughty, R-rated, list (such as the top ten reasons dorm life sucks), police, religious, and blond jokes. At another site,[11] Clinton jokes were among many categories: animal jokes, blond jokes, Christmas jokes, computer humor, forms and tests, lawyer jokes, lists, humor about men and women, miscellaneous humor, quick jokes, real life jokes, school humor, and sports jokes. In the absence of other kinds of evidence, one might presume that Clinton jokes were included as merely another topic of contemporary humor and not because of any particular antipathy to the person or presidency of Bill Clinton. In contrast, when a site posts jokes on only a very few topics, it seems they are more likely to reflect genuine attitudes toward Bill Clinton.

Such was the case at one site, where only Clinton jokes, sick jokes, and an admixture of antireligious jokes and serious quotes appeared.[12] The Web master provided detailed information about his employment, Idaho home, his family, politics, and association memberships. He was a Libertarian with very strong feelings about the right to bear arms. He was a member of the National Rifle Association, Jews for the Preservation of Firearm Ownership, the Second Amendment Foundation, and the International Practical Shooting Association. He claimed to belong to no militias, and he announced no antiminority agendas. In fact, he applauded gays for coming out of the closet and showing others how to protect their rights. His advertised membership in Jews for the Preservation of Firearm Ownership—even though he stated that he was not Jewish—was probably intended to thwart attempts to conceive of him as a militia-based racist. He was strongly against organized religion and the follow-the-crowd mentality that it promotes. His feelings about Bill Clinton—expressed to me in an e-mail message—was that Clinton should be "given a fair trial, then, if convicted, executed for treason." In short, the curious selection of Clinton jokes, antireligion jokes, and sick jokes purveyed at the site (many of the sick jokes involve gun use and references to self-defense) were closely aligned with the Web master's own political and philosophical stances.

Sites often have links to other sites. A perusal of these links may reveal the interests and attitudes of the Web master. If a joke site has numerous links to right-wing conservative sites, it likely reflects significant opposition to Bill Clinton and his politics. A single link may not be indicative of political persuasion, however. One site,[13] which featured a large number of Clinton jokes, also had a link to the Vast Right Wing Conspiracy site. The Vast Right Wing Conspiracy—the site name is taken from a remark of Hillary Rodham Clinton's on January 27, 1998, about the conspiracy directed against her husband—is a site that uses satire to promote politically conservative values and an antiliberal agenda.[14] It has links to serious conservative sites. Yet the Web master of the site with the link to the Vast Right Wing Conspiracy identified herself as a Democrat and a great supporter of Bill Clinton. It seems that a number of links at her site were requested by these other sites, and so the Vast Right Wing Conspiracy was added although it did not seem to reflect the values of the Web master who posted the list of Clinton jokes.

The sites themselves frequently give some indication of the propensities and antipathies of the Web masters. Out of the twenty sites that I studied that contained Clinton humor, five (25 percent) gave some fairly direct indication of anti-Clinton sentiments. These sentiments might be a mild warning, like "Offensive to Democrats and Clinton supporters, read at your own risk";[15] a venomous tag, like "Bill Clinton is a Rapist, a Violent Rapist";[16] or a list attributing the deaths of scores of people—including, of course, Vincent Foster—to a conspiracy orchestrated by Bill Clinton.[17] The other fifteen sites (75 percent) did not display any obvious predilections or antipathies. Of nine e-mail messages I sent to Web masters asking about their politics and attitudes toward Clinton (to which I eventually received eight responses, although two provided no helpful information), I discovered an additional Web master with strong Clinton antipathies, two who claimed to be Clinton supporters, and another three who expressed mixed feelings about the president. Some examples: "Some good, some bad, pretty embarrassing";[18] "I don't really have an opinion on Clinton. I don't follow politics that much at this point, but there are some things that I think he should do differently";[19] "He's about average as presidents go. Above average in lack of responsibility."[20] In other words, in this small sample, 30 percent of the sites at which Clinton humor could be found were promoted by people with strong Clinton antipathies, 10 percent were run by Clinton supporters, and 15 percent seemed to have mixed feelings. The attitudes of the Web masters could not be determined in the remaining 45 percent of the cases.

It is also possible to learn something about the people who log onto humor sites. Some Clinton joke sites permitted the rating of Clinton jokes. JokesandHumor.com, for example, had a collection of 308 jokes in their database divided up into fourteen categories. The category of Bill Clinton jokes included sixteen examples. Viewers were invited to rate jokes on a scale of one to ten, with ten being best. Unfortunately, not all visitors rated all jokes and there were large differences in the numbers of votes cast for different jokes—ranging from 44 to 3,360. Nevertheless, some information may be retrievable from such sites about joke preferences and tastes. The highest rated joke on June 18, 1999, received an average of 7.74 with 1097 people voting. The joke was as follows:

> Bill Clinton steps out onto the White House lawn in the dead of winter. Right in front of him on the White House lawn he sees, "The President Must Die" written in urine across the snow. Well, old Bill is pretty pissed off. He storms into his security staff's HQ and yells, "Somebody wrote a death threat in the snow on the damn front lawn! And they wrote it in urine. Son-of-a-bitch has to be standing right on the porch when he did it! Where were you guys?" The security guys stay silent and stare ashamedly at the floor. Bill hollers, "Well dammit, don't just sit there! Get out and FIND OUT WHO DID IT! I want an answer and I want it TONIGHT!" The entire staff immediately jump up and race for the exits. Later that evening, his security officer approaches him and says, "Well Mr. President, we have some bad news and we have some really bad news. Which do you want first?" Clinton says, "Oh Hell, give me the bad news first." The officer says, "Well, we took a sample of the urine and tested it. The

results just came back, and it was Al Gore's urine." Clinton says, "Oh my god, I feel so . . . so . . . betrayed! My own vice president! Damn. . . . Well, what's the really bad news?" The officer replies, "Well, it's Hillary's handwriting."

The joke with the lowest rating, of 5.27 on the basis of 400 votes cast, follows:

> Bill went jogging one morning and came upon the Washington Monument. He said, "George, what should I do?" After a few seconds George replied, "Abolish the IRS and start over." Bill thought about this for a few seconds and continued jogging. Shortly he came upon the Jefferson Memorial and stopped. He said, "Tom, what should I do?" After a few seconds Tom replied, "Abolish welfare and start over." Bill continued jogging after thinking about this and came upon the Lincoln Memorial. He said, "Abe, what should I do?" After a few seconds Abe replied, "Why don't you take the night off and go to the theater."

The joke that scored so highly is an old chestnut collected by Vance Randolph in the Ozarks from informants in 1945 and 1950, both of whom remembered first hearing it in the 1890s. The joke has been told about a number of American presidents, often in a bad-news/worse-news format.[21] The joke about Clinton jogging past various monuments and memorials goes back, at least, to the 1970s and the presidency of Jimmy Carter.[22] One might suspect that the allusion to an assassination of Bill Clinton reduced the appreciation of this joke by its readers; but the first joke also refers to a death threat against the president. There were other jokes, rated higher than the jogging joke, that also alluded to the assassination or death of the president. Without further data, it would be pointless to speculate about why the first joke was appreciated so much more than the second. Although it is impossible to determine who is doing the rating at these sites, the ratings may provide some sense of the differences in appreciation of the particular jokes in a repertoire—especially if consistent patterns are noted in ratings across joke sites.[23]

One joke site solicited the opinions of their readers about President Clinton.[24] Respondents were asked to submit their comments accompanied by their real names, e-mail addresses, cities, and states. Only the city and state, however, were posted with the respondent's comments. There were over 100 responses. Two sample responses follow:

> Bill could have ended it long ago with an ounce of character. The supporters of Bill Clinton seemed to be obsessed with the sex details; BC's problems revolve around his willingness to lie under oath and thus commit perjury. That is his crime, not sex. While morally wrong, no one is convicting him of his indiscretions.

> Who really gives a s—t what the president did with Monica? Kennedy did the same thing, the only difference is that back then the media knew that the private affairs of the president wasn't [*sic*] anyone else's business! As for the "he lied, so he should be impeached," name ONE president who hasn't lied.

Of 119 opinions registered,[25] 44.5 percent could be categorized as anti-Clinton and 29.4 percent could be categorized as pro-Clinton or otherwise supportive of the president. The latter include statements that suggested that Clinton is human, that we should not judge him, and that his private life is his own affair. Seven and a half percent made positive comments about the joke site and 3.4 percent made negative comments about the joke site. Comments on matters that did not have to do with either the support of the president or the evaluation of the Web site were offered by 15.1 percent Such responses may prove useful in gauging the temper of those who sign on, although it might be expected that individuals willing to register their opinions on the Web tend to be those with strong, well-defined views and a willingness to express them publicly (although, in most cases, anonymously).

These responses, on occasion, also revealed something else. Sometimes respondents not only registered their feelings about the scandal but conceptualized their sense of the relationship of joking to its motives and consequences.[26] These responses can be organized in six categories.

Category 1: Indexical

> Clinton clearly obstructed justice and committed perjury. . . . The jokes are great but they show how far down the presidency has sunk with him in office.

> This site represents to me [the] only way that we as the people can voice our disgust and resentments about a person like Clinton. He is a national disgrace. . . . Your "jokes-stories" etc. hit home and voice the honest opinions of the people. Please keep this site going. But watch your back, many Clinton detractors and defectors in the past have died under very strange circumstances.

Category 2: Distracting

> Hi . . . You guys are great! I needed a laugh, sorry it is at the President's expense but I guess he brought it on himself. . . . Thanks for a brighter day.

> I think he should be booted out of office. It is just one disgusting embarrassment to this country. There ARE some funny jokes though!!!

> I love the jokes, but the saddest part is the message we are sending our young people. If you are stubborn enough, and deny it long enough, you can get away with anything.

Category 3: Tendentious

We need some more Clinton crap. I love this stuff.

I despise Clinton, that stupid freak that can smoke without inhaling, B.S., so I love stuff that puts him down.

Clinton should be impeached . . . and you should keep up the funny jokes. . . . You're so funny I laugh my ass off.

Category 4: Offensive

Stop this rubbish. It is high time that you stopped doing such silly things and started doing some good things. The people who have hosted and created this website represent the worst in the country.

I think most of your jokes are funny, others are extremely mean spirited and pitiful in a country such as this with so-called moral, understanding, forgiving Christian people, you guys are silly.

I love my President, and I do not like anyone to make a joke of him, his family, his wife or our country.

I don't think its right to make jokes over this situation. That's the whole trouble with this world today no respect. No one is perfect. Would you like it if your private life was known. I'm sure you wouldn't.

Thank God that Clinton is human, which makes him a sinner like all of us. I know these jokes are funny, I guess. I am not really into it, but to be hateful about anyone is scary.

I don't know if I can make you laugh, but I can tell you that it is pretty sad that all you can do is kick a man when he's down.

Category 5: Harmless

It's funny. Even though you're pretty much over the line on the Clinton thing, I'm from Canada, so I don't really care. We get a TV show about political comedy, they make fun of Jean Chrétien, and Lucien Bouchard, but Chrétien and Bouchard have both wished them luck. Why? Cause they don't care if they're made fun of. So ClintonJokes.com is basically a net version of our political comedy TV show, except it's American. So don't take these jokes seriously people! THEY ARE JOKES!!! Thank you and happy Clinton bashing!!!

Anyone who plans on being in the public eye knows full well that they are opening themselves up to any and all public ridicule. JOKES included. Besides, I think their annual salaries include the damages to and for their egos.

Love the jokes! There is no harm in having a little laugh about politics; it's better than bitchin' and complainin' and sayin' "Oh ain't it awful."

Category 6: Perilous

Even though the jokes are funny, you shouldn't forget that Bill's the best (and certainly most presentable) president you Americans have had in a long time now—and if you kick him out, it will be a long time until another one comes your way [from Sofia, Bulgaria].

Always make jokes, you will lost [*sic*] your excellent president [from Beijing, China].

The responses in category 1 suggest that jokes reflect the authentic "voice of the people" or otherwise index the prestige of the office of president. The prevalence of the jokes themselves speaks to the "disgust" that all Americans feel about Clinton's behavior. They suggest, perhaps, that even those who defend the president reveal their true attitudes when they read and enjoy these jokes. The responses in category 2 suggest that the jokes are funny, although the affair itself is disgusting and embarrassing. That is to say, the jokes are being enjoyed but with a sense that there is a disjunction between the humor of the jokes and the reality to which they allude. Respondents in category 3 see the jokes as pure aggressions and appreciate them as such. Unlike the previous respondents, they do not sense the tension between the humor of the jokes and the seriousness of the situation. The jokes are enjoyed because they are appropriately directed against a despised target. The responses in category 4 regard the joking as hostile and offensive, and the people who engage in it as mean-spirited and un-Christian. In a sense, they agree with respondents in category 3 about the aggressiveness of the jokes but disagree about whether the president—or anyone, for that matter—merits such hostility. Category 5 responses stress the fact that Clinton jokes are simply political jokes and are to be enjoyed as such. They are basically harmless. Politicians should expect, and be prepared to weather, such ridicule. Category 6 responses suggest that it is time to leave the president alone, that he has been a target long enough, or that it would be a loss if he were expelled from office. The last response in the category actually suggests that it is the jokes themselves—rather than impeachment by the House of Representatives and trial in the Senate—that will drive the president from office.[27]

What is particularly interesting is how each group of respondents articulated the frivolity of the humor in the jokes with the seriousness of the situation to which they referred. The comments in categories 1, 3, and 4 register no tension between humor and reality. Humor is reality. The jokes are clear and unambiguous communications. The comments in categories 2, 5, and 6 suggest that the jokes were at odds with reality—whether that reality called for impeaching the president or saving his presidency. In categories 2 and 5, humor is play. It does not, or should not, count.

What then, if anything, can be learned from this survey? For one, that it is not possible to attribute the posting of Clinton jokes and other forms of humor to people with a single political perspective. Clinton humor was posted by Democrats, Republicans, Independents, Libertarians, and those with no allegiances to or affiliations with any of these parties. It was posted by avid Clinton supporters as well as rabid Clinton haters. Nor was it exclusively sought out and read by people opposed to Bill Clinton. It was consumed by supporters and opponents alike. The reason that people with diametrically opposed political views can enjoy Clinton humor is that people's conceptions of humor vary. Humor may be aggression or it may be entertainment. As entertainment, it is at variance with and may even ameliorate the situation to which it refers. The underlying situation is evaluated independently of the humor itself.

Nevertheless, it would appear that a greater percentage of Clinton humor was both purveyed and consumed by people with fairly strong Clinton antipathies. Does this lend credence to the proposition that humor is basically hostile? Clinton jokes were directed against a president of the United States who had had a sexual affair with an intern in the White House, and who had lied about the affair to his wife, to his daughter, and to the American public. He also had lied—or at least assiduously concealed the truth—about the affair under oath in a legal deposition. The specific details of the sexual escapade were eventually revealed as well. Not even the most avid supporter of the president or the most accomplished spin doctor could view these developments as positive. Whatever defenses of the president were marshaled—that he was the target of a vicious attack by a partisan independent prosecutor, that his sex life was his own concern, that no one could weather such scrutiny of their personal lives, that he had lied only about his private and not governmental affairs, that he had repeatedly apologized for his indiscretions, that various conservative members of Congress also had had inappropriate sexual relationships—they could not entirely excuse the president's behavior nor could the details of his sexual escapade once revealed be reconcealed. Even if the behaviors of the president escaped being legally wrong, they were unpresidential, and the revelation of the particulars of his sexual encounters were unambiguously embarrassing.

Clinton supporters might enjoy the jokes without their affecting their overall assessment of his presidency, but they could hardly use the jokes to advertise his virtues or competencies. One can see them either as jokes that speak to serious flaws in the president or as jokes that focus upon peccadilloes that are embarrassing and humorous but ultimately of little account. However, there is little "up side" to the jokes.[28] They have a negative valence. Consequently, those who held negative views of Bill Clinton could easily ally themselves with such materials. It is therefore not surprising that a greater percentage of anti-Clinton views are expressed by the purveyors and consumers of Clinton humor. At the same time, those who supported—or even "loved"—President Clinton could enjoy the jokes as well. Appreciation of many of these jokes did not depend upon an anti-Clinton stance. That the jokes were frequently marshaled for hostile purposes does not decide the motives or functions of these jokes or of humor in general.

A Web site for humor is not like the oral repertoire of an individual or group. Oral tradition operates editorially. Those jokes that do not meet the standards of an individual or group tend to be transformed or eliminated from the repertoire. Jokes on the Internet are another matter entirely. A Web site over which a Web master does not exercise strict artistic control is more like an archive than a repertoire. The site may be managed for quantity rather than quality. It is an accumulation that may not reflect the aesthetics or ideology of any particular individual or group. Consequently, anything that might qualify as Clinton humor might be posted at the site.[29]

In addition to the narrative and riddle jokes that were posted at ClintonJokes.com dealing with the president's sexual appetite, oral sex, cigars, honesty, White House interns, and his relations with his family, there were many jokes that bore no direct relationship to the scandal. For example, several recycled blond and Polish jokes alluded to the stupidity of Clinton, his staff, and supporters. One joke emphasized that he was cheap, another suggested that he was gay, and another that he was a transvestite. Others targeted his economic policies. Older jokes about smoking marijuana and being a draft dodger appeared, as well as some jokes that addressed his liberalism. Older jokes about Hillary Clinton were also prominent. There were recently composed song and poetry parodies, bumper stickers, lists, speeches, letters, and limericks[30] that also targeted the president. In other words, the contents of a joke site are determined by the individuals who contribute and the degree of editorial intervention. When there is little intervention, there is bound to be something for everyone.

Perhaps the most important lesson to be learned from this survey of joke sites is that there is much that can be learned about the values and attitudes of those who post and read humor on the World Wide Web. The Web is not as anonymous as we are sometimes led to believe. The Web sites that posted Clinton humor also posted personal photographs, political manifestos, recreational interests, organizational memberships, original poetry and fiction, film reviews, listings of computer skills and equipment, personal and family data, rating surveys, e-mail addresses, and reader feedback. The Web provides an arena where with care—though with difficulty—correlations between humor and the people who purvey and consume it might be established; perhaps even in greater detail and with greater precision than we are accustomed to in the analysis of humorous expression in face-to-face interaction.

Afterword

THE CHAPTERS IN THIS BOOK have focused upon three major issues: the *structure* of humor, the *motives* of humor, and the *meanings* of humor. Humor depends upon the apprehension of a particular structure of ideas that I call "appropriate incongruity." This sense of what is humorous has been recognized by a number of scholars for several centuries, but unfortunately it has come in recent times to be conceptualized as "incongruity resolution." This term is unfortunate, because incongruities are never truly resolved. At best, certain kinds of connections between the incongruous domains are detected. Also, as a conceptualization of humor, "incongruity resolution" is too programmatic. It can easily lead to erroneous assumptions about how humor is processed. It suggests that humor is perceived only when first an incongruity is registered, and then connections between the incongruous categories are discovered.[1] While this is often the case, it is not always so. What at first seems perfectly appropriate may later come to be regarded as incongruous. Such is the psychiatrist's response, "You're kidding," to the patient who complained that no one believed anything he said. Unlike incongruity resolution, the conceptualization of humor as the apprehension of an appropriate incongruity does not presume a necessary sequence in the processing of a joke.

Incongruity resolution has also led some analysts to divide jokes into those that have their incongruities completely resolved and those that have them only partially resolved and to interpret differences in the appreciation of these types of jokes as reactions to differences in their structures. Since incongruities are never resolved in humor, however, the distinction between such types is anything but clear. There may be, and probably are, ways in which we might differentiate degrees of appropriateness in jokes, but a notion of appropriateness is unlikely to divide naturally into categories of "complete" and "incomplete" or "full" and "partial."

The greatest virtue of a notion of humor as the apprehension of an appropriate incongruity is its *imprecision.* It defines the structure of humor in only the loosest terms. It captures a greater range of humorous speech and behavior than incongruity resolution does. It does not assume that incongruities in humor are resolved, it does not presume a sequence for the processing of humor, and it does not suppose that degrees of appropriateness can be easily distinguished. In humor, appropriateness is *always* partial.

Although I am uncertain whether the perception of an appropriate incongruity will stand as a characterization of all humor in all times and places, I am still willing, at present, to defend the notion against straight incongruity (sans resolution) theories; superiority, aggression, and disparagement theories; or some combination of the above. The criticism directed against appropriate incongruity are often based upon faulty analyses of humorous examples. The structure of humor is not always so easy to analyze, and even scholars make mistakes.[2] Nor am I willing, at this point, to concede that humor is the response to many different kinds of stimuli rather than to a single one.

All this said, it should be recognized that my engagement with the structure of humor is less a concern with a universal definition of humor than it is a concern with grasping how humorous expressions are organized. If we are to understand what jokes communicate beyond their own funniness, then we are bound to attend to the manner in which jokes structure the verbal and visual materials from which they are constructed. Because in humor an incongruity is never resolved, both the incongruous categories and aspects of appropriateness remain active and bear upon the humor's meaning. Appropriateness does not obliterate incongruity. Humor is an oxymoronic formation—and its messages depend upon the whole of its structure. This is evidenced by the use of jokes as glosses. Glosses employ the whole of the joke. The analogy between a joke and the conversation or interaction in which it is embedded embraces both its incongruity and its appropriateness. For example, the message in the "Lenin in Poland" joke, that fictions may prove unsuitable even when they are crafted to achieve very specific aims, depends upon the Politburo's effort to have a monumental piece of art created to commemorate Lenin's visit to Poland *and* the painting of a naked man and woman lying in bed together that appropriately fulfills this commission. When the joke is explicitly employed to convey meaning, the whole of the joke is engaged. Structure matters.

If I am unhappy with the way that the structure of humor has often been conceived, I am unhappier still with the way that the motivations of humor have been identified. I believe that the motivations for humor are varied and that humor is not the product of any single motive—no matter how powerful or prevalent that motive might be. Consequently, I challenge the frequent presumption that humor is motivated by aggression.[3] One analyst of humor has declared that to argue against an aggression theory of humor is to beat a dead horse.[4] However, disclaiming aggression is easier in principle than when confronted with specific instances of humor. The very same analyst regarded jokes about Asian drivers as a way to "criticize people, holding them up to ridicule, [and] reinforcing prejudice against them." He also regarded a joke about a man who says, "Thank you, Paine Webber"[5] when his wife jumps out the window after he tells her that he is financially ruined as an "aggressive, violent, and even vicious" joke against women.[6] The analyst claims that he found the joke funny when he was going through a divorce, but no longer found it funny when he was happily remarried. The anger, pain, and desire for retribution that often attend a divorce probably bore upon the significance and meaning of this joke to him at that time. (Even so, was this joke the most direct and hostile expression directed toward his wife during this period? Can it really be that more visceral and more vicious verbal locutions eluded him so that that whole of his emotional response to his wife at this time was invested in this joke?) Such situational factors may speak to the *use* of a joke, but they do not address the joke itself. What are we to make of people who tell and laugh at the joke who have never gone through a divorce, who remain happily married, or have never been married? What is the joke to them?

I would gladly give up the effort to undermine aggression theory if humor analysts would stop invoking it. In an on-line roundtable discussion involving some twenty humor analysts,[7] I put forward for discussion a joke that had some currency in the 1960s:

Q: What do you call a Negro with a Ph.D.?
A: Nigger!

I tried to point out that the motives informing this joke could not be derived unambiguously from the text. The incongruity lies in the fact that someone who has earned a Ph.D. degree and should merit a title of respect earns only an odious racial epithet. This incongruously assigned epithet can be regarded as appropriate, however, if one recognizes that there are individuals who regard race as a stigma that no achievement can overcome. Tellers and listeners to such a joke may or may not view race in this way. To understand the joke, all that is necessary is the recognition *that such a view exists.* Whether the joke is informed by the view that no amount of education can alter what is regarded as a fundamentally degenerate being, or whether the joke is, in fact, a critical comment on a society in which blacks are not allowed to succeed no matter what they do cannot be determined from the text alone. The text admits both possibilities. Nevertheless, scholars of humor were certain that the joke was hostile and racist. "It is 'funny' because it aggressively slams blacks," declared one scholar. Another agreed: "The ambiguities in that joke are technically feasible but unrealistic, not likely in actual telling and hearing. . . . It only functions as a joke when it is read as [a slam against blacks]."[8] These evaluations were made despite my pointing out that the joke was told by people who were sympathetic to or invested in the civil rights movement at that time.

What I did not reveal in that discussion was that the joke was part of a joke cycle and was regularly followed by another joke:

> Q: What do you call a seven-foot-tall Negro with a bullwhip?
> A: Sir.

It would prove a somewhat torturous exercise to demonstrate that this joke could also serve as a "slam against blacks." Someone might argue that the image of a black man with a bullwhip trades on a stereotype of black men as large and physically intimidating, but this would be to focus on a single image and ignore the joke. The black man is respectfully addressed because of his physical size and his possession of a weapon. The joke suggests that black men can obtain respect only through intimations or overt displays of violence, not by achievement or the content of their character. As a pair, the jokes are a cynical comment on the way our society works: people are racists and will behave accordingly when they feel they can get away with it; people will behave civilly only when they are compelled to do so.

I can imagine that someone might use the "Negro-with-a-Ph.D." joke to "slam blacks," but I do not believe that this is the hypothesis of choice in understanding the joke. Certainly I do not believe this was how the joke was meant by those white student liberals from whom I heard it in the 1960s. These students were estranged from their society and the racism and hypocrisy that they felt characterized it. They used these jokes to unmask that racism and hypocrisy. The jokes served as a criticism of their society and an expression of the liberal values that the tellers and listeners believed they shared.[9]

So to challenge aggression theory is not to beat a dead horse but to attempt to corral a strong and spirited one. As scholars have not abandoned their notions of humor as aggression, I have not abandoned my efforts to show that such views of humor are unnecessarily parochial. Only when the marriage between humor and aggression has been annulled will analysts be free to explore the range of motives that inform humor and decipher a variety of messages that these expressions convey.

Humor is a species of play, and while play may sometimes be aggressive, it is much else besides. Play is expressive. It is auto- and allo-communicative. What play communicates requires a consideration of context. These contexts include the experiences that an individual brings to the humor that he or she hears and performs; the social interaction in which humorous performances are embedded; the social and historical conditions under which jokes arise, proliferate, and disappear; the cultural knowledge upon which humor depends and with which it plays; and the range of expressions, both within and beyond a society's boundaries, with which localized humorous performances may be compared and contrasted. When context is ignored, analysts are left either to consider humor as a form of aggression or dismiss it as mere amusement devoid of import.

People make jokes for different purposes. Sometimes it is merely to pass time and enliven conversation. Humor is a social lubricant. It may fulfill any number of conversational functions—for example, changing topics, democratizing exchange, marking the arrivals and departures of participants, or filling embarrassing silences.[10] Jokes and witticisms may hold a deeper significance as well. They may be used as vehicles for self-expression and presentation. Humor can speak to the character of an individual, the concerns of a community, or the worldview of a society.

Sigmund Freud's Jewish jokes were intimately connected to his sense of self as a Jew and a member of the scientific and intellectual community in fin-de-siècle Vienna. Invited to participate in the new liberal society, yet rejected for doing so, his jokes poignantly reveal the contradiction that he was forced to live. They provide key insights into his identity. The identities of entire nations also were heavily invested in humor. The humor of the frontier served to persuade Americans, Australians, and Israelis that they were new nations composed of an entirely new kind of folk. At the same time, the humor denied that the characteristics of these frontier folk were their own—else they would not have regarded frontier speech and behavior as incongruous and could not have found them humorous. Blond jokes spoke to, and still speak to, a changing workplace in late-twentieth-century and early-twenty-first-century American society. They are efforts to articulate values that should govern a space that was traditionally inhabited and controlled by men, but which has become increasingly inhabited and controlled by women. These are not trivial messages.

There is a joke about a man who describes to his friend a cocktail party he attended. "At the party, I met this guy who just talked, and talked, and talked, and talked." "What did he talk about?" his friend inquired. "I don't know. He didn't say." Too often, humor is treated like this cocktail party conversation. We know it is there, we know who participated, we know it occurred in a particular space and took up time, we know it was funny. Nevertheless, because joke tellers and wit makers don't usually tell us what their comic performances are about, it is easy to assume that they aren't about anything. I presume, however, that humor *means* something. For me, humor studies is fundamentally an interpretive enterprise. It is an attempt to say what people are talking about even when they don't say so themselves. It is an attempt to wrest meaning—sometimes significant meaning—from ludicrous and seemingly discountable expressions. It is the engagement of humor at its most fascinating and consequential levels.

Appendix

This is a collection of joke glosses and associations (there is only one of the latter) not included in chapter 7. It is based upon my own personal use of such jokes, observed use, reported use, and examples from printed literature and other media.

* * *

1. At an academic conference, I met two Japanese scholars who were attending for the first time. I suggested that they try to meet some other scholars who shared their interests. I gave them some names to look for and told them to introduce themselves should they locate these individuals. I also urged them not to be shy about introducing themselves because it was perfectly all right to do so. I then told them the following joke:

> A ship is wrecked and the survivors make it to a small desert island. There are two Germans, two Americans, two Frenchmen, and two Englishmen. Twenty years later a ship arrives and rescues them. The ship's captain is shown around the island to see what they had accomplished over the years. The guide says, "The two Americans have built a factory. And the two Frenchmen over there run a restaurant. The two Germans serve as our police."
>
> The captain notices one person sitting on a log and staring eastward out to sea and another person, at the other end of the log, staring westward out to sea. "Who are they?" the captain asked.
>
> "Oh, those are the two Englishmen; they are still waiting to be introduced."

The two Japanese scholars laughed at the joke. Later that day they told me they had located one of the scholars I had mentioned and had introduced themselves. They cited the joke as the reason for their boldness.

* * *

2. In the context of an e-mail discussion on humor and political correctness, I used a witticism at the end of a particular argument that depends upon a slight modification of a quotation by Thomas de Quincey.

> Of course, humor can be used to express aggression against some target. . . . On the other hand, the joke might be intended to criticize a society in which [the targeting of such groups takes place]. . . .
>
> I don't recall seeing anything that has attempted to assess the harmfulness of jokes—even the "worst" of them. (And harmfulness should be distinguished from the mere objection to them.) While I also think that there is "a lot of suffering out there; war, poverty, exploitation," I await the studies that show how jokes bring these about.
>
> "If once a man indulges himself in murder, very soon he comes to think little of robbing; and from robbing he comes next to drinking and Sabbath-breaking, and from that to incivility and joke telling." This is a joke; it is not the moral order of things.[1]

* * *

3. The following use of a joke was described to me by a Mormon professor who had occasion to speak about his area of scholarship to a Mormon audience. After the lecture he was asked a question that he did not want to answer because it was likely to get him in trouble with the church. He responded to the question with the following J. Golden Kimball story:[2]

> J. Golden Kimball went into a store to buy a hat. When the clerk told him how much it cost, he asked, "Where are the holes?"
>
> "What holes?" asked the clerk.
>
> "The holes for the ears for the jackass who would pay that much for a hat."

The professor reported that the joke deflected the question while communicating why he didn't want to answer. He said that the audience laughed and seemed to understand his intent in telling the story.

* * *

4. The same Mormon professor told me about another incident. The professor stopped by his friend's house on his way back from a trip out of town. His friend worked in the church maintenance program. The friend didn't agree with his superior about something, but the superior said that he was guided by the Spirit. The professor responded with a brief J. Golden Kimball story.

> J. Golden Kimball said at General Conference, "When I talk, I think I am moved by the Holy Ghost. Some of my brethren think I'm not. There you have it. How the hell you gonna know?"

* * *

5. The use of this joke was reported to me by a professor at another university. The school in which the professor's program was housed was being merged with another. There was a party for students, faculty, alumni, and donors to announce the merger. The provost gave a twenty-minute speech that never once mentioned the impact of the merger on the students. After the provost left the party, this professor did get up and say something about the degree programs being preserved.

Later on the professor, the head of the alumni association, a graduate student, and an alumnus were discussing the forthcoming merger. This was a decision made by administration, and very few faculty or students were in favor of it. The professor was thanked for her short speech, since it was the only mention of the impact of the merger on the students.

The alumnus pointed out that he was serving on a committee for city charter reform and that his work on that committee required reviewing the charter that contains information on the relations of the city to the school district. He examined the charter to understand the city's responsibility to the school district and also whether it should be changed. At the bottom of his report he wrote, "There is only one thing that is important here. How what we do affects the quality of education for students—does what we do improve the quality of education?" A discussion followed over whether this shouldn't be true in the university as well. Consolidation should be looked at in terms of what students get out of it. He then referred to a book, *The Peter Principle,* from which he reported the following joke:

> A prospective client was being shown around a stock brokerage. He is taken to a mooring, and the stock broker says, "This is where the yachts of the equity brokers are moored." He is taken further. "This is where the yachts of the bond traders are moored." Further on. "This is where the yachts of the futures traders are moored." The client then says, "This is all very impressive, but where are the yachts of your clients?"

The implication of the joke would seem to be that a university administration's first concern should be the education of students—not economic concerns or administrative convenience.

* * *

6. A friend had come to dinner and, after we had finished the dinner that she had prepared, we were cleaning up. I was teasing her about how many dishes she used and how the mess was so spread out. She then said that I could at least say something nice about the dinner she had prepared. I said that it was a good dinner. She said, "There you go!" I said, "It reminds me of a story":

> An old Jewish man was ill and was being taken care of by his daughter, who did everything for him. One day, after doing a number of difficult things for him, she became exasperated with him and said, "The least you could do is say 'Thank you.'" The man replied, "What! Suddenly you're a stranger?"

The point of the joke was that "thank you" is a form of politeness reserved for people who are distant. For people who are close, it is not necessary, or even appropriate.

* * *

7. At an American Folklore Society meeting in Philadelphia, there was a discussion of whether the field of folklore studies should be renamed to make it more acceptable to other scholars.[3] When comments from the floor were solicited, I rose and opposed the name change. I concluded my remarks with the following joke:

> A little Jewish man appears in front of a judge to request a change of name. "What do you want to change your name to?" asked the judge.
>
> "O'Grady," answered the man.
>
> "And what's your name now," the judge asked?
>
> "O'Reilly," the man replied.
>
> "But you already have a fine Irish name. Why should you want to change it?"
>
> "So I will be able to answer people when they ask me what my name was before I changed it."

The point of telling the joke was to suggest that changing our name would not disguise the fact that we are folklorists, and that it was a ludicrous strategy in addressing the problem of folklore studies in the academy.

* * *

8. After a wedding, I was waiting outside the church with a few people, including one acquaintance. We got to talking about throwing rice at weddings. Someone pointed out that the reason people don't do it anymore is that birds eat the rice but they can't pass it. I then told the following joke:

> A guy walks into a bar with a monkey. He puts him on the bar and orders a drink. After a while, he says to the bartender, "I have to go to the bathroom. Would you mind watching my monkey for a few minutes?" The bartender says okay and the guys goes off. As soon as he leaves, the monkey jumps off the bar and jumps up on the pool table. He picks up the cue ball, examines it closely, and swallows it. Then he jumps back up on the bar. When the guy returns from the bathroom, he asks, "Was the monkey okay?"
>
> The bartender says, "He did something unusual. He went over to the pool table and swallowed the cue ball."
>
> The guy starts apologizing. "Oh, my gosh. I am sorry. What does a cue ball cost?"
>
> The bartender says, "Oh, about fifteen dollars."
>
> The guy peels off a twenty and puts it on the bar. "I hope this covers it, and I am really sorry," and leaves with the monkey.
>
> About a week later the guy comes back to the bar with his monkey. Again he orders a drink and after a few minutes asks the bartender if he would watch his

> monkey while he goes to the bathroom. The bartender agrees, and as soon as the man leaves, the monkey hops down the bar, goes over to the bowl of peanuts, picks one up, looks at it, shoves it up his ass, takes it out, and then eats it. He then hops back to his original place on the bar.
>
> When the man comes back from the bathroom he asks the bartender how his monkey behaved. The bartender says, "Well he did something sort of strange. He went down to the bowl of peanuts, picked one out, shoved it up his ass, took it out, and ate it."
>
> And the man says, "Oh, ever since he passed that cue ball he measures everything he eats."

The joke was not a gloss but an association with the discussion of animals having difficulty passing the things they eat.

* * *

9. I was giving a lecture on male bathroom behavior to my introductory cultural anthropology class. I discussed the idea that bodily waste products are considered dirty and defiling—with one exception. When I asked what that exception was, a student said, "Tears." I asked why tears should be an exception, and another student suggested that they reflected emotion. I said that other waste products could be associated with emotion, and I told the following joke:

> An American man-of-war was patrolling the Mediterranean in the days of the Barbary pirates. One day the captain is standing on the quarterdeck when the first mate comes running up to him, shouting, "Captain, captain! Pirate ship off the starboard bow."
>
> The captain says, "Bring me my telescope." The mate brings the telescope and the captain looks, and sure enough, there is a pirate ship off the starboard bow.
>
> The captain says to his mate, "Bring me my sword and red cape." The mate fetches the sword and cape, and the man-of-war engages the pirate ship and sinks it.
>
> The next day the captain is standing on the quarterdeck when the first mate again runs up to him, shouting, "Captain, captain! Pirate ship off the port bow."
>
> The captain says, "Bring me my telescope." The mate brings the telescope and the captain looks, and sure enough, there is a pirate ship off the port bow.
>
> The captain says to his mate, "Bring me my sword and red cape. The mate fetches them and the man-of-war engages the pirate ship and sinks it.
>
> After the battle the mate asks the captain, "Sir, I understand why you call for your sword before the battle, but why do you wear the red cape?"
>
> The captain says, "If I am wounded in the course of battle, I would not like the wounds to show. The cape will camouflage the blood, and the crew will not become demoralized." The mate nods in understanding.
>
> The next day the captain is standing on the quarterdeck when the first mate

> comes running up to him, shouting, "Captain, captain! There is a pirate *fleet* off the starboard bow."
>
> The captain says, "Bring me my telescope." The mate brings the telescope and the captain looks, and sure enough, there is an entire pirate fleet off the starboard bow. The captain says to his mate, "Bring me my sword and brown pants."

The point of the joke was to suggest that there are excretions other than tears that could be associated with emotion—in this case, the emotion of fear.

* * *

10. In the course of the same lecture on public men's rooms, I had occasion to remark that excretion is associated with sexuality because of the proximity of the sexual organs to the organs of elimination. I then told the following joke:

> Three engineers were arguing about the nature of God. The mechanical engineer said, "God must be a mechanical engineer. Just look at the wonderful structure of bones and muscles that make up the human body. Only a mechanical engineer could have created that."
>
> The electrical engineer says, "No! God is an electrical engineer. Look at the marvel of the human nervous system. The intricate network of nerves linked to a central brain is governed by electrical impulses. God must be an electrical engineer."
>
> The civil engineer says, "You're both wrong. God is a civil engineer."
>
> The other two look at him in amazement. "Why would God be a civil engineer?"
>
> "Because only a civil engineer would run a major sewer outlet right through a prime recreational area."

* * *

11. In an introductory cultural anthropology class, I spoke about the concept of explicit culture—cultural patterns that you are conscious of and capable of describing. I used an example of trying to explain to a student from a very different culture how to negotiate the campus cafeteria. The patterns for cafeteria use are fairly explicit, but even if we tried to give fairly complete instructions on how to use the cafeteria, we would probably leave something out so that a foreign student at some point would be at some sort of impasse. To illustrate the point, I told the following joke:

> An immigrant who spoke no English came to the United States. He went to live with his cousin, who got him a job at the factory where he worked. Every day at lunch he went hungry because he didn't know how to order food in the factory cafeteria. He was getting so hungry at lunchtime that he pleaded with his cousin to teach him some English so that he could order something.
>
> His cousin said, "OK! Memorize this: 'Apple pie and coffee.'"

So the guy repeats to himself, "Apple pie and coffee, apple pie and coffee, apple pie and coffee." He thinks he's got it, and the next day he can't wait to try it.

He goes into the cafeteria, and when the guy behind the counter says, "What'll you have, bub?" he says, "Apple pie and coffee." Lo and behold, he is handed apple pie and coffee. He pays, sits down at a table, and eats it. He is very satisfied.

After three weeks, he is getting very tired of apple pie and coffee. He wants to eat something else. So he asks his cousin, "Teach me something else."

So the cousin says, "OK! Learn this: 'Roast beef sandwich.'" So he starts to memorize, "Roast beef sandwich, roast beef sandwich, roast beef sandwich."

The next day he goes into the cafeteria in great anticipation of eating something new. When he gets to the counter, the guy behind it says, "What'll you have, bub?"

He says, "Roast beef sandwich."

The guy behind the counter says, "On white or rye?"

He freezes for an instant and says, "Apple pie and coffee."

* * *

12. Two jokes with commentary introduce Woody Allen's film *Annie Hall.* Allen appears on screen telling the following jokes:

> There's an old joke. Two elderly women are at a Catskill Mountain resort and one of them says, "Boy, the food at this place is really terrible." And the other one says, "Yeah, I know. And such small portions."
>
> Well that's essentially how I feel about life. Full of loneliness, misery, suffering, and unhappiness, and it's all over much too quickly.

Allen continues,

> The other important joke for me is one that is usually attributed to Groucho Marx, but I think that it appears originally in Freud's *Wit and Its Relation to the Unconscious.*[4] I'm paraphrasing: "I would never want to belong to any club that would have me as a member." That's the key joke of my adult life in terms of my relationship with women.

* * *

13. The following joke ends the film *Annie Hall.* It accompanies the final scene of his parting from Annie after they had met again in New York. Allen does not tell the joke to Annie, but his telling of the joke accompanies the street scene of their parting.

> I thought of that old joke. This guy goes into a psychiatrist and says, "Doc, my brother's crazy. He thinks he's a chicken."
>
> And the doctor says, "Well, why don't you turn him in?"
>
> And the guys says, "I would, but we need the eggs."

Well, I guess that's pretty much now how I feel about relationships. You know, they're totally irrational and crazy and absurd, but I guess we keep going through it because most of us need the eggs.

* * *

14. In "Observations on Transference-Love," Sigmund Freud discusses the problems with transference and how it might be dealt with. He claims that the analyst should not hold social conventions up to the patient in an effort to force her to restrain her love. This would only add to the repression that is the likely cause of the transference in the first place. Nor should the analyst declare his fond feelings while avoiding any physical intimacy so that he can guide the encounter to a higher level. Psychoanalysis is founded on truthfulness, and the worst thing is to get caught in untruthfulness. The love should not be reciprocated either physically or emotionally. Rather, the love should be allowed to persist to make it work to make changes. Her impulses should not be appeased by means of surrogates.

What would happen if the doctor and patient were free and the doctor "were to avail himself of that freedom in order to return the patient's love and to still her need for affection?"

> If he has been guided by the calculation that this compliance on his part will ensure his domination over his patient and thus enable him to influence her to perform the tasks required by the treatment, and in this way liberate her from her neurosis—then experience would inevitably show him that his calculation was wrong. The patient would achieve *her* aim, but he would never achieve *his.* What would happen to the doctor and the patient would only be what happened, according to the amusing anecdote, to the pastor and the insurance agent.
>
> > The insurance agent, a freethinker, lay at the point of death and his relatives insisted on bringing in a man of God to convert him before he died, The interview lasted so long that those who were waiting outside began to have hopes. At last the door to the sick-chamber opened. The freethinker had not been converted; but the pastor went away insured.
>
> If the patient's advances were returned, it would be a great triumph for her, but a complete defeat for the treatment.[5]

* * *

15. In "The Ego and the Id," Freud talks about changing love to hate and the notion of a neutral displaceable energy that can be added to an erotic or destructive impulse. That displaceable libido (for eros is more plastic than the destructive instincts) has an indifference to the path it takes so long as it is discharged. It is often indifferent to the objects it chooses, and it is especially evident in transferences in analysis that develop irrespective of the persons who are their object.

Not long ago Rank published some good examples of the way in which neurotic acts of revenge can be directed against the wrong people.

> Such behavior on the part of the unconscious reminds us of the comic story of the three village tailors, one of whom was hanged because the only village blacksmith had committed a capital offense.[6]

* * *

16. In *The Interpretation of Dreams,* Sigmund Freud discusses the egoism of dream thoughts. Thinking about the death of a friend, he recognized the idea that he was still alive and had survived others who had died and was left in "possession of the field": "I gave expression to my delight with all the naive egoism shown in the anecdote of the married couple one of whom says to the other: 'If one of us should die, I shall move to Paris.' So obvious was it to me that I should not be the one to die."[7]

* * *

17. Hanns Sachs recalled in his memoir of Freud

> one occasion when Freud illustrated a scientific principle by an anecdote from his personal experience which is too characteristic to be omitted. The problem which he treated was that of "overdetermination," that is, the multiple causality which exists everywhere but is especially important for the products of the unconscious. He warned us not to be easily satisfied even when the known causes seemed perfectly sufficient to produce the effect:
>
> > An old professor of medicine died who had ordered in his will that his body should be dissected. The autopsy was performed by a renowned pathological anatomist and I functioned as his assistant. "Look here," the anatomist said to me, "these arteries are as thick as ropes. Of course the man couldn't live with them." I answered him: "All right. But it is a fact that the man did live till yesterday with these blood vessels."[8]

* * *

18. Hanns Sachs also recalled when Freud "discussed with us the psychoanalytic therapy of neurosis [and] . . . used a picture-postcard of the most ordinary kind for making his point. The picture showed a yokel—we would say a hill-billy—in a bedroom trying to blow out the electric light like a candle. 'If you attack the symptom directly, you act in the same way as this man. You must look for the switch.'"[9]

* * *

19. Again, Hanns Sachs recalled how in the relaxed mood of his nightly walks,

> Freud indulged more freely than at other times in his habit of illustrating a difficult point with a story. When he found in his rich treasure of anecdotes one

that answered exactly his purpose, he did not care if it was not "quite nice." Once he discussed with us the curious phenomenon that some people can contemplate a great amount of their moral deficiencies and misdeeds with an unruffled conscience whereas something comparatively little that "hits the spot" may upset them entirely. He quoted Anatole France's *Histoire comique* (later he discussed and explained the same point in his article on "Character-Types" by the analysis of Rebecca West in Ibsen's *Rosmersholm*). He wound up his exposition with this story:

> In the Magnaten-Club in Budapest (at that time the most exclusive club, open only to the high aristocracy) one member made a bet with another that he would eat a goodly portion of fecal matter (monosyllabic among friends). It was served, of course on a golden platter, and he fell to it with a will. Suddenly he paused, spluttered, and could not go on eating. He had found a hair in it.[10]

* * *

20. During the years of World War I, Sachs stayed with Freud in Vienna while Otto Rank, Sandor Ferenczi, Max Eitingon, and Karl Abraham were in the military. Sachs had the best opportunity for intimacy with Freud but he developed tuberculosis and could not take advantage of his proximity to his colleague and teacher. On Armistice Day, he traveled to Switzerland for a cure and stayed nearly two years.

It had been arranged in the months preceding the Convention of 1920 that I should leave Switzerland and go, not back to Vienna, but to Berlin where Abraham and Eitingon, together with Simmel, had founded a Psychoanalytic Institute and Clinic. As it turned out I worked there for twelve years as teacher and training analyst.

When I think back over my career I remember one of those Jewish stories which contains the essential sadness of life (*Sunt lacrimae rerum*) disguised as humor and irony—a story that I heard first from Freud long before it became adaptable to my case. The story is this:

> A very poor youth is befriended by a rich and influential man. The benefactor gives his protégé a letter of recommendation to the Jewish community of a small town—let us call it Rzezow—where the post of schammes [a synagogue functionary] has become vacant. The job is miserably paid, but it protects at least against downright starvation and therefore the man is extremely eager to get it. All seems to go well until it turns out the applicant can neither read nor write. Since the post involves some clerical work and official correspondence he is turned down. He comes home deeply despondent and his protector, out of compassion for his disappointment, lends him a small sum of money so that he can start making a living as a pedlar. He shows excellent business sense and accumulates some capital. When oil is found in the parts of the country where he does business he enters the oil game and in a few years the pedlar has become the owner of a big oil firm. His progress culmi-

> nates in a transaction by which he is to become the chief executive of a big concern. The president of the bank which has managed and financed the deal arranges a sort of celebration; the new chief is asked to read aloud and sign the agreement. When he hears this, he draws the president aside and asks him to drop this part. Pressed for his reason, he finally admits that he can neither read nor write. "What," cries the president, "a man with your financial acumen, illiterate! What would have been your career without such a handicap!" "I can tell you about that," comes the reply. "I would have been schammes in Rzezow."

This was exactly my case. If I had followed the career that was outlined for me and had, like my father and my uncles, studied the law conscientiously and diligently, my lot would have been undernourishment and death by tuberculosis or in a concentration camp.[11]

* * *

21. Sachs wrote of Freud's independence, courage, and character and about not giving in when one is convinced that happiness does not exist. He described Freud's sense of a task and duty that he and everyone must fulfill. For all that, Freud did not think that the meaning of life lay in devotion to the love of mankind in general:

What made him toil to the end of his days amid illness, suffering, and exhaustion, in the very shadow of death, when he had no hope of a reward for himself or for those he loved?

It is as if Freud walked intuitively and unknowingly in the footsteps of his ancestors, and followed one of the oldest Jewish traditions; that is, the belief that all Jews, born and unborn unlike, were present on Mount Sinai and have there taken on themselves "the yoke of the Law." If we set this pious idea free from the narrowness of creed and nationality, it becomes identical with his answer to the problem of life.

The Jews have cultivated a habit of expressing their most serious thoughts—and even their bitterest grievances and their sharpest self-criticisms—by way of jokes. This custom has often been misunderstood and has brought much unjust blame on their heads, but it has produced a series of the profoundest funny stories which the world has seen. Nobody loved them more and appreciated them better than Freud, as his book *Der Witz und seine Beziehung zum Unbewussten* shows. I am in this respect too much of his kin to suppress the joke which gives in its humorous way the same answer.

> A Jewish coachman whips his horse mercilessly. Cruelty to animals is not a Jewish trait and the Jews who stand by entreat him to spare the poor beast; but he answers coolly: "Since he has undertaken to be a horse, he must run" (*As es sich hat ünternümmen ze sejn a Ferd, müss es lejfen*).

Since we take it upon ourselves to be men. . . .[12]

* * *

22. Theodor Reik also wrote about Freud's use of Jewish jokes:

> Here are a few instances which show occasions on which Freud remembered a Jewish story and the special manner in which he used it. I discussed with him once the case of a patient whom he had referred to me for psychoanalytic treatment. The young man suffered from a compulsion neurosis, especially from syphiliphobia, a fear of being infected by a spirochete, and had developed a complicated system of measures which should protect him from the danger of venereal infection in everyday life. He refused for instance to sit down on a chair where a person had sat who could have been acquainted with another whom he suspected of having syphilis. The patient found out that on a certain occasion his parents had taken a man who was the uncle of such a suspected person to the theater in their automobile. The patient refused to use the car of his parents any more. Pointing out the possibility of infection by touch, he insisted that they should buy him a car of his own. In discussing the secondary gains of the neurosis, the different advantages the patient gains from his illness after it is established, Freud told a Jewish anecdote:
>
>> A man in an insane asylum rejects the food there and insists on having kosher dishes. His passionate demand is fulfilled and he is served food prepared according to the Jewish law. On the next Saturday the patient is seen comfortably smoking a cigar. His physician indignantly points out to him that a religious man who observes the dietary laws should not smoke on Saturday. The patient replies: "Then, what am I meschugge (nuts) for?"
>
> Since Freud told me that story I have often quoted it to patients illustrating that they get various secondary compensations in the form of attention, love and even financial support from others from whom they expect help as a result of their neurosis.[13]

* * *

23. Reik recalled another of Freud's use of jokes:

> We were speaking of a group of neurotic cases in whose symptomatology manifestation of instinctual drives are blended with expressions of unconscious guilt feelings. Freud pointed out that such an *entente cordiale* between the demands of the drives and the powers of conscience can often be discovered in the psychology of masochistic and obsessive characters. He told me of a case in which a grossly selfish tendency which was conscious, was put into the foreground disguising an intense unconscious need for atonement and punishment.
>
>> "Do you remember the anecdote of Jacob at the synagogue on Yom Kippur?" Freud asked. The premise of the story is based on the fact that seats for the

service on the High Holidays have to be paid for and poor Jews often cannot afford the price. Jacob pleads with the sexton at the door of the synagogue to let him enter because he has to convey an important business message to Mr. Eisenstein. But the sexton adamantly refuses, saying: "I know you, you *gonnif* (scoundrel)! You only want to get in to *daven* (say your prayers)."[14]

* * *

24. The following appeared in the TV miniseries *Oliver's Travels* broadcast on public television. It starred Alan Bates and Sinead Cusack. Oliver (Bates) is being pursued by people who are trying to kill him. He finds himself in a church and winds up giving a sermon to the congregation. He begins:

> About religious faith and a man in a bowler hat. May I tell it?
>
> A man was walking through a forest one day when in a clearing he met another man. The second man was stark naked except for a bowler hat.
>
> "Excuse me," said the first man. "But you're not wearing any clothes."
>
> "Nobody walks in this part of the forest."
>
> "So why are you wearing a bowler hat if nobody walks in this part of the forest?"
>
> "Well," said the second man, "you never know. Somebody might."
>
> Religion is, I suggest, a bowler hat which we choose to wear or not as the case may be in case it turns out there's somebody in the depths of the forest.

* * *

25. I was talking to a department chair in my university about faculty activity reports for merit raises. The deadline for submissions had just been postponed by the chancellor after all the hurry to submit by the original deadline. The memo from the dean indicated that those faculty who had not met the first deadline still had the chance to submit their reports. The chair complained that people who hadn't even tried to meet the first deadline now had time to hand in their reports. I told the following joke:

> In the Soviet Union, there was a rumor that a large shipment of meat was coming to the local meat market and everybody lined up for it. After two hours, the store manager came out and said that the shipment was not going to be as large as anticipated and that all the Jews should go home. So the Jews left the line and went home. After another two hours he came out and said that the shipment would be even less than anticipated and that people who were not members of the Communist party should go home. So nonmembers left the line and went home. After another two hours he said the shipment would be smaller still and that those who had not fought in the Great War should go home. So nonveterans left the line and went home. After another two hours the manager came out

> and said that there would be no shipment of meat and everyone should leave. As the remaining people left, they said, "Goddamn Jews."

The point of the joke was to suggest that the chair was complaining about certain people for something that was not, in fact, of their doing. The administrators were responsible for the change, and he should direct his dissatisfaction to them.

* * *

26. I was talking to a friend and said that I probably could see her on her balcony from my own home if I used a telescope. She said the telescope would invert the image and she would appear upside down. I said it didn't matter because of "Zachary Syndrome." The reference was to a joke that she had told me some time before. The joke itself was not repeated.

> A woman had no luck with men. She thought there was something wrong with her, so she went to a doctor, but he couldn't find anything wrong with her. She goes from doctor to doctor, but none can find anything wrong with her. Finally it is recommended that she see a Chinese herbalist. She is reluctant, but she finally consents. She goes to him, and he tells her to completely undress. She undresses.
>
> He says, with a Chinese accent, "Okay, crawl toward me on your hands and knees." She thinks this is strange but she does it. Then he says, "Crawl away from me on your hands and knees." Again she does so. He says, "As I suspected, you have Zachary Syndrome."
>
> "Zachary Syndrome? What's that?" the woman asks.
>
> He looks at her and says, "Your face rook zachary rike your ass."

* * *

27. A colleague consulted a cardiologist after an episode of cardiac arrhythmia. The cardiologist said that tests showed everything to be normal and that such arrhythmias were common among older people. Nevertheless, the cardiologist suggested that my friend "avoid anything stimulating." The patient then told the cardiologist the following joke:

> A guy had a heart attack and, after he was released from the hospital, he went to see a cardiologist. The cardiologist told him to give up drinking, smoking, staying up late at night, and running after women. "Will that make me live longer?" the patient inquired. "No, but it will seem like it."

* * *

28. A friend was talking about his interest in learning how to do computer graphic layouts. I pointed out that he didn't even own a computer. He responded, "Taste the soup," which is the punch line of the following joke:

> A guy in a restaurant ordered a meal. The waiter brought him his soup. After a minute he called the waiter over and said, "Taste the soup."
>
> The waiter says, "The soup was made this morning, it's excellent, and it is steaming hot. What's the problem?"
>
> The guy said, "Taste the soup."
>
> The waiter said, "I had that soup for lunch today. I happen to know it is delicious. I know that there isn't any problem with it."
>
> The guy says again, "Taste the soup."
>
> The waiter says, "All right. All right. I'll taste it. Where's the spoon?"
>
> And the guy says, "Aha!"

The point of my friend's joke allusion was ambiguous. He might have been agreeing with me and suggesting that he would never learn the things that he wanted to learn without the appropriate utensil—in this case, a computer. Or he might have been suggesting that if he got a computer, he could learn what he needed to learn. Just as the man's difficulties with the soup would evaporate once the waiter brought him a spoon, he could learn what he needed to learn once he bought a computer. The obstacle was not insurmountable.

* * *

29. A professor delivered the closing remarks at a conference on the performance of oral epic, ballad, and song. He employed the following joke:

> A guy goes to visit his cousin in Ireland. He is very keen to visit a pub, as he has heard so much about the camaraderie of the drinkers in Irish pubs. When his cousin picks him up, he conveys his wish about visiting the pub, but his cousin says that they can't go to his pub until Wednesday night because that is the night when all his friends will be there. It's Thursday, so they will have to wait a whole week, but in the meantime they can visit any other pub they like.
>
> So each night they go to a different pub, but it isn't what he expects because his cousin isn't really known in any of them and he doesn't get the feeling of community that he expected.
>
> As Wednesday approaches, he is getting excited. On Wednesday night, he and his cousin go to the pub and he immediately sees how close the group is and how well they know one another. One of the lads at the bar says, "Thirty-seven," and everybody laughs. Someone else responds with "Sixty-four," and everybody laughs again. The guy is befuddled by what is going on so he asks his Irish cousin what is going on. His cousin tells him that they all know the same one hundred fifty jokes, and that to save time, they just give the number rather than tell the joke since everyone already knows them so well.
>
> The cousin is excited about trying to tell a joke himself, and he asks his cousin if it is all right. His cousin assures him that it is, so he takes a few swallows of Guinness to fortify himself and shouts, "Eighty-nine." There is dead silence. The

guy is humiliated, and he turns to his cousin and asks, "Why didn't anyone laugh?"

His cousin says, "You have to know how to tell them."

The professor went on to say that the conference was concerned with reanimating old texts with meaning and vitality. It was about making them come alive by exploring the conditions under which these texts would have been told and the oral and social dynamics that attended their expression. It was a conference not about literary text but about performance.

Notes

Preface

1. The term "humor" in English has a history, and its meaning has changed rather dramatically over the course of several centuries. I mean by "humor" an amusement-provoking stimulus that is recognized as such by someone who smiles or laughs, is disposed to smile or laugh, or even rejects the enticement to smile or laugh.

2. Childhood also succumbs to notions of triviality as noted by Brian Sutton-Smith in "Psychology of Childlore: The Triviality Barrier," *Western Folklore* 29 (1970): 1–8.

Chapter 1: Appropriate Incongruity Redux

1. For a broader discussion of this concept, see Elliott Oring, *Jokes and Their Relations* (Lexington: University Press of Kentucky, 1992), pp. 1–15.

2. This is a distinction that is often made, for example, by Sigmund Freud in *The Standard Edition of the Complete Psychological Works of Sigmund Freud,* trans. under the general editorship of James Strachey in collaboration with Anna Freud, 24 vols. (London: Hogarth Press and the Institute for Psycho-Analysis, 1953–74) (hereafter cited as *SE*), 8:90–91.

3. Admittedly this is a weak joke, since nothing about payment had been previously established.

4. For the sake of brevity, I often refer to the perception of appropriate incongruity simply as "appropriate incongruity." However, appropriate incongruity always depends upon a perception and is not to be construed as an objective quality of the percept. If appropriate incongruity is not perceived, there is no humor.

5. James Beattie, *Essays: On Poetry and Music, as They Effect the Mind; On Laughter and Ludicrous Composition; On the Utility of Classical Learning* (Edinburgh: W. Creech, 1778), p. 347.

6. Jerry M. Suls, "A Two-Stage Model for the Appreciation of Jokes and Cartoons: An Information-Processing Analysis," in *The Psychology of Humor: Theoretical Perspectives and Empirical Issues,* ed. Jeffrey H. Goldstein and Paul E. McGhee (New York: Academic Press, 1972), p. 84; Jerry M. Suls, "Cognitive and Disparagement Theories of Humor: A

Theoretical and Empirical Synthesis," in *It's a Funny Thing, Humour,* ed. Antony J. Chapman and Hugh C. Foot (Oxford: Pergamon, 1977), p. 41.

7. Suls, "Cognitive and Disparagement Theories."

8. Freud, *SE,* 8:31.

9. For example, Paul E. McGhee, *Humor: Its Origin and Development* (San Francisco: W. H. Freeman, 1979), p. 42; John Morreall, ed., *The Philosophy of Laughter and Humor* (Albany: State University of New York Press, 1997), p. 187.

10. Such incongruities also excite laughter in the case of absurd humor, which will be considered in the next chapter.

11. McGhee, *Humor,* pp. 131–33.

12. Brian Sutton-Smith, "A Developmental Structural Account of Riddles," in *Speech Play: Research and Resources for the Study of Linguistic Creativity,* ed. Barbara Kirshenblatt-Gimblett, (Philadelphia: University of Pennsylvania Press, 1976), p. 118.

13. McGhee, *Humor,* p. 133.

14. Thomas R. Schultz discovered that children often create their own incongruities and resolutions to cartoon humor that are not in keeping with those intended by the artist. See "The Role of Incongruity and Resolution in Children's Appreciation of Cartoon Humor," *Journal of Experimental Psychology* 13 (1972): 474–75.

15. We are speaking of American children or, at most, children in English-speaking or Western countries, and then only some subset of these.

16. The issue of Aristotelian definition was raised by Gregory Schrempp in "Our Funny Universe: On Aristotle's Metaphysics, Oring's Theory of Humor, and Other Appropriate Incongruities," *Humor* 8 (1995): 219–28. See also Kanavillil Rajagopalan, "Austin's Humorous Style of Philosophical Discourse in Light of Schrempp's Interpretation of Oring's 'Incongruity Theory' of Humor," *Humor* 13 (2000): 287–311.

17. Except, perhaps, in those cases in which the fraudulence of human rationality is intimated.

18. See Ted Cohen, "Metaphor and the Cultivation of Intimacy," *Critical Inquiry* 5 (1978): 10. See also Joseph Stanley, ed., *Dictionary of World Literature* (Totowa N.J.: Littlefield Adams, 1968), s.v. "metaphor."

19. Actually, the two senses of *spring* are related, as they stem from a notion of "moving or rising suddenly." Conventional usage of these words, however, has suppressed this semantic connection.

20. It would not be difficult to generate numerous humorous definitions of people by utilizing the same spurious technique: "Man is the only animal to paint its toenails"; "Man is the only animal to think it looks good in Bermuda shorts"; "Man is the only animal to pay eight dollars for a movie ticket."

21. It should be noted that Gary Larson's mother is named Doris, and she apparently takes photos at all family gatherings. See Gary Larson, *The PreHistory of the Far Side: A Tenth Anniversary Edition,* (Kansas City, Mo.: Andrews and McMeel, 1989), p. 72.

22. This joke contains a paradox of the type formulated by Epimenides, in that the patient's statement is itself a member of the class of statements to which it refers. The paradox itself does not engender humor, for if it did, laughter should occur at the point when the patient states, "No one believes anything I say."

Although humor and paradox are related, it does not seem that paradoxes are perceived as humorous. For those who engage paradox, they are serious and disturbing. See William F. Fry, Jr., "Humor and Paradox," *American Behavioral Scientist* 30 (1987): 42–71. For most people, paradoxes need to be elaborated upon and not merely stated. For example, it is not sufficient to state Epimenides' paradox that "All Cretans are liars." It needs to be *shown* that the Cretan's statement is false when it is true, and true when it false. (Actually this latter formulation is only achieved by the improper negation of the statement "All Cretans are liars" as "All Cretans tell the truth." The proper negation of "All Cretans are liars" is "Some Cretans are not liars." The statements "I am lying" or "This statement is false" do constitute genuine paradoxes, however.) Explaining a paradox is likely to have the same effect that explaining a joke has. It is not funny. On the relation between paradox and humor, see Gregory Bateson, *Steps to an Ecology of Mind* (New York: Ballantine, 1972), pp. 177–93; and John Allen Paulos, *Mathematics and Humor* (Chicago: University of Chicago Press, 1980), pp. 41–55.

23. Joel Sherzer, "Puns and Jokes," in *Handbook of Discourse Analysis,* ed. Teun A. Van Diyk (London: Academic Press, 1985), p. 3:219.

24. The use of the word "corny" to characterize humor should be differentiated from the use of the word to characterize excessive sentimental expression (see chapter 6). But the uses of the term are similar to the extent that too much is outwardly displayed: sentiment in one case, spurious technique in the other.

25. Freud, *SE,* 8:46.

26. Ibid., 120. See also Arthur Schopenhauer, *The World as Will and Representation,* trans. E. F. J. Payne, 2 vols. (New York: Dover, 1966), 2:92, and Noël Carroll, "On Jokes," *Midwest Studies in Philosophy* 16 (1991): 289–90.

27. What is considered spurious may well vary between cultures and classes (and what is perceived as humor may consequently vary as well). It may be that in one culture sound resemblances between words are generally discounted as accidental and meaningless unless some specific historical connection between words has been demonstrated. In another culture, such sound resemblances may be regarded as substantive and the basis for magical and religious speculation and practice. See, for example, Victor Turner, "Symbols in African Ritual," *Science* 179 (1973): 1100–1105.

28. Gabriella Eichinger Ferro-Luzzi, "On Unnecessary Incongruities," *Humor* 10 (1997): 117–19. This point had been made before. See Michael Clark, "Humour and Incongruity," *Philosophy* 45 (1970): 20.

29. Gabriella Eichinger Ferro-Luzzi, "Tamil Jokes and the Polythetic-Prototype Approach to Humor," *Humor* 3 (1990): 147–58. See also her book *The Taste of Laughter: Aspects of Tamil Humor* (Wiesbaden, Germany: Otto Harrassowitz, 1992).

30. Mahadev Apte seems also to have accepted Eichinger Ferro-Luzzi's claim that incongruity is not sufficient to define humor. See his review of her book in *Humor* 8 (1995): 299–305.

31. Tamil refers to the speakers of Tamil, one of the principal Dravidian languages of southern India, among whom Eichinger Ferro-Luzzi has done extensive research. She claims that she could illustrate her point with examples from Western humor but that Tamil humor adds an exotic note to the discussion. In challenging definitions and theories, it is advisable to employ the most accessible forms of humor to demonstrate claims. This allows scholars to easily evaluate the examples and the persuasiveness of the overall

argument. Tamil humor should be used to challenge general definitions of humor among Tamil-speaking scholars or when Tamil humor provides the only available counterexamples to the propositions in question. What Tamil humor (or any other esoteric humor) adds to the theoretical discussion is not an exotic note but an equivocal one.

32. Eichinger Ferro-Luzzi, "On Unnecessary Incongruities," p. 118.

33. In urban India it is common to have one's lunch shipped from home to one's place of work, but even then, the meal remains whole. One portion is not sent to one place and the remainder to another.

34. Eichinger Ferro-Luzzi, "Tamil Jokes," p. 154.

35. Similar criticisms may be leveled at other examples in Eichinger Ferro-Luzzi's works in which she claims that incongruity is absent.

36. Eichinger Ferro-Luzzi, "Tamil Jokes," p. 156.

37. Eichinger Ferro-Luzzi, "On Unnecessary Incongruities," p. 118.

38. Wittgenstein's metaphor of the rope made up of overlapping strands is also curious, since the rope is made up of overlapping strands that are similar and overlap in exactly the same way. The resemblances and relations are identical, unlike the resemblances in a family. Moreover, while overlapping strands make up the rope, they do not determine the concept of rope or what belongs to the category. Ludwig Wittgenstein, *Philosophical Investigations,* trans. G. E. M. Anscombe (New York: Macmillan, 1953), para 66–67.

39. Unless one is a professional athlete or one is betting on these contests. If one is betting, the outcome may have significant consequences, but that would be true no matter what one was betting upon. It is the winning or losing of the bet that is significant, and not the outcome of the contest per se.

40. While it is true that not everything that is called humorous is necessarily laughed at, I would think that the things that one categorizes as humorous might appropriately be laughed at, and that one would not be surprised if someone actually laughed at them.

Chapter 2: The Senses of Absurd Humor

1. Evan Esar, *The Humor of Humor* (New York: Bramhall, 1952), pp. 271–73.

2. John Morreall, ed., *The Philosophy of Laughter and Humor* (Albany: State University of New York Press, 1987), p. 197.

3. Esar refers to these as "nonsensisms," a term that includes every kind of absurdity. See *The Humor of Humor,* p. 271.

4. The old Latin sense of "absurd" is "unmelodious"; in the more contemporary and conventional sense, "irrational," "impossible," or "impracticable."

5. Mary K. Rothbart and Diana Pien, "Elephants and Marshmallows: A Theoretical Synthesis of Incongruity-Resolution and Arousal Theories of Humor," in *It's a Funny Thing, Humour,* ed. Anthony J. Chapman and Hugh C. Foot (Oxford: Pergamon, 1977), pp. 38.

6. Hot chocolate is often served with a marshmallow floating in it.

7. Rothbart and Pien, "Elephants and Marshmallows," p. 37. Why the interchangeability of "a wafer" for "away for" is not similarly cited as a piece of nonsense escapes me.

8. Not all incongruity-resolution theorists regard resolution in this fashion. For many, resolution merely involves finding some level of fit between incongruous elements. See

Jerry Suls, "Cognitive Processes in Humor Appreciation," in *Handbook of Humor Research,* ed. Paul E. McGhee and Jeffrey H. Goldstein (New York: Springer-Verlag, 1983), 1:42.

9. Robert L. Latta makes much of this point in *The Basic Humor Process: A Cognitive-Shift Theory and the Case against Incongruity* (Berlin: Mouton de Gruyter, 1999), but he overlooks that many incongruity-resolution theorists mean by "resolution" only a sense of fit between categories. See my review of Latta's book in *Humor* 12 (1999): 457–64.

10. Henny Youngman, *Take This Book, Please* (New York: Gramercy, 1984), p. 97.

11. Immanuel Kant, *Critique of Judgement,* trans. Werner S. Pluhar (Indianapolis: Hackett, 1987), p. 203.

12. Michael Mulkay, *On Humour* (Oxford: Basil Blackwell, 1988), p. 19.

13. Walter Nash, *The Language of Humour: Style and Technique in Comic Discourse* (London: Longman, 1985), p. 107.

14. Mulkay, *On Humour,* p. 19.

15. Although many expressions might be nonhumorous *and* absurd.

16. H. Paul Grice, "Logic and Conversation," in *Syntax and Semantics,* vol. 3, *Speech Acts,* ed. Peter Cole and Jerry L. Morgan (New York: Academic Press, 1975), pp. 45–46.

17. It should be noted that the "What am I, a milliner" joke is taken from a joke book by Henny Youngman—a Jewish comedian. Among the stereotypes of Jews is that they answer questions with other questions: "'Why do you Jews answer a question with another question?' a Gentile asks. 'Why should we not answer a question with a question?'" (Theodor Reik, *Jewish Wit* [New York: Gamut, 1962], p. 117.) For that reason, answering a question with a question can allude to a Jewish style of discourse that may add to the appropriateness of the "What am I, a gardener" response.

18. Sigmund Freud, *The Standard Edition of the Complete Psychological Works of Sigmund Freud,* trans. under the general editorship of James Strachey in collaboration with Anna Freud, 24 vols. (London: Hogarth Press and the Institute for Psycho-Analysis, 1953–74) (hereafter cited as *SE*), 8:138–39, n. 1.

19. Freud (ibid.) goes on to explain the source of the pleasure, which he would not need to do if the joke produced no laughter response. I have personally observed this joke producing sustained and hearty laughter.

20. Ibid.

21. Ibid., 139. If the joke is seen as a practical joke, then the incongruity is to some extent appropriate, because the listener recognizes the teller's intent to deceive the listener into trying to locate a textual appropriateness that is not there. The humor is appropriate extratextually.

22. Ibid.

23. Were the punch line in the mayonnaise joke changed to "I'm sorry, I thought it was Brylcream" (the brand name of a men's hair styling cream), the mistaken identity might be comprehensible. Brylcream does, or did, resemble mayonnaise in color and texture, but why someone should think Brylcream would be offered at dinner, or why it would be appropriate to apply it at the table if it were, would remain a mystery.

24. See Alan Dundes, "Metafolklore and Oral Literary Criticism," *Analytic Essays in Folklore* (The Hague: Mouton, 1975), pp. 53–54, and Noël Carroll, "On Jokes," *Midwest Studies in Philosophy* 16 (1991): 293–94.

25. Freud, *SE,* 138, n. 1.

26. This interpretation is also offered by Reik, *Jewish Wit,* p. 117. The history of this joke, its variants, and interpretations are discussed in Richard Raskin, *Life Is like a Glass of Tea: Studies of Classic Jewish Jokes* (Aarhus, Denmark: Aarhus University Press, 1992), pp. 131–65. The suspension-bridge joke used by Freud can be found there in a more elaborate form:

> On another occasion, after the later services on a Sabbath afternoon, the pious men sit around their wise rabbi at the Sabbath meal. Again he sinks into deep meditation. As the men become aware of this, they stop their debates and disputes and wait for the moment when the holy man will awaken from his mediation. When this doesn't happen, the eldest member of the congregation touches the rabbi's shoulder, and as he gives a start, the rabbi is asked what thoughts had preoccupied him to such a degree.
>
> The great man then raises his thoughtful gaze and speaks: "Life . . . life is like a suspension bridge." Then he falls silent once again.
>
> "What did he say? . . . What did he say?" the men whisper, and after they have reverently murmured the statement to one another, they begin to discuss it eagerly and with passion. And so great is their eagerness in interpreting the statement that one after another their minds and finally also their fists intervene in the dispute. An agreement as to the meaning of the enigmatic statement cannot be reached, and they finally agree to ask the rabbi, still withdrawn in meditation, what he meant by it.
>
> "Rabbi," they say, "you can see we haven't understood you. Give us the meaning, tell us the significance. How is life like a suspension bridge?
>
> Once again the rabbi raises his thoughtful gaze and speaks: "How should I know?" (p. 137).

27. Freud deals with a similar formulation of G. C. von Lichtenberg: "How is it that cats have two holes cut in their skin precisely at the place where their eyes are." *SE,* 8:59–60. Freud does not feel that the question is entirely absurd, since it captures the "great problem of teleology in the structure of animals"; ibid., 93–94. This teleological problem is not resident in the joke about plumbing, however.

28. This confusion often erupts in verb agreement with relative pronouns. Thus the sentence "This is only *one* of the local papers *that prints* a daily horoscope" is correct because "that" refers to only one paper. See John C. Hodges and Mary E. Whitten, *Harbrace College Handbook,* 10th ed. (San Diego: Harcourt Brace Jovanovich, 1986), p. 63.

29. Morreall has claimed that this joke lacks "resolution" and that it evidences his claim that incongruity alone is sufficient to produce humor. I agree that there is no second scheme that makes the question coherent, but the question is framed in such a way that the concatenation of the first part and the second part gives a measure of appropriateness to an otherwise nonsensical whole. Latta disagrees with Morreall and sees the humor as the result of puzzling over the sense of the question to arrive at the conclusion that it simply does not make sense. While it is true that the nonsense of the expression must be recognized, this is a joke and not just any piece of nonsense. The question is puzzling because of the way it is structured. The structure delays recognition of the nonsense by conjoining parts that are in themselves appropriate. See Morreall, *Philosophy of Laughter,* pp. 197–99; and Latta, *Basic Humor Process,* p. 138.

30. One search engine produced 2,800 "hits" for the phrase "eat their young." Most

did not relate to animal behavior. It was used as a metaphor for business, nurse training, and chiropractic and was even applied to the French because of their lack of a child-centered culture. It is also the title of a rock lyric.

31. Thomas R. Shultz also sees humor as "resolvable or meaningful" incongruity. Irresolvable incongruity, however, is genuine "nonsense." "A Cognitive-Developmental Analysis of Humour," in *Humor and Laughter: Theory, Research and Applications,* ed. Anthony J. Chapman and Hugh C. Foot (London: John Wiley, 1976), p. 13.

32. John C. Paolillo, "Gary Larson's *Far Side:* Nonsense? Nonsense!" *Humor* 11 (1998): 264, 271, regards Gary Larson's cartoon of runners handing off ducks to one another in a race and captioned "Duck relays," as having no resolution. The incongruity is appropriate, however. The joke simply depends upon the substitution of ducks for batons. In a baton relay, a baton is passed from runner to runner; ergo, in a duck relay a duck would be passed. If there were no resolution, the cartoon would be nonsense and puzzling rather than funny. Furthermore, while the scenario is implausible, it is not contrary to reality. One could hold a duck relay. Stranger things have been done (e.g., cow pie–tossing contests; races to see how fast one could swallow a string of spaghetti and make it emerge from one's nose). If there is humor, there is appropriateness or resolution.

33. A similar example would be "Why is there a stain on my car seat? Because there are two of them." The answer is "definitionally correct" because if there are two stains, there is necessarily a single stain. The answer will not, however, satisfy the inquirer, who is likely to be interested in how the stain got there and not in the arithmetic implications of the number two.

34. Grice, "Logic and Conversation," pp. 45–46.

35. Based on Mr. J., *Giant Book of Dirty Jokes* (Seacacus, N.J.: Castle, n.d.), p. 12.

36. Types 1–299 in Antti Aarne and Stith Thompson, *The Types of the Folktale,* FF Communications no. 184 (Helsinki: Suomalainen Tiedeakatemia, 1964).

37. The elephant-and-sparrow joke requires mapping human traits onto animal characters, but this does not make the incongruity in the joke any less appropriate or "resolvable."

38. Elephant jokes first circulated in the United States in the mid-1960s. See Ed Cray and Marilyn Eisenberg Herzog, "The Absurd Elephant: A Recent Riddle Fad," *Western Folklore* 26 (1967): 27–36.

39. One could also create the joke "Q: How do you know when an elephant has been in your refrigerator? A: After eating leftovers, you have the overwhelming urge to vote Republican." The joke is equally absurd, but a connection between the refrigerator and the elephant is established, since leftovers are kept in the refrigerator and the elephant is the symbol of the Republican party.

40. For a discussion of other principles of riddling that elephant jokes violate, see Elliott Oring, *Jokes and Their Relations* (Lexington: University Press of Kentucky, 1992), pp. 16–28.

41. James Manns, in "Two Faces of the Absurd," *Humor* 1 (1988): 262–63, maintains that, unlike absurdist drama, absurd humor does not refer to anything beyond itself. Interpreters of elephant jokes would not agree: see Mac E. Barrick, "The Shaggy Elephant Riddle," *Southern Folklore Quarterly* 28 (1964): 266–90; Oring, *Jokes and Their Relations,* pp. 16–28; and Joseph Boskin, *Rebellious Laughter: People's Humor in American Culture* (Syracuse, N.Y.: Syracuse University Press, 1997), pp. 66–70.

42. While it is certainly on the boundaries of possibility that an elephant could be a nun, it is within the realm of possibility that an elephant could be dressed in nun's habit, since animals in circuses are dressed in human-style clothing all the time. So would the joke-riddle "What is black and white and gray? An elephant in nun's habit" be qualitatively different from one whose answer is "Sister Mary Elephant"? It would seem that the only difference is that the latter requires the listener to do more work to apprehend the appropriateness of the incongruity.

43. Rothbart and Pien make a strong distinction between possible and impossible incongruities and complete and incomplete resolutions. These distinctions seem arbitrary. See "Elephants and Marshmallows," pp. 37–40.

44. WD = *Witz-Dimensionen* (humor dimensions). For more about the test and its findings, see the references cited in Willibald Ruch, "Assessment of Appreciation of Humor: Studies with the 3 WD Humor Test," in *Advances in Personality Assessment,* ed. Charles D. Spielberger and James N. Butcher (Hillsdale, N.J.: Lawrence Erlbaum, 1992), pp. 9:27–75.

45. Ibid., p. 32. Rosemary Staley and Peter Derks regard the distinction as between incongruity-resolution humor and pure incongruity. See "Structural Incongruity and Humor Appreciation," *Humor* 8 (1995): 99.

46. Paul E. McGhee, Willibald Ruch, and Franz-Josef Hehl, "A Personality-Based Model of Humor Development during Adulthood," *Humor* 3 (1990): 130.

47. Ibid., pp. 132–33.

48. Ruch, "Assessment of Appreciation of Humor," p. 29. Only the sexual humor category is based on content, although this content will also be structured as incongruity resolution or nonsense.

49. The original cartoon, which was translated from German, employs the verb *brummen,* which can mean both "growling" and "buzzing." Thus there is an added measure of appropriateness in the German version, since one can understand why a bear might have entered and succeeded in such a contest. However, the joke still works in English without the double meaning.

50. As Ruch states: "We referred to the model of Rothbart and Pien (1977) who propose to distinguish between possible and impossible incongruities and between complete and incomplete resolutions. They argue that possible incongruities can be resolved completely while for impossible incongruities, there is always a residue of incongruity left." Ruch, "The Sense of Nonsense Lies in the Nonsense of Sense," *Humor* 12 (1999): 76.

51. Paolillo also questioned the categorizations of nonsense and incongruity-resolution humor employed in the 3 WD studies. He argued that Gary Larson's *Far Side* cartoons might earn the same funniness ratings as nonsense humor because German experimental subjects did not have the requisite cultural knowledge to resolve the incongruities in many of those cartoons. Unfortunately, Paolillo accepts the basic distinction between nonsense humor and incongruity-resolution humor promoted by Rothbart and Pien and utilized in the 3 WD taxonomy. He disagrees only with the assignment of particular jokes to these categories. See Paolillo, "Gary Larson's *Far Side,*" pp. 282–83.

52. McGhee, Ruch, and Hehl, "Personality-Based Model," pp. 133, 135; Willibald Ruch and Franz-Josef Hehl, "A Two-Mode Model of Humor Appreciation: Its Relation to Aesthetic Appreciation and Simplicity-Complexity of Personality," in *The Sense of Humor:*

Explorations of a Personality Characteristic, ed. Willibald Ruch (Berlin: Mouton de Gruyter, 1998), pp. 109–42. Unfortunately, the 3 WD Humor Test does not assess a subject's understanding of the humor stimulus. For that reason it is difficult to ascertain the degree to which comprehension difficulty is a factor in humor assessment. Ruch is aware of this; see "Assessment of Appreciation of Humor," pp. 48–49.

53. One wonders what differences psychologists might measure in audiences that prefer the film *High Noon* to *Outland.* Narratively, the latter is a remake of the former, but the former is set in the Old West and the latter is situated in a futuristic space colony.

Chapter 3: Joke Thoughts

1. For an example of such a revision, see Elliott Oring, "Victor Turner, Sigmund Freud, and the Return of the Repressed," *Ethos* 21 (1993): 273–94.

2. Sigmund Freud, *The Standard Edition of the Complete Psychological Works of Sigmund Freud,* trans. under the general editorship of James Strachey in collaboration with Anna Freud, 24 vols. (London: Hogarth Press and the Institute for Psycho-Analysis, 1953–74) (hereafter cited as *SE*), 8:21, 60–61, n. 1, 70, 110–11.

3. Ibid., 15:149–69.

4. Melford E. Spiro, "Tropes, Defenses, and Unconscious Mental Representation: Some Critical Reflections on the 'Primary Process,'" *Psychoanalysis and Contemporary Thought* 16 (1993): 185.

5. Freud's discussions of symbols appear in the 1909, 1911, and 1914 editions of *The Interpretation of Dreams* and in part 1 of *Introductory Lectures on Psycho-Analysis,* first published in 1916. If the explicit discussion of these kinds of symbols only came after the publication of *Jokes and Their Relation to the Unconscious* in 1905, there is nevertheless every indication that the concept was known to Freud long before. In 1900 Freud already grasped the sexual significance of such objects as boxes and snakes; a significance he recognized as being confirmed in "linguistic usages, superstitions, and customs"; *SE,* 4:154–55, 347. J. Laplanche and J.-B. Pontalis also hold that this sense of symbol was evident in Freud's earliest work. See *The Language of Psychoanalysis,* trans. D. Nicholson-Smith (New York: W. W. Norton, 1973), pp. 443–44.

6. In truth, the number of categories to which Freud consigns the techniques of jokes often varies. He also mentions unification, absurdity, faulty reasoning, representation by the opposite, overstatement, allusion, analogy, and representation by something small. Overstatement would seem to be a subcategory of representation by the opposite (*SE,* 8:72), and allusion and analogy a form of indirect representation (pp. 74, 81). Faulty reasoning may be a form of displacement (pp. 60, 164). Elsewhere he characterizes condensation, displacement, and indirect representation as the "most striking" technical methods (p. 165).

7. Ibid., p. 166.

8. Ibid., p. 179.

9. This is generally the case, but Freud equivocates. First, he suggests that cynical jokes may have unconscious purposes or purposes reinforced by the unconscious (ibid., pp. 176–77). Indeed, in his analysis of the *schadchen* (marriage broker) jokes, Freud proposes that they are not directed at the figure of the *schadchen* but at the institution of marriage itself (pp. 105–9). In other words, the *schadchen* stands for the institution in

which he participates and serves as some sort of "symbol" of it; a symbol not readily deciphered. The *schadchen* jokes engage in two kinds of concealment, according to Freud: the concealment of what they have to say and the concealment of what they are forbidden to say (p. 106).

10. Spiro, "Tropes," p. 176.

11. Laplanche and Pontalis, *Language of Psychoanalysis,* p. 443.

12. Consequently, such propositions as "Colorless green ideas sleep furiously" or "Bengal tigers take their tea at five" would not be acceptable as joke thoughts. My definition of a joke thought, however, begs the question of thoughts that might underlie absurd or nonsense jokes. The whole issue remains a matter for discussion.

13. Yan Zhao, "The Information-Conveying Aspect of Jokes," *Humor* 1 (1988): 279–98.

14. After Mildred Meiers and Jack Knapp, *Fifty-six Hundred Jokes for All Occasions* (New York: Avenel, 1980), p. 256.

15. A script is a large chunk of semantic information surrounding a word or evoked by it. Loud and domineering is part of the comic conception of the wife. See Victor Raskin, *Semantic Mechanisms of Humor* (Dordrecht, Holland: D. Reidel, 1985), pp. 80–81.

16. It is wives, rather than women in general, who are conceptualized as loud and overbearing talkers. "The only chance I get to open my mouth around my wife is when I yawn"; "A cynic said recently of his wife: 'At the evening's end, she was so tired she could scarcely keep her mouth open'"; "Was your wife outspoken? Not by anyone I know"; "I'm a man of few words." "I know—I'm married, too." See Meiers and Knapp, *Jokes for All Occasions,* pp. 154–57.

17. It is important to note that jokes, unlike puzzles, demand immediate solution. Too much delay, too much intellectual expenditure, ruins the joke. P. A. Schiller, "A Configurational Theory of Jokes and Puzzles," *Journal of General Psychology* 18 (1937): 217–34.

18. Freud, *SE,* 8:37.

19. Ibid., p. 37.

20. Ibid., p. 30.

21. Ibid., p. 33.

22. Ibid., p. 31.

23. Ibid., p. 33.

24. Evan Esar, *The Humor of Humor* (New York: Bramhall, 1952), pp. 83–84.

25. After Meiers and Knapp, *Jokes for All Occasions,* p. 295.

26. Freud, *SE,* 8:33, n. 2.

27. Ibid., p. 16.

28. Ibid., p. 19.

29. Freud prefers to consider double meaning a kind of condensation (*SE,* 8:42). Undoubtedly, this had something to do with Freud's determination to demonstrate that the mechanisms of jokes were homologous with the mechanisms he had previously identified for dreams. I prefer to think of condensation as a species of double meaning.

30. Ibid., p. 19.

31. However, in contexts where the semantic domain "milliner" is richer than it is likely to be for us, and where some conceptual linkage with "familiar" could be forged to establish a joke thought, it would be possible for the "famillinerily" joke to be equally deep.

32. Freud recognized this distinction between "verbal jokes" (*Wortwitz*) and "concep-

tual jokes" (*Gedankenwitz*); see *SE,* 8:90. The "famillionairely" joke, while rooted in language play, has a conceptual component as well, since the linkage between "familiarly" and "millionaire" also depends upon an understanding of how millionaires behave.

33. After Murray S. Davis, *What's So Funny: The Comic Conception of Culture and Society* (Chicago: University of Chicago Press, 1993), p. 114.

34. Freud, *SE,* 8:51.

35. Freud recognized three kinds of thoughts; "trivial" and lacking in substance; "innocent," asserting something of substance; and "tendentious," in conflict with an inhibition and normally forbidden direct expression. Ibid., p. 92.

36. See Davis, *What's So Funny,* p. 1; and Hugh LaFollette and Niall Shanks, "Belief and the Basis of Humor," *American Philosophical Quarterly* 30 (1993): 334.

37. It might be argued that jokes never teach us anything valuable; at best, they merely direct our attention to some piece of knowledge that is already in our possession.

38. I have borrowed this joke from Davis, *What's So Funny,* p. 241, but I have altered it to bear multiple interpretations. Davis's version admits only one interpretation.

39. These ancillary thoughts, however, are not what Freud would have conceptualized as joke thoughts, since none of these propositions can be transformed into the joke in question merely through the operation of condensation, displacement, or indirect representation. These thoughts are too removed from the elements of the joke itself.

40. Which is actually the formulation of the joke as presented by Davis in *What's So Funny.*

41. Ibid., p. 195.

42. Richard Raskin characterizes jokes that bear multiple interpretations as "reversible" and has claimed that reversible jokes are better jokes than those that are "closed." I don't agree. In any event, I believe it is dangerous for joke analysts to allow qualitative evaluations to enter their discussions, since they are likely to promote their own preferences. Qualitative data is meaningful if it reflects the preferences of informants. Quality, however, should not be considered as some intrinsic feature of a joke. See *Life Is like a Glass of Tea: Studies of Classic Jewish Jokes* (Aarhus: Aarhus University Press, 1992), pp. 29–30; and Elliott Oring, "Review of *Life is Like a Glass of Tea,*" *Humor* 6 (1993): 415–19.

43. William A. Wilson, "Documenting Folklore," in *Folk Groups and Folklore Genres: An Introduction,* ed. Elliott Oring (Logan: Utah State University Press, 1986), p. 239. The thought and the comic device in this joke are ancient. See William Hansen, "The Seer and the Computer: On *Philogelos* and Modern Jokes," *Classical Bulletin* 77 (2001): 98–102.

44. The joke would be improved were the husband not "hooked up" to the pain machine. It would be better if the machine were described as beaming, in some way, the woman's pain into the father.

45. Wilson, "Documenting Folklore," p. 239.

46. It is unfortunate that there are so few descriptions in the literature of such discrepancies in joke interpretation. Differences in the articulation of the thought underlying a riddle joke about Sammy Davis Jr. are noted in Elliott Oring, "Everything Is a Shade of Elephant: An Alternative to a Psychoanalysis of Humor," *New York Folklore* 1 (1975): 152–53.

47. Actually, a person who could not formulate such a thought might be considered schizophrenic. See K. Goldstein, "The Significance of Special Mental Tests for Diagnosis and Prognosis in Schizophrenia," *American Journal of Psychiatry* 96 (1939): 575–88.

48. "Proverbs are the simplest of the metaphorical genres of folklore," according to Peter Seitel, "Proverbs: A Social Use of Metaphor," in *The Wisdom of Many: Essays on the Proverb,* ed. Alan Dundes and Wolfgang Mieder (New York: Garland, 1981), p. 137.

49. Neal R. Norrick has discussed how proverb figures carry meaning, but his discussion does not seem directly applicable to the interpretation of jokes. See *How Proverbs Mean: Semantic Studies in English Proverbs* (Berlin: Mouton, 1985).

50. Proverbs have what Norrick calls "standard proverb interpretations," or SPIs. This is not the case for jokes. See *How Proverbs Mean,* pp. 155–64.

51. Barbara Kirshenblatt-Gimblett, "Toward a Theory of Proverb Meaning," in *The Wisdom of Many,* pp. 112–15.

52. Freud considered such proverbs as "Traduttore traditorre" [a translator is a traitor] to be jokes; *SE,* 8:34. Many proverbs seem to employ the techniques of jokes; for example, "The grumbler does not work, the worker does not grumble"; "A dull-edged plow furrows your brow"; "Marry in haste, repent at leisure"; "Be true to your teeth or they will be false to you." See Wolfgang Mieder, *A Dictionary of American Proverbs* (New York: Oxford University Press, 1992), pp. 270, 273; and Jan Harold Brunvand, *The Study of American Folklore* (New York: W. W. Norton, 1986), p. 76.

53. See chapter 7 in this volume.

54. Elliott Oring, *The Jokes of Sigmund Freud: A Study in Humor and Jewish Identity* (Philadelphia: University of Pennsylvania Press, 1984), pp. 11, 23.

55. Among many others, see Jonathan Gutman and Robert F. Priest, "When Is Aggression Funny?" *Journal of Personality and Social Psychology* 12 (1969): 60–65; Jacob Levine, "Approaches to Humor Motivation," in *Motivation in Humor,* ed. Jacob Levine (New York: Atherton, 1969), pp. 127; and Jay M. Davis and Amerigo Farina, "Humor Appreciation as Social Communication," *Journal of Personality and Social Psychology* 15 (1970): 175–78.

56. Alan Dundes, "Metafolklore and Oral Literary Criticism," *Monist* 50 (1966): 505–16.

57. Even Dundes, who introduced the notion of oral literary criticism in 1966 in folklore studies, has made very little use of it in his own work. However, he did include an essay that relied heavily on such commentary in his reader on African American folklore. See Paulette Cross, "Jokes and Black Consciousness: A Collection with Interviews," in *Mother Wit from the Laughing Barrel: Readings in the Interpretation of Afro-American Folklore,* ed. Alan Dundes (Englewood Cliffs, N.J.: Prentice-Hall, 1973), pp. 649–69.

Chapter 4: The Humor of Hate

1. Stuart M. Kaminsky, *A Fine Red Rain: An Inspector Porfiry Rostnikov Mystery* (New York: Charles Scribner's Sons, 1987), pp. 189–90.

2. Actually, in many instances an initial laugh is supplanted by an expression of rejection and disgust at the underlying joke image or thought. To the extent that such a transformation in affect is possible, it might serve to substantiate rather than undermine Freud's theory of the joke form. That it does happen (and with some regularity) would also suggest that the joke is far from a totally successful vehicle for the communication of disreputable ideas.

3. Sigmund Freud, *The Standard Edition of the Complete Psychological Works of Sigmund Freud,* trans. under the general editorship of James Strachey in collaboration with Anna

Freud, 24 vols. (London: Hogarth Press and the Institute for Psycho-Analysis, 1953–74) (hereafter cited as *SE*), 8:103.

4. Freud does not speak of jokes being more sophisticated but of being more "refined" [*feiner*]. Ibid., p. 100.

5. Ibid., pp. 99–100. Freud's discussion of smut is as much directed to elucidating the sources of pleasure derived from both smut and jokes as it is to the power of joke techniques to forestall criticism. However, it is solely with this rhetorical function of the joke that this chapter is concerned.

6. *The Web of Hate: Extremists Exploit the Internet* (n.p.: Anti-Defamation League, 1996), p. 11. As of November 2001, the address was <http://www.resist.com>.

7. A term common in the Identity Church movement for ethnic and racial minorities.

8. "White Aryan Resistance Positions," *WAR*, March 1995, p. 12.

9. The government is usually referred to as ZOG, an acronym for Zionist Occupied Government.

10. James Mason, "What on Earth Is a Jew," *WAR*, March 1996, p. 10.

11. "Happy Mud Flood Day America!" *WAR*, July 1986, p. 1.

12. "Hate group" is not merely an etic designation. The White Aryan Resistance explicitly promotes itself as a "hate" group. The Web site advertises itself as "The White Aryan Resistance Hate Page." See *WAR*, February 1996, p. 4.

13. After the title of a Beatles song. See *WAR* 6:5 (1987): 10.

14. The commonplace response of comedian Oliver Hardy to Stanley Laurel in the various Laurel and Hardy movies. See *WAR* 6:4 (1987): 1.

15. *WAR*, May 1995, p. 5.

16. All are mentioned by Freud in *Jokes and Their Relation to the Unconscious*, see *SE*, vol. 8.

17. This action line has been called a "waftarom." See Randall P. Harrison, *The Cartoon: Communication to the Quick* (Beverly Hills, Calif.: Sage Publications, 1981), pp. 63–64.

18. Caricature has been used in this way for centuries and is not peculiar to the cartoons printed in *WAR* or other recent hate publications. See Bohun Lynch, *A History of Caricature* (Boston: Little Brown, 1927), pp. 32–45.

19. *WAR*, April 1996, p. 10.

20. The suggestion not to laugh is probably ironic. The implication is that one can only laugh at the incongruous idea that the odious figure depicted would have more opportunity than does a white man.

21. I agree with Noël Carroll, "On Jokes," *Midwest Studies in Philosophy* 16 (1991): 295.

22. "Nigger Heaven" was also a slang term used to designate the cheap balcony seats in a theater. See Ed Cray, "Ethnic and Place Names as Derisive Adjectives," *Western Folklore* 21 (1962): 33. Other jokes utilize ethnic stereotypes to define heaven. For example, see Alan Dundes and Carl R. Pagter, *Never Try to Teach a Pig to Sing: Still More Urban Folklore from the Paperwork Empire* (Detroit: Wayne State University Press, 1991), p. 232.

23. *WAR*, November 1995, p. 5.

24. *WAR*, July 1995, p. 6.

25. *WAR*, October 1995, p. 4. The cartoon curiously shows the alien monster standing next to a pump at a Mobil gas station where the cost of gas is listed as 10 cents a gallon for regular and 12 cents for high-test.

26. "What Makes a Fuhrman?" *WAR,* November 1995, p. 10.

27. "An Asocial World," *WAR,* August 1996, p. 7.

28. Mason, "What on Earth Is a Jew?" p. 10.

29. "Declaration of War," *WAR,* February 1995, p. 1.

30. "Walls Are Replacing Open Borders," *WAR* 5:3 (1986): 7.

31. *WAR,* June 1995, p. 2.

32. Despite *WAR*'s statement that homosexuality poses no particular threat to the Aryan race (March 1995, p. 12), the spread of AIDS seems to have altered this position. See "AIDS Anyone," *WAR* 6 (1987): 4.

33. Morris Dees and Steve Fiffer, *Hate on Trial: The Case against America's Most Dangerous Neo-Nazi* (New York: Villard, 1993), pp. 144–45.

34. The jury eventually found for the plaintiffs in the sum of $12.5 million. The trial hinged not on violence promoted by the Metzgers in their publications but on the fact that they had sent an agent to organize and incite the Portland skinhead group. The plaintiffs did not argue that the Metzgers' publications incited the violence against Seraw. See Dees and Fiffer, *Hate on Trial,* pp. 78, 97, 102, 104, 106, 233, 255, 272.

35. One might argue that "striking back," which may be used as a generalized term for a reaction, is here used in its more literal and physical sense and thereby constitutes a "double meaning." Nonetheless, since the meaning of "striking back" is primarily a physical one, and since this notion is preconditioned by the graphic (which is likely to be scanned before the caption is read), I would think that the sense of a double meaning would be very weak.

36. "Berg" means "mountain" or "hill" in both Yiddish and German and is a common element of Jewish (but also German) names—e.g., Goldberg, Weinberg, Steinberg.

37. The White Aryan Resistance denies that the extermination of millions of Jews in gas chambers ever took place. Nevertheless, they use the image either because of its offensive nature to Jews or because their Holocaust denial is expedient rather than sincere.

38. Indeed, they are not suppressed: "The Jew is a parasite. . . . 'As the potato bug destroys crops and fields, as it is his nature to do, so the Jew destroys people and nations.'" Mason, "What on Earth Is a Jew," p. 10.

39. "White Aryan Resistance Positions," p. 12.

40. *WAR* 4:5 (1985): 10.

41. "A Passing Thought," *WAR* 5:1 (1986): 9.

42. Edward Kerling, "Whitey Revolutionary: The Potential Terrorist," *WAR,* November 1995, p. 8.

43. Edward Kerling, "Whitey Revolutionary: Terrorism Defined," *WAR,* October 1995, p. 8.

44. For example, *WAR* 5 (1986): 6–7, 10; 7:2 (1988): 1.

45. For example, John Jewell, "Kill the Governor: White Revolt of 1676, Virginia," *WAR* 6:2 (1987): 6–7, 9; and John Jewell, "Green Corn Rebellion," *WAR* 6:4 (1987): 6–7, 10.

46. See the five-part series by Edward Kerling, "Whitey Revolutionary," in various issues of *WAR* in 1995.

47. "Revolution? Let er' [*sic*] Rip!" *WAR,* October 1995, p. 8.

48. Carlos W. Porter, "Looking at Stalin," *WAR,* May 1995, p. 5.

49. See chapter 1. See also Noël Carroll, "On Jokes," *Midwest Studies in Philosophy* 16 (1991): 295.

50. Raphael S. Ezekiel, *The Racist Mind: Portraits of American Neo-Nazis and Klansmen* (New York: Penguin, 1995), p. 81.

51. *WAR* promotional flyer (Fallbrook, Calif.: n.d.).

52. Nevertheless, *WAR* was mailed in a plain white envelope with no indication of its source or contents. In 1997 the envelope began to carry the name John Metzger in the return address, but without the name of the organization—White Aryan Resistance. Many, but by no means all, of the letters and e-mail messages received from readers are published or listed without attribution.

53. Ezekiel sees a distinction between the motives of leaders and followers and notes the necessity of leaders taking risks. See *Racist Mind,* pp. 144–46.

54. "Laughter always implies a kind of secret freemasonry, or even complicity, with other laughers, real or imaginary." Henri Bergson, *Laughter* in *Comedy,* ed. Wylie Sapher (Garden City, N.Y.: Anchor Doubleday, 1956 [1900]), p. 64. See also Ted Cohen, "Jokes," in *Pleasure, Preference, and Value: Studies in Philosophical Aesthetics,* ed. Eva Schaper (Cambridge: Cambridge University Press, 1983), pp. 124–26.

55. Kathleen Stokker suggests that anti-Nazi humor was instrumental in reducing the sense of isolation and creating a feeling of solidarity among Norwegians during the occupation. The humor demonstrated "that others shared similar perceptions of the circumstances." Stokker thinks that the humor served to create an image of Norwegian resistance as more pervasive than it really was. This image of the resistance helped strengthen actual resistance to the Nazis. See *Folklore Fights the Nazis: Humor in Occupied Norway, 1940–1945* (Madison, N.J.: Fairleigh Dickinson University Press, 1995), pp. 137, 208, 212–13. Freud also sees the building of alliances as central to obscene and hostile humor. See *SE,* 8:100.

56. Ezekiel's study of neo-Nazis in Detroit starkly portrays the isolation of the membership and the fragility of the group. See *Racist Mind,* pp. 171–326.

57. Tom Metzger has deliberately avoided recruiting his readers into any kind of formal organization. Like some other racist movement leaders, he advocates "leaderless resistance," which keeps White Aryan Resistance sympathizers free from government harassment and allows them the greatest latitude for action (Ezekiel, *Racist Mind,* p. xxxii). He lost the Seraw case in Oregon because the plaintiffs were able to convince the jury that he had sent an agent to organize and incite Portland skinheads.

58. Freud, *SE,* 8:103.

Chapter 5: Blond Ambitions and Other Signs of the Times

1. Marty Rosen, "Dumb Blonde Joke Troubles Recipients," *St. Petersburg Times,* 2 October 1992, city edition, Community Times, p. 1; Stephen Nohlgren, "Women Sue, Claim Boss Told Lewd Jokes," *St. Petersburg Times,* 5 April 1994, city edition, Clearwater Times, p. 3; Lance Williams, "A Slap on the Wrist in Capitol Sex Case," *San Francisco Examiner,* 26 February 1996, 2d ed., p. A1; Elizabeth Walker Mechling and Jay Mechling, "Shock Talk: From Consensual to Contractual Joking Relationships in the Bureaucratic Workplace," *Human Organization* 44 (1985): 339–43.

2. From a sexual harassment report at the University of California, Davis, cited in Mechling and Mechling, "Shock Talk," p. 339.

3. William Petrocelli and Barbara Kate Repa, *Sexual Harassment on the Job,* 2d ed. (Berkeley, Calif.: Nolo Press, 1994), pp. 3/14–17.

4. See chapter 1.

5. Gregory Bateson, *Steps to an Ecology of Mind* (New York: Ballantine, 1972), p. 180.

6. As of March 2002, "Weed's Enormous List of Blonde Jokes" could be found at <http://r.empstudios.com/Humor/Jokes/blonde.jok>.

7. A possibility that has become less incongruous given in vitro fertilization.

8. A script is "a large chunk of semantic information surrounding a word or evoked by it. The script is a cognitive structure internalized by the native speaker and represents the native speaker's knowledge of a small part of the world." See Victor Raskin, *Semantic Mechanisms of Humor* (Dordrecht, Holland: D. Reidel, 1985), p. 81. A script is not a stereotype, which is a belief that rationalizes conduct in relation to that category. See Gordon W. Allport, *The Nature of Prejudice,* abr. ed. (Garden City, N.Y.: Doubleday Anchor, 1958), p. 187.

9. "Q: What is foreplay for a blonde? A: Thirty minutes of begging" (#246) is a recycled JAP joke. In the JAP joke, it is the man who does the begging. In this joke, it seems to be the blond.

10. Evan Esar, *The Humor of Humor* (New York: Bramhall, 1952), p. 24.

11. Ibid., pp. 253–54.

12. Alan Dundes and Carl R. Pagter, *Never Try to Teach a Pig to Sing: Still More Urban Folklore from the Paperwork Empire* (Detroit: Wayne State University Press, 1991), p. 25.

13. Weed's list includes 416 numbered jokes, although joke #331 has 11 parts, which were counted as separate jokes. Joke #342, which deals with blond definitions of medical terminology, has more than forty parts. It was counted only as a single joke and assigned to the stupidity script. Some 22 jokes on the list were regarded as repetitions and eliminated from the total. Nineteen jokes (4 percent) resisted convenient classification. Other categories used (for a total of 9 percent) included dirt/sex, other sex, blond mannerisms, end of sexual activity, feminist/bitch, and male stupidity.

14. Judith Martin, "The Laugh, Thank You, Is Not on Me," *Chicago Tribune,* 17 May 1992, final edition, Womanews, p. 6.

15. The eighth-grader was not herself a blond. Editorial, "Shattering Stereotypes—Teenager Strikes a Blow for Smart-Blonde Jokes," *Seattle Times,* 22 February 1992, final edition, p. A15.

16. Joan Beck, "Blonde Jokes May Be Telling Us to Lighten Up about Political Correctness," *Houston Chronicle,* 25 November 1991, star edition, Opinion, p. 17.

17. Martha Sherrill, "Those Dumb Dumb-Blonde Jokes," *Washington Post,* 22 September 1991, final edition, Living, p. E1; Elizabeth Snead, "Blonde Bashing," *USA Today,* 30 December 1991, final ed., Life, p. 1D.

18. Yet the terms "fool" and "numbskull" are generally thought to designate males. In folk literature, fools and numbskulls are predominantly male figures. Motifs J1700–J1729 in Stith Thompson, *Motif-Index of Folk-Literature,* rev. enlrgd. ed. (Bloomington: Indiana University Press, 1955) indicate that fools are overwhelmingly male. Clever persons (motifs J1100–J1249) are as likely to be females.

19. Sherrill, "Those Dumb Dumb-Blonde Jokes."

20. Snead, "Blonde Bashing."

21. Frances Bula, "Teenage Girls Learn about Abuse; Course Gets Them to Examine Belief that Jealousy Equals Love," *Montreal Gazette,* 1 June 1992, final edition, Woman News, p. C1. Petrocelli and Repa employ a blond joke as an example of harassment. See *Sexual Harassment,* p. 3/15.

22. There seems to be a link between being a redhead and susceptibility to endometriosis, which causes infertility. Patrick Howington, "Scientists: Redheads More Prone to Infertility Disease," *San Bernardino Sun,* 27 December 1995, p. A6.

23. Eric Berne, "The Mythology of Dark and Fair: The Psychiatric Use of Folklore," *Journal of American Folklore* 72 (1959): 1–13.

24. Wendy Cooper, *Hair: Sex, Society, and Symbolism* (New York: Stein and Day, 1971), p. 76.

25. In addition to the stupidity script, the jokes about Dan Quayle focused on his avoiding the draft by joining the National Guard and the influence of his family's wealth. See Michael Kramer, Gloria Borger, Donald Baer, Andy Plattner, Kenneth T. Walsh, and Gordon Witkin, "Can Bush Survive Quayle?" *U.S. News and World Report,* 29 August–5 September 1988, p. 24. Jeannie B. Thomas also considered blond jokes in the light of jokes about Dan Quayle, but she considered them to be different because most Quayle jokes and blond jokes were not interchangeable. Of course, Quayle is a real person with a particular history and not merely a sign. Consequently, many jokes that were told about him could not be told about blonds. I believe nevertheless that the repeated emphasis in Quayle jokes on his stupidity were engendered by his blondness and the highlighting of his physical attractiveness. See Jeannie B. Thomas, "Dumb Blondes, Dan Quayle, Hillary Clinton: Gender, Sexuality, and Stupidity in Jokes," *Journal of American Folklore* 110 (1997): 277–313.

26. Robert Andrews, *The Columbia Dictionary of Quotations* (New York: Columbia University Press, 1993), p. 391.

27. Cooper, *Hair,* p. 98.

28. *The Oxford Dictionary of English Proverbs,* comp. William George Smith, 2d ed., rev. Sir Paul Harvey (London: Oxford University Press, 1948), p. 185.

29. Eugene E. Brussell, ed., *Webster's New World Dictionary of Quotable Definitions,* 2d ed. (Englewood Cliffs, N.J.: Prentice-Hall, 1983), p. 52.

30. This is usually achieved in the jokes by contrasting head hair with pubic hair; for example, "Q: What do you get when you turn three blondes upside-down? A: Two brunettes" (#301).

31. Bob Dyer, "Have You Heard the One," *Chicago Tribune,* 6 November 1991, North, sports final edition, Style, p. 21.

32. Elliott Oring, *Jokes and Their Relations* (Lexington: University Press of Kentucky, 1992), pp. 122–34.

33. She also added, "And I also know I'm not blonde." Aleene MacMinn, Morning Report: People watch, *Los Angeles Times,* 19 May 1992, home edition, p. F2.

34. Gordon Smith, "Joke's on Men, Women to Men, 'Take that Buddy!'" *San Diego Union-Tribune,* 24 September 1992, Lifestyle, p. C1.

35. Charles Bremner, "The Fun Goes Out of Being Blonde," *Times,* 7 November 1991, Overseas News.

36. "Blonde Jokes Get Dander Up," *Arizona Republic,* 30 May 1993, Final Chaser, Comics.

37. Elliott Oring, "Hey, You've Got No Character: Chizbat Humor and the Bound-

aries of Israeli Identity," *Journal of American Folklore* 86 (1973): 358–66; Christie Davies, "Ethnic Jokes, Moral Values, and Social Boundaries," *British Journal of Sociology* 33 (1982): 383–403.

38. Christie Davies, *Ethnic Humor around the World: A Comparative Analysis* (Bloomington: Indiana University Press, 1990), pp. 45, 70.

39. As suggested by Joseph Boskin in *Humor and Social Change in the Twentieth Century* (Boston: Public Library of the City of Boston, 1979), p. 35. Whatever antagonism might have arisen against Poles in local American settings, it cannot account for the broad dissemination and national popularity of the Polish joke cycle.

40. Davies, *Ethnic Humor,* p. 189.

41. This sense of success existed within as well as outside the Jewish community. It was accentuated by a concurrent perception of religious and spiritual decline. See Bernard Rosenberg and Gilbert Shapiro, "Marginality and Jewish Humor," *Midstream* 4 (1958): 74–75. A recent article in the Jewish press identifies materialism as one of the key causes of spiritual decline. A joke emphasizing this materialism is cited in the article: "What did one mink say to another on the way to the slaughterhouse? See you in *shul* [synagogue]." Ira Stoll, "Report on Jewish Women Greeted with Gasps, Ire," *New York Forward,* 24 November 1995, pp. 1–2.

42. Camille Paglia characterizes the conflict a bit more floridly: "The prostitute, seductress, and high-glamour movie star wield woman's ancient vampiric power over men. That power is neither rational nor measurable. The Apollonian rules we pass to govern the workplace will never fully govern the demonic impulses of Dionysian night. . . . Professional functioning in the Apollonian capitalist machine—which I laud as the vehicle of woman's modern liberation—must not be confused with full human identity. Nor can office politics dictate our understanding of sexuality, which begins as a force of nature outside the sexual realm. . . . Office manners grind down and homogenize all . . . differences." *Vamps and Tramps: New Essays* (New York: Vintage, 1994), pp. ix–xi.

43. In the contest between sex and reason, sex seems to always win out. Now the image of the intelligent and competent female—pressed suits, sensible shoes, glasses—has become sexy. Kaylee, "If She Only Had a Brain," *Jakarta Program What's On Magazine,* March 1996, pp. 32–33.

44. Liesl Schillinger, "Blonde Bondage; Now That I'm a Brunette, I've Discovered What Gentlemen Truly Prefer," *Washington Post,* 24 July 1994, final edition, Outlook, p. C1.

45. Joan Riviere has described the pathological condition of otherwise competent women who retreat behind the masquerade of sexuality and incompetence to gain approval and mollify men with whom they are competing. While I believe the childhood etiology that she hypothesizes at the root of this behavior to be questionable, the syndrome highlights the conflict that blond jokes address. See "Womanliness as Masquerade," in *Formations of Fantasy,* ed. Victor Burgin, James Donald, and Cora Kaplan (London: Methuen, 1986), pp. 35–44, orig. pub. in 1929 in *International Journal of Psychoanalysis.*

46. A significant collection of these can be found in the folklore archives at Brigham Young University in Provo, Utah, and at Utah State University in Logan.

47. This is similar to the logic that required Dan Quayle to be stupid because he was handsome.

48. See the "Canonical List of Sorority Girl Jokes," as of March 2002 at <http://r.empstudios.com/Humor/Jokes/sorority.jok>.

49. Michael Fagan gained entry to the queen's bedroom in Buckingham Palace on 9 July 1982. She spoke to him for about ten minutes until police arrived.

50. Basil Don [pseudonym], ed., *The Very Best of Essex Girl Jokes* (London: Attica, 1991), pp. 15–16, 23, 65.

51. Simon Heffer, "A Year in the Life of Essex Man," *Sunday Telegraph* (London), 10 November 1991, p. 101.

52. Andrew Brown, "How Do You Tell an Essex Girl from a West Coast Blonde?" *Independent*, 5 November 1991, Home News Page, p. 3.

53. Susannah Richmond, "It Is Wise to Woo Essex Man," *Campaign*, 1 November 1991, p. 17.

54. See John H. Goldthorpe, David Lockwood, Frank Bechhofer, and Jennifer Platt, *The Affluent Worker in the Class Structure* (Cambridge: Cambridge University Press, 1969), pp. 103, 127, 158–59; and Peter Willmott, *The Evolution of a Community: A Study of Dagenham after Forty Years* (London: Routledge and Kegan Paul, 1963), pp. 30, 82–83, 102, 126.

55. "Q: Why does Essex girl get on so well with Dagenham man? A: Because they spend so much time in Fords." Don, *Very Best of Essex Girl Jokes*, p. 67. The implication is that Essex girls are in Fords for sex; Dagenham men are in Fords because they work in the nearby Ford plant. Dagenham is a large working-class community to the east of London, although not as far east as the heart of Essex Man/Girl country, which is defined by the triangle of Brentwood, Basildon, and Romford. Nevertheless, the two are paired in the joke, and the joke may acknowledge the likelihood of an Essex girl "getting on with" and marrying a man of her class. See Heffer, "A Year in the Life of Essex Man," p. 101; See also Christie Davies, "Review of *The Very Best of Essex Girl Jokes*," *Humor* 5 (1992): 435–36.

56. Christie Davies, *Jokes and Their Relation to Society* (Berlin: Mouton de Gruyter, 1998).

Chapter 6: Humor and the Suppression of Sentiment

1. G. Legman, *Rationale of the Dirty Joke: An Analysis of Sexual Humor*, 1st ser. (New York: Grove, 1968), p. 9; Ann Nietzke, "Hostility on the Laugh Track," *Human Behavior* 3 (1974): 64; William Keough, *Punchlines: The Violence of American Humor* (New York: Paragon House, 1990), p. xi.

2. Sigmund Freud, *The Standard Edition of the Complete Psychological Works of Sigmund Freud*, trans. under the general editorship of James Strachey in collaboration with Anna Freud, 24 vols. (London: Hogarth Press and the Institute for Psycho-Analysis, 1953–74) (hereafter cited as *SE*), 8:97.

3. When the sexual aim is frustrated, smutty and obscene expressions become humorous and serve as a means of *exposure*—that is, a means of aggression. Jokes, in other words, are motivated only by a single impulse. Freud, *SE*, 8:97–100.

4. Ibid., 97–102.

5. Fred Kaplan, *Sacred Tears: Sentimentality in Victorian Literature* (Princeton: Princeton University Press, 1987), p. 17.

6. Louis I. Bredvold, *The Natural History of Sensibility* (Detroit: Wayne State University Press, 1962), pp. 15–23.

7. Ibid., pp. 8–10.

8. Kaplan, *Sacred Tears,* pp. 14–15.

9. A change from "I think, therefore I am" to "I feel, therefore I am." Erik Erämetsä, *A Study of the Word "Sentimental" and Other Linguistic Characteristics of Eighteenth-Century Sentimentalism in England,* ser. B, nide-tom 74 (1) (Helsinki: Suomalainen Tiedeakatemian Toimituksia, 1951), p. 14.

10. Kaplan draws the distinction (*Sacred Tears,* pp. 19–20, 32–33), and while the contrast is noted by others (e.g., Erämetsä, *Study,* p. 15), the terminology seems to be distinctly his own. Indeed, a number of authors use "sensibility" and "sentimentality" interchangeably.

11. Not that sentimental writers were beyond attributing the noble sentiments to pagans and aborigines. See Herbert Ross Brown, *The Sentimental Novel in America, 1789–1860* (New York: Pageant, 1959), pp. 143–45.

12. Kaplan, *Sacred Tears,* pp. 19, 116.

13. Bredvold, *Natural History of Sensibility,* pp. 53–73.

14. Jane Tompkins, *Sentimental Designs: The Cultural Work of American Fiction, 1790–1860* (New York: Oxford University Press, 1985), pp. 128–29.

15. Brown, *Sentimental Novel in America,* pp. 124–26.

16. Ibid., pp. 29–30.

17. Quoted in ibid., p. 156.

18. Ibid., p. 25.

19. Ibid., pp. 170–71.

20. Kaplan, *Sacred Tears,* p. 14.

21. Bredvold, *Natural History of Sensibility,* p. 18.

22. Brown, *Sentimental Novel in America,* p. 33.

23. Carl Bode, *The Anatomy of American Popular Culture, 1840–1861* (Berkeley: University of California Press, 1960), p. 157.

24. Brown, *Sentimental Novel in America,* p. 95.

25. Kaplan, *Sacred Tears,* pp. 122–43.

26. Ibid., p. 121.

27. Winfried Herget, "Towards a Rhetoric of Sentimentality," in *Sentimentality in Modern Literature and Popular Culture,* ed. Winifried Herget (Tübingen: Gunter Narr, 1991), p. 3.

28. Philip Rieff, *Freud: The Mind of the Moralist* (Garden City, N.Y.: Anchor, 1961), p. 361.

29. Freud, *SE,* 7:200, 207, 223.

30. Ibid., 17:88.

31. Ibid., 13:61, 14:251.

32. Ibid., 9:119.

33. Ibid., 7:231.

34. Rieff, pp. xxiii, 361.

35. Freud, *SE,* 2:305.

36. Rieff, *Freud,* p. 389.

37. Ibid., p. xxiii.

38. Thomas Hobbes, *Leviathan, or the Matter, Forme and Power of a Commonwealth Ecclesiasticall and Civil* (New York: Collier, 1962 [1651]), p. 52.

39. Hobbes, like Freud, believed love sprang from desire, and goodness to be merely what men love. Pity and compassion originated in self-pity (ibid., pp. 48, 53). And both rooted their understanding of society in an image of "civil war" (ibid., p. 100; Freud, *SE*, 23:173).

40. His face is known to all as well. Note the use of Freud as an icon in contemporary popular culture. His portrait can be found on T-shirts, coffee mugs, calendars, tote bags, kitchen aprons, and dozens of other objects. I doubt that there is any other psychologist, philosopher, or scientist whose face is so recognizable or so frequently appropriated. To the extent that Freud's image can be considered a symbol of modernity, these playful appropriations seem to reflect a self-consciousness about, and perhaps a rebellion against, modernity itself.

41. Frederick Lewis Allen, *The Big Change: America Transforms Itself, 1900–1950* (New York: Harper, 1952), p. 134; Henry F. May, *The End of American Innocence: A Study of the First Years of Our Own Time, 1912–1917* (New York: Alfred A. Knopf, 1959), p. 235. At first, Freudian psychology found favor among intellectuals in the United States because they believed it could be made to defend Victorian idealism and humanism (see May, pp. 232–35). This belief proved mistaken.

42. I see the repudiation of sentimentality as part and parcel of a modernist stance. Robert C. Solomon suggests that class, gender, and ethnic biases motivate the attack. See "On Kitsch and Sentimentality," *Journal of Aesthetics and Art Criticism* 49 (1991): 9.

43. Matei Calinescu, *Five Faces of Modernity: Modernism, Avant-Garde, Decadence, Kitsch, Post-Modernism* (Durham: Duke University Press, 1987), pp. 41–42, 125.

44. Winfried Fluck, "Sentimentality and the Changing Function of Fiction," in *Sentimentality in Modern Literature*, p. 15. The terminology used to negatively characterize sentimentality invariably stresses its enfolding, entrapping, "undistanced" qualities—that is, sentimentality is "sticky," "sloppy," or "mushy." See Dagmar Buchwald, "Suspicious Harmony: Kitsch, Sentimentality, and the Cult of Distance," in *Sentimentality in Modern Literature*, pp. 42–44.

45. Buchwald, "Suspicious Harmony," p. 47.

46. Mark Jefferson, "What Is Wrong with Sentimentality?" *Mind* 92 (1983): 527–29. The passing of the Victorian era in the United States is often referred to as the "end of innocence" (see May, *End of American Innocence*).

47. Mary Midgely, "Brutality and Sentimentality," *Philosophy* 54 (1979): 385–89.

48. Calinescu, *Five Faces of Modernity*, p. 230; Buchwald, "Suspicious Harmony," p. 41.

49. Quoted in Allen, *Big Change*, p. 271.

50. These terms are reserved for the sunnier sentiments. Mourning and melancholy are dismissed as "morbid," "macabre," or "sick."

51. Of course, modernity has not vanquished sentimentality. Hollywood movies, popular music, television news, and national political conventions all attest to the vitality of Victorian sentimental values at the close of the twentieth century. Though widespread, these values are not dominant. They are not the values of the culturally elite.

52. See chapter 1.

53. Joan P. Emerson, "Negotiating the Serious Import of Humor," *Sociometry* 32 (1969): 169–70.

54. Brown, *Sentimental Novel in America*, p. 94.

55. Doris Kerns Quinn, "What Makes a Good Sentimental Greeting?" *Writer* 77 (October 1964): 22.

56. Although the poem was included in popular anthologies of the time, probably few people would know it today:

> Werther had a love for Charlotte
> Such as words could never utter;
> Would you know how first he met her?
> She was cutting bread and butter.
> Charlotte was a married lady,
> And a moral man was Werther,
> And for all the wealth of Indies
> Would do nothing for to hurt her.
> So he sighed and pined and ogled,
> And his passions boiled and bubbled,
> Till he blew his silly brains out,
> And no more was by it troubled.
> Charlotte, having seen his body
> Borne before on a shutter,
> Like a well-conducted person,
> Went on cutting bread and butter.

See Hazel Felleman, ed., *The Best Loved Poems of the American People* (Garden City, N.Y.: Anchor, 1936), pp. 457–58.

57. The verse would seem to have been specifically directed at Julia A. Moore's *Sentimental Songbook* published in 1877. See Kenneth Lynn, ed., *Huckleberry Finn: Text, Sources, and Criticism* (New York: Harcourt, Brace and World, 1961), pp. 156–60.

58. Ambrose Bierce, *The Devil's Dictionary* (Cleveland: World, 1944 [1906]).

59. The poem, reprinted in E. B. White and Katherine S. White, *A Subtreasury of American Humor* (New York: Coward-McCann, 1941), p. 713, is identical to Percy Bysshe Shelley's 1817 original until its close:
And on the pedestal these words appear:

> "My name is Ozymandias, king of kings:
> Look on my works, ye Mighty, and despair!"
> And also the names of Emory P. Gray,
> Mr. and Mrs. Dukes, and Oscar Baer
> Of 17 West 4th St., Oyster Bay.

60. Ibid., p. 342.

61. Elliott Oring, *Jokes and Their Relations* (Lexington: University Press of Kentucky, 1992), pp. 135–44.

62. Paola Tavarelli, "Dyadic Traditions in Mixed Couples," *Folklore and Mythology Studies* 11–12 (1987–88): 72.

63. Regina Bendix, "Marmot, Memet, and Marmoset: Further Research on the Folklore of Dyads," *Western Folklore* 46 (1987): 185.

64. George A. Test, "The Roast: American Ritual Satire and Humor," in *Rituals and*

Ceremonies in Popular Culture, ed. Ray Browne (Bowling Green, Ohio: Bowling Green University Popular Press, 1980), p. 161.

65. Quoted in ibid., p. 162.

66. Quoted in George A. Test, "Hot Foots for the High and Mighty: The American Roast," *American Humor: An Interdisciplinary Newsletter* 10 (1983): 13.

67. Test, "The Roast," pp. 167–70.

68. The roasts apparently increased the ratings for the show significantly. See "TV Roasts: A Crazy Way of Telling People You Love Them," *TV Guide,* 11 May 1974, p. 15.

69. Robert A. McCarl, "Occupational Folklore," in *Folk Groups and Folklore Genres: An Introduction,* ed. Elliott Oring (Logan: Utah State University Press, 1986), pp. 85–86.

70. Detective Harry Callahan ("Dirty Harry") was given to saying "Go ahead, make my day!" when pointing his gun at an armed criminal and daring him to shoot first.

71. "TV Roasts," p. 14. The roast is a fairly complicated event and not only a manifestation of the suppression of sentimentality. It bears some resemblance to the ritual insults and status reversals described by anthropologists and to the value in American culture of having a good sense of humor and being able to take a joke. See Max Gluckman, *Custom and Conflict in Africa* (New York: Barnes and Noble, 1967), pp. 109–36; and Mahadev Apte, "Ethnic Humor vs. 'Sense of Humor,'" *American Behavioral Scientist* 30 (1987): 28–30.

72. Ernest Dudley Chase, *The Romance of Greeting Cards* (Detroit: Tower, 1971 [1926]), p. 36.

73. "Freud Pays Off," *Fortune,* February 1947, 133–34.

74. Ibid., p. 134.

75. At the turn of the nineteenth century, there were Valentine cards known as "penny dreadfuls" or "vinegar" cards that included an insulting verse directed at their recipient. It would seem that these cards were meant to be insulting rather than humorous. There were also books containing Valentine verse that one might copy that included such selections as "To a Bad Dancer," "To a Conceited Man," "To an Old Maid," "To a Stingy Fellow," "To a Coxcomb," To a Lady with Bad Teeth" (Chase, *Romance of Greeting Cards,* pp. 62, 68).

76. "Greetings . . . 'You Bum,'" *Newsweek,* 16 February 1959, 82.

77. *Greetings Dearie! A Connoisseur's Collection from Hallmark's Contemporary Cards* (Kansas City, Mo.: Hallmark Cards, 1962), pp. 82, 125, 143, 145.

78. Ibid., pp. 100, 122.

79. Catholic magazines seem to have been particularly disturbed by the proliferation of studio-type cards and took their aggressive expressions at face value. See "Greetings," *Commonweal* 66 (July 1957): 414; and Norbert Muhlen, "The Canned-Emotion Industry," *America,* January 1959, 426.

80. Robert Solomon's defense of sentimentality, Frank D'Angelo's apology for sentimental greeting card verse, Suzanne Clark's attempt to reclaim sentimentality as a distinctly female rhetoric, as well as changes in fictional styles—for example, Robert Grudin, *Book* (New York: Random House, 1992)— suggest that a postmodern rehabilitation of sentimentality is under way. If this rehabilitation succeeds at the popular level, we might expect to see some changes in the use of humor as a kind of sentimental discourse. See Robert C. Solomon, "In Defense of Sentimentality," *Philosophy and Literature* 14 (1990):

304–23; Frank D'Angelo, "The Rhetoric of Sentimental Greeting Card Verse," *Rhetoric Review* 1 (1992): 337–45; and Suzanne Clarke, *Sentimental Modernism: Women Writers and the Revolution of the Word* (Bloomington: Indiana University Press, 1991).

Chapter 7: The Joke as Gloss

1. The former emphasis has been particularly evident in the works of folklorists, sociologists, and semanticists; see, for example, Christie Davies, *Ethnic Humor around the World: A Comparative Analysis* (Bloomington: Indiana University Press, 1990); Murray S. Davis, *What's So Funny: The Comic Conception of Culture and Society* (Chicago: University of Chicago Press, 1993); Alan Dundes, *Cracking Jokes: Studies of Sick Humor Cycles and Stereotypes* (Berkeley: Ten Speed Press, 1987); Elliott Oring, *Israeli Humor: The Content and Structure of the Chizbat of the Palmah* (Albany: State University of New York Press, 1981); and Victor Raskin, *Semantic Mechanisms of Humor* (Dordrecht, Holland: D. Reidel, 1985). The latter approach has been emphasized in the work of sociolinguists and conversational analysts; see, for example, Paul Drew, "Po-faced Receipts of Teases," *Linguistics* 25 (1987): 219–53; Joan Emerson, "Negotiating the Serious Import of Humor," *Sociometry* 32 (1969): 169–81; Michael Mulkay, Colin Clark, and Trevor Pinch, "Laughter and the Profit Motive: The Use of Humor in a Photographic Shop," *Humor* 6 (1993): 163–93; and Neal R. Norrick, *Conversational Joking: Humor in Everyday Talk* (Bloomington: Indiana University Press, 1993).

2. Most notably in the work of Harvey Sacks, "An Analysis of the Course of a Joke's Telling," in *Explorations in the Ethnography of Speaking,* ed. Richard Bauman and Joel Sherzer (Cambridge: Cambridge University Press, 1974), pp. 337–53; also Norrick, *Conversational Joking,* pp. 104–27.

3. Good work that has been done includes Barbara Kirshenblatt-Gimblett, "The Concept and Varieties of Narrative Performance in East European Jewish Culture," in *Explorations in the Ethnography of Speaking,* pp. 283–308; Barbara Kirshenblatt-Gimblett, "A Parable in Context," in *Folklore: Performance and Communication,* ed. Dan Ben-Amos and Kenneth S. Goldstein (The Hague: Mouton, 1975), pp. 105–30; and Anat Zajdman, "Contextualization of Canned Jokes in Discourse," *Humor* 4 (1991): 23–40.

4. Salvatore Attardo, "Humor," in *Handbook of Pragmatics,* ed. Jef Verschueren, Jan-Ola Östman, Jan Blommaert, and Chris Bulcaen (Amsterdam: John Benjamins, 1996), p. 6.

5. Zajdman, who has explored this spectrum of joke contextualization, has, to some extent, conflated two different aspects of context. There is the embeddedness of the joke in the exchange so that a joke is linguistically modified to appear as a spontaneous piece of conversation rather than as a performance. The semantic relevance of the joke to the conversational exchange would seem to be a separate and somewhat independent dimension of context. While it might be expected that a joke linguistically altered to fit the conversation would be the most semantically relevant, this is not necessarily the case. It is not clear that her example of what she terms Type A, or "Supplier," discourse is semantically less relevant than her example of Type D, or "Merger," discourse. The two may communicate very similar messages within the interaction. See Zajdman, "Contextualization," pp. 28–29, 34–35.

The conversational embeddedness in Type D discourse may obscure that a joke text is canned. Joker and audience might both recognize the use of a preexisting text. It is possible, however, that a joker is aware of using a canned text but the audience is not; or that the audience might recognize the use of a preexisting text of which the joker is unaware. It is even possible that both the teller and audience are unaware that a preexisting text (identified by the analyst) has been employed. In this last case, it may be difficult to articulate what bearing the preexistence of a text has upon the communication.

6. What Zajdman calls a password. This password, however, is more than a signal of a forthcoming digression; there is an explicit or implicit claim that the digression is relevant to the preceding interaction and hence, perhaps, not a digression at all. See Zajdman, "Contextualization," p. 26; and Robert A. Georges, "Do Narrators Really Digress? A Reconsideration of Audience 'Asides' in Narrating," *Western Folklore* 40 (1981): 245–52.

7. The joke teller learned this joke from Joseph Telushkin, *Jewish Humor: What the Best Jewish Jokes Say about Jews* (New York: William Morrow, 1992), pp. 117–18.

8. As it was entitled in the book from which it was learned; ibid.

9. The narrator reported having once coined a proverb: "Tell lies about your friends and the truth about your enemies." It would seem that he had previously contemplated issues of fiction and realism.

10. The period since his usage of the joke as a gloss and the time of this publication is some five years.

11. Raskin, *Semantic Mechanisms of Humor,* pp. 148–79.

12. The dampening and even outright suppression of elements in a joke gloss has been remarked upon by Kirshenblatt-Gimblett. In the example she studied, the social situation depended upon an accumulation of offenses of exactly the same type, whereas the joke depended upon a hierarchical chain of offenses in which each sin in the chain was more serious than its predecessor. See Kirshenblatt-Gimblett, "A Parable in Context," p. 126. For another discussion of a seeming deviation from the central features of a narrative in the creation of a gloss, see William F. Hansen, "The Applied Message in Storytelling," in *Folklorica: Festschrift for Felix J. Oinas,* ed. Egle Victoria Žygas and Peter Vorheis, Indiana University Uralic and Altaic Series, vol. 141 (Bloomington: Research Institute for Inner Asian Studies, 1982), pp. 99–109.

13. I had totally overlooked the parallelism until a late stage in the analysis of the joke.

14. The database for this chapter is some thirty-five joke glosses. Those not discussed within the chapter can be found in the Appendix.

15. It is true that "Lenin's in Poland" also constitutes the punch line of the joke, but it is not clear that this invalidates the observation. In any event, the use of a whole joke to establish an association regularly occurs as illustrated by text 8 in the Appendix.

16. In the case of text 8 in the Appendix, no gloss on the situation is ventured. The narrator's attempt is merely to establish a topical link between the joke and the conversation. In the case of this joke, the topic of "not being able to pass something you eat" is revealed only in the punch line and consequently requires reference to the whole joke.

17. Philip J. Reilly, *Old Masters of Retailing* (New York: Fairchild, 1966), p. 135.

18. There is another Jewish joke with a similar punch line:

> In the early twenties, three Jews immigrated to the United States. As so often happened in those days, the American immigration officials at Ellis Island simplified

their complicated names on the official records. In this case, the three were recorded as Diamond, Gold, and Taylor. Many years later they met and asked how each of them had done.

Diamond: "Oh, I've done pretty well. With my name I started a jewelry store. Right from the start it was successful. Now there are Diamond Jewelers all over the country."

Gold: "Well, brother Diamond. I too have succeeded. Same idea. Gold? So I started a Gold Ornament Shop. The shop succeeded wonderfully. The branches spread. Now I'm a millionaire."

Taylor: "With me it wasn't so simple. My name is Taylor so I started a clothing store. I worked very hard, but it failed. So I started another, but it also failed. So what could I do but pray to God? 'O Lord,' I said. 'Help me to prosper. If you do I promise to give you fifty percent of the profits.'"

Diamond and Gold: "Well, tell us. Did it work?"

Taylor: "Did it work? You never heard of Lord and Taylor?"

Although the punch line is similar, this joke could not be used to gloss the same situation as the "Jesus and Finkelstein" joke.

19. More than five years have passed since I told her the joke. She has yet to make use of it. It suggests that prepared glosses rarely find the occasion to be performed.

20. This last function seems to result from the author's occupation as a university professor. I am likely to use, hear, and read of jokes being used in this way.

21. Barbara Kirshenblatt-Gimblett, "Toward a Theory of Proverb Meaning," in *The Wisdom of Many: Essays on the Proverb,* ed. Wolfgang Mieder and Alan Dundes (New York: Garland, 1981), p. 111.

22. This is what Zajdman calls Type C discourse or "Joint Venture." See "Contextualization," pp. 31–34.

23. The joke was originally told in Spanish, and the punch line was "asalto es asalto" (literally, "an assault is an assault"). "Robbery" was the informant's translation. It is also known as a Jewish joke with the punch line "a pogrom is a pogrom." See Ralph L. Marquard, *Jokes and Anecdotes for All Occasions* (New York: Hart, 1977), p. 273.

24. The amount of explanation of terms and practices within the text of this joke suggests that the text was not recorded at the time of its use as a gloss but as a report after the event. This was, indeed, the case. See Kirshenblatt-Gimblett, "A Parable in Context," pp. 109–10.

25. Norrick, *Conversational Joking,* pp. 14–18.

26. See Elliott Oring, review of *Conversational Joking* by Neal R. Norrick, *Language and Society* 23 (1994): 449–50.

27. Raskin, *Semantic Mechanisms of Humor,* pp. 100–104.

28. Attardo, "Humor," pp. 5–6.

29. Yan Zhao, "The Information-Conveying Aspects of Jokes," *Humor* 1 (1988): 270–98.

30. Attardo, "Humor," p. 6.

31. See Peter Seitel, "Proverbs: A Social Use of Metaphor," *Genre* 2 (1969): 143–61.

32. This is true in most cases, but not all. There are a number of examples in the Appendix in which the joke text is closely related to the events or circumstances of the conversation or interaction. No metaphor is involved. See, for example, texts 11 and 27.

Chapter 8: Colonizing Humor

1. For one example of many, see Lawrence Mintz, "American Humor and the Spirit of the Times," in *It's a Funny Thing, Humour,* ed. Anthony J. Chapman and Hugh C. Foot (Oxford: Pergamon, 1977), p. 17.

2. A recent exception to this trend can be found in the work of Christie Davies; see *Ethnic Humor around the World* (Bloomington: Indiana University Press, 1990) and *Jokes and Their Relation to Society* (Berlin: Mouton de Gruyter, 1998). There is also the comparative work of anthropologists on the figure of trickster, ritual humor, and joking relationships. For references and discussion, see Mahadev Apte, *Humor and Laughter: An Anthropological Approach* (Ithaca, N.Y.: Cornell University Press, 1985).

3. In a passing comment, Avner Ziv noted the similarity between the United States, Australia, and Israel in the prevalence of the tall tale, but he still emphasized the differences between national humor styles based upon their differences in language, history, and tradition. Avner Ziv, "Introduction," in *National Styles of Humor,* ed. Avner Ziv (New York: Greenwood Press, 1988), p. xi.

4. There are many other differences as well, but here I would note only that unlike Australia, Palestine lacked free land, and the greatest majority of those who settled on the land were often educated or well read.

5. Israel has no navigable rivers.

6. Ray A. Billington, *America's Frontier Culture: Three Essays* (College Station: Texas A&M University Press, 1977), pp. 20–21.

7. Ibid., pp. 56–73.

8. In Australia, for example, the argot of convicts proved enormously influential in the early Australian vocabulary.

9. W. S. Ramson, "Nineteenth-Century Australian English," in *English Transported: Essays on Australasian English,* ed. W. S. Ramson (Canberra: Australian National University Press, 1970), p. 34.

10. Bill Wannan, *A Treasury of Australian Humor* (London: Angus and Robertson, 1962), pp. 33–36.

11. There are more terms than these. Sidney J. Baker, *The Australian Language* (Sydney: Currawong, 1966 [1945]), pp. 38–39; Bill Wannan, *A Dictionary of Australian Folklore* (Ringwood, Australia: Viking O'Neil, 1970), pp. 67–68.

12. J. S. Gunn, "Twentieth-Century Australian Idiom," in *English Transported,* p. 50; Baker, *The Australian Language,* p. 93. Hyram Davis and Peter Crofts also acknowledge the humor of the language in "Humor in Australia," in *National Styles of Humor,* pp. 4–5, 8, 16.

13. See also Walter Blair, *Native American Humor, 1800–1900* (New York: American, 1937), pp. 24, 37.

14. "The nearer sundown, the more original the character and odd the expression," wrote John S. Robb in 1847. Quoted in Billington, *America's Frontier Culture,* p. 73.

15. Mody C. Boatright, *Folk Laughter on the American Frontier* (New York: Macmillan, 1949), p. 152.

16. Ibid., pp. 146–50.

17. Cathy M. Orr, "Folk Comparisons from Colorado," *Western Folklore* 35 (1976): 175–208; Gunn, "Twentieth-Century Australian Idiom," p. 52; Boatright, *Folk Laughter,* p. 156.

18. I myself witnessed and recorded in a Galilean village an extended performance in Hebrew, Arabic, and Yiddish in which the admixture of languages was itself the focus of the comedy.

19. The reverse was true in the Diaspora. In Europe, the Jewish lingua franca was Yiddish, a form of German which was littered with Hebrew vocabulary. In North Africa and the Near East, Jews often spoke Judaeo-Arabic, which likewise incorporated Hebrew words. Ladino, a Judeo-Spanish language spoken in communities in North Africa, Turkey, Greece, and Bulgaria also employed Hebrew terms.

20. Dahn Ben-Amotz and Netivah Ben-Yehudah, *Milon Olami Le-Ivrit Meduberet* [Universal Dictionary of Spoken Hebrew] (Jerusalem: A. Lewis Epstein, 1975). The authorship of Ben-Amotz and Ben-Yehuda was intended to allow the dictionary to be characterized as "the Ben-Yehuda dictionary," in a parody of the great Hebrew dictionary *Complete Dictionary of Ancient and Modern Hebrew,* compiled by lexicographer and Hebrew language advocate Eliezer Ben-Yehuda. That dictionary was begun in 1910 and comprised seventeen volumes, but it was only completed in 1959 (thirty-seven years after Ben-Yehuda's death). Eliezer Ben-Yehuda immigrated to Palestine in 1881 and spoke only Hebrew in his home. His son was the first modern Hebrew-speaking child. See *Encyclopaedia Judaica,* ed. Cecil Roth (Jerusalem: Keter, 1972), s.v. "Ben-Yehuda, Eliezer." In terms of its authorship, therefore, the dictionary of Hebrew colloquial speech was also intended in part as a joke, since it too could legitimately be referred to as "the Ben-Yehuda dictionary," like its formidable predecessor.

21. Boatright, *Folk Laughter,* p. 153.

22. John O. West, *Cowboy Folk Humor: Life and Laughter in the American West* (Little Rock, Ark.: August House, 1990), pp. 19–20.

23. Bill Wannan, *My Kind of Country: Yarns, Ballads, Legends, Traditions* (Sydney: Rigby, 1967), pp. 186–87.

24. Bill Wannan, *The Australian: Yarns, Ballads, Legends, Traditions* (Adelaide: Rigby, 1974 [1954]), p. 83; Bill Scott, *The Penguin Book of Australian Humorous Verse* (Ringwood, Australia: Penguin, 1984), p. 89.

25. W. S. Ramson, "Nineteenth-Century Australian English," pp. 35–36.

26. A censorious person; a killjoy. G. A. Wilkes, *A Dictionary of Australian Colloquialisms* (Sydney: Sydney University Press, 1978), s.v. "wowser."

27. Wannan, *My Kind of Country,* p. 11.

28. Wilbur G. Howcroft, *Black with White Cockatoos or Mopokes and Mallee Roots* (Melbourne: Hawthorne, 1977), pp. 7, 17–18, 31.

29. Avner Ziv, "Humor in Israel," in *National Styles of Humor,* p. 430.

30. In Elliott Oring, *Israeli Humor: The Content and Structure of the Chizbat of the Palmah* (Albany: State University of New York Press, 1981), I could document few jokes or anecdotes that were profane or obscene.

31. See Oz Almog, *The Sabra: The Creation of the New Jew,* trans. Haim Watzman (Berkeley: University of California Press, 2001), pp. 209–25. In addition, isolated groups of males were less likely to be found in Palestine than on the American and Australian frontiers.

32. See Oring, *Israeli Humor,* pp. 149, 188, 224, 236. These and more obscene curses appear in Ben-Amotz and Ben-Yehuda; for example, see p. 116.

33. Almog, *The Sabra,* pp. 198–99.

34. Wannan, *My Kind of Country,* p. 43.

35. Wannan, *The Australian,* p. 47.

36. Benjamin A. Botkin, *A Treasury of Western Folklore* (New York: Crown, 1975), p. 13.

37. Oring, *Israeli Humor,* p. 171.

38. This is one version of the tale of an encounter that is often known as "The Arkansas Traveler." See Gene Bluestein, "The Arkansas Traveler and the Strategy of American Humor," *Western Folklore* 21 (1962): 153–60.

39. Boatright, *Folk Laughter,* p. 51. For a similar Australian conversation, see Wannan, *The Australian,* pp. 48–49. Billington gives an example of purported mountain man taciturnity; see *America's Frontier Culture,* p. 43.

40. The American frontiersman was also depicted as a boaster and braggart. The frontier boasts of such characters as Mike Fink and Davy Crockett and other "ring-tailed roarers" are poetically related to the kinds of invective cited above: "I'm . . . half-horse, half-alligator, a little touched with snapping-turtle; can wade the Mississippi, leap the Ohio, ride upon a streak of lightning and slip without a scratch down a honey locust; can whip my weight in wild cats,—and if any gentleman pleases, for a ten dollar bill, he may throw in a panther,—hug a bear too close for comfort, and eat any man opposed to Jackson." Boasting has some resemblance to tall talk. See Boatright, *Folk Laughter,* p. 28; and Jan Brunvand, ed., *American Folklore: An Encyclopedia* (New York: Garland, 1996), s.v. "boast."

41. Oring, *Israeli Humor,* p. 232.

42. Ibid., pp. 191–92. The word *dugri* came to denote this direct speech style in Israel. See Tamar Katriel, *Talking Straight: Dugri Speech in Israeli Sabra Culture* (Cambridge: Cambridge University Press, 1986).

43. Howcroft, *Black with White Cockatoos,* p. 87.

44. Both are cited in Carolyn S. Brown, *The Tall Tale in American Folklore and Literature* (Knoxville: University of Tennessee Press, 1987), pp. 18, 24.

45. For example, telling of a man who carried five one-hundred-pound bags of flour two hundred yards though admitting that three of the bags were tied together; Bill Scott, *Complete Book of Australian Folklore* (Sydney: Summit, 1978), p. 219; Boatright, *Folk Laughter,* pp. 87–90; Brown, *Tall Tale,* p. 18.

46. Ernest W. Baughman documents the abundance of tall tale motifs in the United States relative to England, but it may be that tall tales were more deliberately sought out and recorded; *Type and Motif-Index of the Folktales of England and North America* (The Hague: Mouton, 1966), pp. xv–xvi. Rudolf Erich Raspe's book *Baron Munchausen's Narrative of His Marvellous Adventures and Campaigns in Russia* was first published in England in 1785 and appeared in an American edition only two years later. It was exceedingly popular and went through two dozen editions in the United States before 1835, but most of the tales in it could already be found in oral circulation before its publication. See Walter Blair, *Essays on American Humor,* comp. Hamlin Hill (Madison: University of Wisconsin Press, 1993), p. 63. The association of tall talk with American humor has been remarked upon at least since the 1850s. See "American Humor," *Eclectic Magazine,* September 1854, 38.

47. Bill Wannan, *Crooked Mick of the Speewah and Other Tall Tales* (Melbourne: Landsdowne, 1965), pp. 71, 73, 88. In the United States one could become crooked by standing too long on its overly fertile soil. See Botkin, *A Treasury of Western Folklore,* p. 517.

48. See Ron Edwards, *The Australian Yarn* (Adelaide: Rigby, 1978 [1977]), pp. 216–26; Scott, *Complete Book of Australian Folklore,* pp. 217–66; Howcroft, *Black with White Cockatoos,* pp. 93–96; Wannan, *The Australian,* pp. 84–88; Wannan, *A Treasury of Australian Humor,* pp. 171–74; and Bill Scott, *The Penguin Book of Australian Humorous Verse,* pp. 107–41.

49. The American acronym WASP is also used in Israel to designate a class having special rights and privileges. In English it is an acronym for White Anglo-Saxon Protestant. In Hebrew it is pronounced "VASP" (there is no *W* in Hebrew) and is an acronym for Vatik (oldtimer), Ashkenazi (of European-Jewish origin), Sotzialist (socialist), and Palmach. See Ziv, "Humor in Israel," p. 124.

50. For more about the *chizbat* and the Palmach, see Oring, *Israeli Humor.*

51. Ibid., pp. 241–42. I cite this tale because Crooked Mick healed his broken ribs in a similar fashion. Wannan, *Crooked Mick of the Speewah,* p. 88.

52. Brown, *Tall Tale,* p. 34.

53. Roger L. Welsch, *Catfish at the Pump: Humor and the Frontier* (Lincoln: University of Nebraska Press, 1982), p. 39. Ron Edwards has claimed that in all his experience in living in country towns he has only rarely encountered tall tales, and these seemed to be the reworking of material published in Bill Wannan's column in the *Australian Post.* Bill Scott feels that the teller of tall tales, though rare, is to be found. In any event, what is important is that the tall tale became a *symbol* of outback, and hence authentic Australian, narration (as it did in the United States and Israel). Whether it is a statistically predominant form is another matter. See Scott, *Complete Book of Australian Folklore,* p. 262.

54. Richard S. Tallman, "A Generic Approach to the Practical Joke," *Southern Folklore Quarterly* 38 (1974): 260–61.

55. Boatright, *Folk Laughter,* pp. 60–61; *The Cowboys* (New York: Time-Life, 1973), pp. 29, 144, 220; Hennig Cohen and Williams B. Dillingham, eds., *Humor of the Old Southwest* (Athens: University of Georgia Press, 1975), pp. xxiv–xxv; Oring, *Israeli Humor,* pp. 80–85; Edwards, *Australian Yarn,* pp. 55–65; Wannan, *The Australian,* pp. 188–89; Wannan, *My Kind of Country,* pp. 82–83.

56. Howcroft, *Black with White Cockatoos,* p. 2.

57. Oring, *Israeli Humor,* p. 90.

58. Boatright, *Folk Laughter,* p. 53.

59. Ibid., p. 1; *Cowboys,* p. 220.

60. *Zanhan* in Hebrew means "paratrooper." The newcomer is viewed as someone who dropped from the sky.

61. Boatright, *Folk Laughter,* p. 70.

62. Oring, *Israeli Humor,* p. 245.

63. Howcroft, *Black with White Cockatoos,* p. 52.

64. Gwenda Beed Davey and Graham Seal, eds., *The Oxford Companion to Australian Folklore* (Melbourne: Oxford University Press, 1993), p. 214.

65. Stan Hoig, *The Humor of the American Cowboy* (Lincoln: University of Nebraska Press, 1958), pp. 190–91.

66. Oring, *Israeli Humor,* p. 197.

67. A similar anecdote was told about a Jewish shepherd who was told about the wonders of the socialist revolution in Russia. He asks the very same question as the Bedouin youth; ibid.

68. Ibid., p. 176.

69. Of course, we have only the humor that has been recorded and printed as the basis for this impression, and what is printed is not a random sample of humorous tradition. It might be argued that the benign view of indigenous peoples in humor occurs only after their subjugation, when they are no longer a serious threat. While this might be true for America and Australia, it is doubtful in the Israeli case. The *chizbat* of the Palmach was at its height in the 1940s, that is, before the outcome of a major conflict with the Arabs had been decided.

70. For example, Botkin, *A Treasury of Western Folklore,* p. 161.

71. There are other instances in which relations of hostility fail to be mirrored in a people's joke repertoire. In Ethelyn G. Orso's *Modern Greek Humor: A Collection of Jokes and Ribald Tales* (Bloomington: Indiana University Press, 1979), there are jokes about Americanized Greeks, Mexicans, and Scots, but there are no joking slurs about Turks. In one of the few texts in which a Turkish character appears, the Turk winds up sodomizing a Greek who had attempted to seduce his wife; see pp. 176–77. This may be another indication that jokes are not a significant means for registering antipathy and expressing aggression. See also Christie Davies, *Ethnic Humor around the World,* pp. 7–8, 87–88.

72. This same kind of feeling was expressed to me by a former American soldier who had fought in Vietnam. He said that he felt more kinship with the Vietcong that he was fighting than with the rear-echelon members of his own army. The antipathy toward rear-echelon troops is discussed in Elliott Oring, "Totemism and the A.E.F. Revisited," in *Folk Groups and Folklore Genres: A Reader,* ed. Elliott Oring (Logan: Utah State University Press, 1989), pp. 308–14.

73. See Russel Ward, *The Australian Legend* (Melbourne: Oxford University Press, 1958), pp. 186–87; and Oring, *Israeli Humor,* pp. 28–29, 99–92.

74. Ward, *Australian Legend,* p. 49; Edwards, *Australian Yarn,* p. 78.

75. Oring, *Israeli Humor,* pp. 188, 234.

76. Boatright, *Folk Laughter,* pp. 89, 50.

77. Davey and Seal, *Oxford Companion to Australian Folklore,* p. 213.

78. Billington, *America's Frontier Culture,* p. 91.

79. Sigmund Freud, *The Standard Edition of the Complete Psychological Works of Sigmund Freud,* trans. under the general editorship of James Strachey in collaboration with Anna Freud, 24 vols. (London: Hogarth Press and the Institute for Psycho-Analysis, 1953–74), 8:80–81, 113.

80. Almog, *The Sabra,* pp. 108–12.

81. Ibid., pp. 105, 109, 131.

82. Oring, *Israeli Humor,* p. 167, see also pp. 214, 265. Even so, officers did not hold the same place in the Israeli military as in the U.S., British, or Australian militaries. For one thing, Israeli officers did not direct their troops into battle, they *led* them into battle. Anecdotes similar to the one about the steamroller are found about the Australian soldier or "Digger." See Wannan, *The Australian,* pp. 80–81.

83. Wannan, *The Australian,* p. 92. Dad, Dave, Joe, and Sally were characters in a series

of short stories published by Steel Rudd in the *Sydney Bulletin* at the turn of the century. Dad and Dave became a radio show that included Dave's girlfriend Mabel whom Dave never wanted to marry. There was also a series of Dad and Dave jokes. Many of these are based on older oral tales about cocky farmers. See Wannan, *A Dictionary of Australian Folklore,* p. 167.

84. Oring, *Israeli Humor,* p. 185.

85. Botkin, *A Treasury of Western Folklore,* p. 12.

86. See Ferdynand Zweig, *Israel: The Sword and the Harp* (London: Heinemann Educational Books, 1969), pp. 3–12; Ward, *Australian Legend,* pp. 1–2; and Frederick Jackson Turner, *The Frontier in American Society* (New York: Henry Holt, 1920), p. 37.

87. Turner, *Frontier in American Society,* pp. 1–38.

88. Mark Twain's literary achievements depended on such sources. See Frank J. Meine, ed., *Tall Tales of the Southwest: An Anthology of Southern and Southwestern Humor, 1830–1860* (New York: Alfred A. Knopf, 1936 [1930]), pp. xv–xvi, xxix.

The humorous sketch and novel based on folk sources and styles can be found in Australia and Israel as well. See Wannan, *A Treasury of Australian Humor,* and Shaul Beber's picaresque sketches serialized in the Israeli periodical *Bamahaneh Nahal* from 1959 to 1963. See also Binyamin Tammuz, *Hayye Elyakum* [The Life of Elyakum] (Tel Aviv: Am Oved, 1968); Puchu [pseud.] *Havurah Shekazot* [Such a Gang] (Tel Aviv: Masada, n.d.).

89. Turner, *Frontier in American Society,* p. 3.

90. For the use of double vision to explain a serious expressive form, see Barre Toelken, "Ballads and Folksongs," in *Folk Groups and Folklore Genres: An Introduction,* ed. Elliott Oring (Logan: Utah State University Press, 1986), pp. 162–65.

91. For example, Blair, *Native American Humor*; Meine, *Tall Tales of the Southwest*; and Constance Rourke, *American Humor: A Study of the National Character* (New York: Harcourt Brace, 1931).

92. A humor becomes a national humor in the same way that a folk song becomes a national song. A locally collected song is published in books and included on records that are characterized as compilations of authentic American song. This published humor may have considerable longevity. Treasuries and anthologies of such humor are published and republished. The humorous exploits of Davy Crockett and Mike Fink that first appeared in newspapers and almanacs of the 1830s, 1840s, and 1850s in the United States are rediscovered in the 1920s and 1930s and reprinted again in popular anthologies of the mid- and late twentieth century. The same can be said of Australian humor. As for native Israeli humor, the first major collection was published in 1956. By 1970 it had gone through eight printings, and in 1979 it was published in a new, enlarged edition. See Dahn Ben-Amotz and Hayim Hefer, *Yalkut Ha-Kezavim Ha-Male Ve-Ha-Shalem* [The Complete Unabridged Sack of Lies] (Tel Aviv: Metsiut, 1979). There are other collections as well. See, for example, Uri Sellah, *Kifak Hey* [Hurrah!] (Tel Aviv: Afrasamon, 1967).

93. It is instructive to look at Edward Gibbon Wakefield's physical description of native Australians. Wakefield never visited Australia and based his book on the writings of others. See his *Letter from Sydney and Other Writings* (London: J. M. Dent, 1929 [1829]), pp. 61–68. Descriptions that similarly emphasize the radical physical transformation of Americans and Israelis also can be found, for example, in Almog, *The Sabra,* p. 78.

94. In 1814 the British inflicted a particularly severe blow to American pride when they invaded and burned the nation's capital.

95. Robert Hughes, *The Fatal Shore* (New York: Alfred A. Knopf, 1987), pp. xi–xiii. The word "convict" was not used in Australia. "Government man," "expiree," and "emancipist" were among the preferred euphemisms. See Baker, *The Australian Language*, pp. 24–25.

96. The frontier experience in Canada does not seem to have become part of its self-image. Unlike the Americans, the Canadians did not revolt against the British. Unlike the Australians, they did not repudiate British social structure. They tried, instead, to emulate the British. See Seymour Martin Lipset, *The First New Nation: The United States in Historical and Comparative Perspective* (New York: Basic Books, 1963), p. 258.

97. "The American frontier gives birth to a humorous literature and a comic mythology." Richard M. Dorson, *Davy Crockett: American Comic Legend* (New York: Spiral Press for Rockland, 1939), p. xv.

98. Wakefield, *A Letter from Sydney*, pp. 51, 66–67. Ziv also noted that tall tales may be characteristic of newer rather than older societies. See Ziv, "Introduction," xi.

99. H. W., "Slick, Crockett, Downing, Etc.," *London and Westminster Review* (December 1838): 136–45.

100. One thinks of the provision proposed in the 1853 constitution to establish hereditary titles in Australia. Derisively labeled the "*bunyip* aristocracy"—the bunyip being a human-eating monster in Aboriginal mythology—by its opponents, the clause was withdrawn. See Wannan, *A Dictionary of Australian Folklore*, pp. 106–7.

101. For an interesting discussion of the development of the sense of humor as a concept and its relationship to the sense of personhood, see Daniel Bernard Wickberg, "The Sense of Humor in American Culture" (Ph.D. diss., Yale University, 1993). Humor as self-representation is an idea that has spread to "old" societies. At the 2000 conference of the International Society for Humor Studies in Osaka, Japan, a number of Japanese scholars either tried to overcome the notion that the Japanese had no humor, or argued that the social constraints against laughter that made them seem humorless were disappearing. In both cases, they were indicating that they had absorbed the idea that humor was an important basis for self-representation and identification. See *Abstracts: 2000 International Humor Conference* (Osaka: Kansai University, 2000). In a bid to host a future humor conference in Nepal, the proposal of the Nepalese committee claimed that the purpose of the meeting was "to inform that Nepal is a beautiful country . . . and to show [the] 500 year old tradition of humor in which all people participate and how [the] people of Nepal smile."

Chapter 9: Sigmund Freud's Jewish Joke Book

1. Freud in fact characterizes a joke about a tour through a waxwork show that von Falke reports from Ireland as an "Irish joke," but no further mention or characterization of Irish jokes is attempted (*The Standard Edition of the Complete Psychological Works of Sigmund Freud*, trans. under the general editorship of James Strachey in collaboration with Anna Freud, 24 vols. [London: Hogarth Press and the Institute for Psycho-Analysis, 1953–74] [hereafter cited as *SE*], 8:71).

2. Although he was not the first to use the phrase, comedian Jackie Mason once complained that his Jewish audience found his act "too Jewish." This phrase became the title of a traveling museum exhibit that appeared at the Armand Hammer Museum in Los Angeles in 1997. See Dwight Hemion, dir., *Jackie Mason on Broadway,* HBO Video, Van Manoff/Mason Productions, 1988; and Norman L. Kleeblatt, ed., *Too Jewish? Challenging Traditional Identities* (New York: Jewish Museum; New Brunswick, N.J.: Rutgers University Press, 1996).

3. "A Gentile would have said that Freud had few overt Jewish characteristics, a fondness for relating Jewish jokes and anecdotes being perhaps the most prominent one." Ernest Jones, *The Life and Work of Sigmund Freud,* 3 vols. (New York: Basic Books, 1953–57), 1:22.

4. There is one other joke that Freud hints is Jewish since "dialect or skill" is "necessary." There are others that Freud probably considered Jewish but did not explicitly identify. In calculating percentages, I have used the conservative figure of twenty.

5. The total number of witticisms and jokes in *Jokes and Their Relation to the Unconscious* is slightly inflated because some texts were added in the 1912 edition of the book, and these have been included in the count. No Jewish jokes were added, however. They all appeared in the 1905 edition.

6. Not true riddles, but linguistic puzzles; for example, see Freud, *SE,* 8:237–38.

7. See *The Encyclopedia of Language and Linguistics,* 10 vols. (Oxford: Pergamon; Aberdeen: University of Aberdeen Press, 1994), s.v. "joke."

8. Jews from the province of Galicia tended to be more traditional, poorer, less likely to convert or intermarry, and more likely to live in Jewish neighborhoods and be active in Jewish movements. There had been a mass wave of Jewish emigration from Galicia just before the writing of *Jokes and Their Relation to the Unconscious.* See Marsha L. Rozenblit, *The Jews of Vienna, 1867–1914: Assimilation and Identity* (Albany: State University of New York Press, 1983), pp. 40–44, 96–97, 140–41.

9. Elliott Oring, *The Jokes of Sigmund Freud: A Study in Humor and Jewish Identity* (Philadelphia: University of Pennsylvania Press, 1984).

10. Freud, *SE,* 8:49. Freud earlier (p. 33) introduces the anecdote about Herr N.'s (Felix Unger's) comment to a converted Jew who was making a spiteful remark about Jews, but he does not characterize it as a "Jewish joke."

11. Ibid., p. 72.

12. Ibid., p. 111.

13. Ibid., pp. 111–12.

14. Jews are viewed as comic figures in and of themselves. Comedy is discovered in the comparison of some other with oneself. Jokes are made. Comedy is also concerned with the ugly. Ibid., pp. 10, 181.

15. Ibid., pp. 80–81.

16. Ibid., p. 112.

17. Ibid., pp. 112–13.

18. Nevertheless, according to Freud, the jokes constitute a *criticism* of this morality. The Jews cannot claim to live up to it.

19. Ibid., pp. 106–8.

20. I would agree with Freud that the joke in which the *schadchen* characterizes a suit-

or's desire for a woman who is beautiful, rich, and educated as requiring "three matches" (Freud, *SE,* 8:108) constitutes a clear comment on the unrealistic expectations of the suitor. If one did not recognize these expectations as unrealistic, the *schadchen*'s comment would not be amusing but puzzling.

21. As Peter Gay has also noted. See *Reading Freud: Explorations and Entertainments* (New Haven: Yale University Press, 1990), pp. 139–40.

22. Freud, *SE,* 8:142.

23. Otto Weininger, *Sex and Character,* trans. from the 6th German ed. (London: William Heinemann, 1906), pp. 301–30.

24. He makes reference to it in a footnote and outlines Weininger's neurotic constitution. See Freud, *SE,* 10:36, n. 1.

25. Freud was to come to some grief over his connection with Weininger because the notion of bisexuality, which Freud had gotten from his friend Wilhelm Fliess, became a central thesis in Weininger's book. See, for example, Frank Sulloway, *Freud, Biologist of the Mind: Beyond the Psychoanalytic Legend* (New York: Basic Books, 1979), pp. 223–29.

26. It is true that Freud employs no example of an obscene Jewish joke and thus avoids the charge that Jews are inevitably concerned with sexual things (although his own scientific discourse certainly betrays this concern). In fact, Freud gives no example of an obscene joke of any kind. Some joke examples are employed that depend upon sexual allusion, and these also are not Jewish.

27. Freud, *SE,* 8:229.

28. This conception Freud was to elaborate twenty-two years later in his essay "Humour," *SE,* 21:161–66.

29. Freud, *SE,* 8:228.

30. Ibid., pp. 49, 51–52, 55–58, 61–65, 72, 78, 80, 105–13, 115.

31. Sander L. Gilman, *Jewish Self-Hatred: Anti-Semitism and the Hidden Language of the Jews* (Baltimore: Johns Hopkins University Press, 1986); Sander Gilman, *The Jew's Body* (New York: Routledge, 1991); Sander L. Gilman, *The Case of Sigmund Freud: Medicine and Identity at the Fin de Siècle* (Baltimore: Johns Hopkins University Press, 1993).

32. Gilman, *Jewish Self-Hatred,* pp. 18, 47, 97, 92, 112, 127, 203, 245.

33. Freud, *SE,* 8:61–65. A question arises why in the jokes the male is marked with corrupt speech and the female with a corrupt body. Nineteenth-century stereotypes emphasize the degenerate male body and duplicitous female speech. Gilman, *Case of Sigmund Freud,* pp. 23, 172; Gilman, *The Jew's Body,* pp. 5, 134.

34. Gilman, *Case of Sigmund Freud,* pp. 23, 172.

35. He termed this *Kuppelei,* which has the sense of "procuring."

36. This commitment to sexuality is not selfish and individual but idealized and abstract (Weininger, *Sex and Character,* p. 260).

37. Weininger, *Sex and Character,* pp. 259–60, 276–77, 279, 282–84, 286. Yet the matchmakers in the jokes all seem to be males.

38. Ibid., 311–41.

39. Richard M. Meyer, review of *Jokes and Their Relation to the Unconscious* by Sigmund Freud, *Deutsche Literaturzeitung* 43 (1905): 2630–32, in *Freud without Hindsight: Reviews of His Work (1893–1939),* ed. Norman Kiell, trans. Vladimir Rus and Denise Boneau (Madison, Conn.: International Universities Press, 1988), p. 331. This was not the only objection to

Freud's use of these Jewish jokes; A. A. Brill also reports that he received angry letters about them. See *Freud's Contributions to Psychiatry* (New York: Norton, 1944), p. 195.

40. Gilman, *Jewish Self-Hatred,* p. 139.

41. Ibid., p. 268.

42. Richard M. Dorson, "Jewish-American Dialect Stories on Tape," in *Studies in Biblical and Jewish Folklore,* ed. Raphael Patai, Frances Lee Utley, and Dov Noy (Bloomington: Indiana University Press, 1960), pp. 111–74; Dan Ben-Amos, "The 'Myth' of Jewish Humor," *Western Folklore* 32 (1973): 123–25; Alan Dundes, *Cracking Jokes* (Berkeley, Calif.: Ten Speed Press, 1987), pp. 76–66.

43. Freud, *SE,* 8:15. Freud's personal interest in Jewish jokes is confirmed in his correspondence, where he "confesses" to having made a collection of "profound" Jewish jokes at the very time he began his self-analysis. See Sigmund Freud, *The Origins of Psycho-Analysis: Letters to Wilhelm Fliess, Drafts and Notes, 1887–1902,* ed. Marie Bonaparte, Anna Freud, and Ernst Kris, trans. Eric Mosbacher and James Strachey (New York: Basic Books, 1954), p. 211.

44. Freud actually provides a parenthetical translation of *schadchen,* but he leaves it to the reader to grasp the term *schnorrer* (*SE,* 8:55, 112). *Schnorrer* is a German word and appears in German dictionaries, but it definitely had a Jewish connotation at the end of the nineteenth century in German-speaking countries. See F. Flügel, I. M. Schmidt, and G. Tanges, *A Dictionary of the English and German Language for Home and School,* 2 vols. (Brunswick, N.J.: George Westermann, 1897), s.v. "schnorrer." *Schadchen* entered Yiddish from Hebrew.

45. Freud comments that when the techniques of a joke are weak, dialect can enhance their comic effects. See *SE,* 8:108, 114.

46. Ibid., pp. 16, 23, 36–37, 39–41, 46–48, 69–70, 77–79, 85, 87, 114.

47. See Jefferson S. Chase, *Inciting Laughter: The Development of "Jewish Humor" in Nineteenth-Century German Culture* (Berlin: Walter de Gruyter, 2000), pp. 139–92.

48. Freud, *SE,* 8:72, 78.

49. This quotation comes from ibid., p. 81, but I have included the language of the baroness as it appears in the original German edition. This delineates the progression from French to German to Yiddish more clearly.

50. This is a joke that Freud does not explicitly identify as Jewish. That the joke is Jewish is revealed by "*waih geschrien.*" See also Theodor Reik, *Jewish Wit* (New York: Gamut, 1960), p. 34.

51. Freud, *SE,* 1:283–397. Actually it goes back to his work with Josef Breuer in *Studies on Hysteria* (*SE,* 2:185–92) but is more fully developed in the *Project.*

52. Sulloway, *Freud,* pp. 118–20.

53. Freud, *SE,* 8:42; elsewhere, *Ersparung;* e.g., ibid., p. 118.

54. Ibid., p. 236.

55. Ibid., pp. 103, 118–19, 132–33.

56. Ibid., pp. 156–57.

57. Sulloway, *Freud,* pp. 65–67.

58. Freud's use of an economic metaphor parallels Heine's use of the economic metaphor for Catholic clerics (*SE,* 8:87).

59. Gilman sees Freud's scientific discourse compromised by the charge that, as with Weininger, it is just another case of Jewish anti-Semitism; *Jewish Self-Hatred,* p. 286. In fact, Freud's scientific discourse appears a deliberate attempt to rescue the Jewish jokes from the charge of self-hatred. Freud's scientific discourse is more fundamentally compromised, as described above.

60. Gilman, *The Case of Sigmund Freud,* p. 221.

61. Freud, *SE,* 8:142.

62. Gilman, *The Case of Sigmund Freud,* pp. 53, 88, 124; Peter Gay, *A Godless Jew: Freud, Atheism, and the Making of Psychoanalysis* (New Haven: Yale University Press, 1987), p. 135.

63. Freud, *SE,* 8:203.

64. These were Freud's own words to Karl Abraham on 3 May 1908. *A Psycho-Analytic Dialogue: The Letters of Sigmund Freud and Karl Abraham, 1907–1926,* ed. Hilda C. Abraham and Ernst L. Freud, trans. Bernard Marsh and Hilda C. Abraham (New York: Basic Books, 1965), p. 34. See also Gay, *A Godless Jew,* pp. 117–54.

65. Variously translated. See, for example, Frederic V. Grunfeld, *Prophets without Honor: A Background to Freud, Kafka, Einstein and Their World* (New York: Holt, Rinehart and Winston, 1979), p. 56.

66. Gilman, *Jewish Self-Hatred,* p. 2.

Chapter 10: The Context of Internet Humor

1. The years of the Monica Lewinsky scandal and the impeachment of the president.

2. *Los Angeles Times,* Saturday home ed., calendar, 30 January 1999, F2.

3. Even at the date of this writing, 31 March 2002, a major search engine was yielding almost six thousand hits from a search for "Bill Clinton jokes."

4. Alfred A. Kroeber, "The Superorganic," *American Anthropologist* 19 (1917): 163–213.

5. Joseph Boskin, *Rebellious Laughter: People's Humor in American Culture* (Syracuse, N.Y.: Syracuse University Press, 1997), p. 1.

6. Students of folklore and humor have not published much on cyberspace folklore or humor. Nevertheless, the assumption seems to be that such materials are largely anonymous and without "clearly identifiable performers and audiences." See John Dorst, "Folklore in the Telectronic Age," *Journal of Folklore Research* 27 (1990): 182–83.

7. Whether they respond is an entirely different matter, but quite a few did respond to my inquiries.

8. <http://members.xoom.com/DRFerrai/Clinton.html>. This site existed on 24 January 1999, but could not be located on 17 June 1999.

9. <http://www.his/%&Ekuster/ego/home.htm>.

10. <http://www.4degreez.com/jokes>.

11. <http://www.jokesandhumor.com>.

12. <http://www./personal.palouse.net/joeh/index.htm>.

13. <http://www.best.com/valerieh/toc.htm>.

14. <http://home.att.net/joserojas/conspiracy.html>.

15. <http://www.bedford.k12.ia.us/StudentPages/96.97Pages/shannon/ Page3.html>. A middle-school student posted this on the Bedford Community School's Web site. I found

it on 23 May 1999, but it was no longer there on 24 June 1999. The page was probably cleared to make room for more current student sites.

16. <http://www.io.com/%7Ecjburke/bwords/bww990226.html>.

17. <http://www.personalsingles.com/bubbaland/impeachbill.htm>. Curiously, this Web site also attempted to lead viewers to a dating service.

18. <http://www.rust.net/%7Ecomedy/index/htm>.

19. <http://sdcc13.ucsd.edu/bbrickey/clinton.htm>.

20. <http://printers devil.com/hypoc/clinton.htm>.

21. Vance Randolph, *Pissing in the Snow and Other Ozark Folktales* (New York: Avon, 1976), pp. 37–38.

22. Duane De Witt recalls hearing the joke in the late 1970s in Texas and California when he was serving in the military. President Carter, DeWitt reported, was distrusted by the military because he was a "peacenik" and too liberal (personal communication, 17 November 2000).

23. <http://www.4degreez.com/jokes> is another site where visitors can rate jokes, but it is not clear how the scores are computed.

24. <http://www.clintonjokes.com>.

25. At ibid. on 24 January 1999.

26. I have corrected the spelling in the following comments, but I have not corrected the grammar or punctuation.

27. Although there were only a handful of respondents from outside the United States, they were unanimously supportive of Clinton.

28. Except, perhaps, for a group of men who might regard sexual conquest as positive, regardless of the price paid for it.

29. The Web master of ClintonJokes.com even posted in a separate listing those jokes he rejected from inclusion in the main Clinton joke listing. He also included his own humorous responses to these pathetic efforts.

30. Of the type that one would find in the volumes of photocopy lore. See, for example, Alan Dundes and Carl Pagter, *Never Try to Teach a Pig to Sing: Still More Urban Folklore from the Paperwork Empire* (Detroit: Wayne State University Press, 1991).

Afterword

1. Jerry M. Suls, "A Two-Stage Model for the Appreciation of Jokes and Cartoons: An Information-Processing Analysis," in *The Psychology of Humor: Theoretical Perspectives and Empirical Issues,* ed. Jeffrey H. Goldstein and Paul E. McGhee (New York: Academic Press, 1972), p. 82.

2. Certainly not only Gabriella Eichinger Ferro-Luzzi, mentioned in chapter 1. For example, Rosemary Staley and Peter Derks ("Structural Incongruity and Humor Appreciation," *Humor* 8 [1995]: 98) are a bit hasty in their analysis of the following joke: "How many academics does it take to change a lightbulb?—None, that is why they have graduate students." They claim that the incongruity lies in "the relationship between an academic and changing a lightbulb." It is true that there is an incongruity in the question, since it should take only one person, *regardless of occupation,* to perform this task. Once the formula for these lightbulb jokes is learned, however, the incongruity lies in the num-

ber given in the answer, which almost invariably is more or less than the one person needed for the job. In the above example, the incongruity is created by the number zero. The incongruity is appropriate, because graduate students supposedly free the academic from having to do anything at all. For another example of misanalysis, see my review of *The Basic Humor Process: A Cognitive-Shift Theory and the Case against Incongruity* by Robert L. Latta, *Humor* 12 (1999): 462. There are other examples as well.

3. I am equally skeptical of other theories rooted in emotional catharsis. The criticism has been formulated by Gabriella Eichinger Ferro-Luzzi, *The Taste of Laughter: Aspects of Tamil Humor* (Wiesbaden, Germany: Otto Harrassowitz, 1992), xvii–xviii.

4. Larry Mintz, review of *Jokes and Their Relations* by Elliott Oring, *Western Folklore* 54 (1995): 165.

5. The joke is based on television commercials for the stock brokerage Paine Webber that conclude with the expression "Thank you, Paine Webber."

6. Paul Lewis, ed., "Humor and Political Correctness," *Humor* 10 (1997): 456–57.

7. Ibid., pp. 453–513.

8. Ibid., pp. 465–66.

9. Very much like, I am sure, the journalist in South Africa who "laughed herself silly" when one of her antiapartheid friends commented on an ANC poster that showed a black pair of hands breaking a set of shackles, "Stupid kaffirs—they break everything" (ibid., p. 468).

10. For a catalogue of these, see Neal R. Norrick, *Conversational Joking: Humor in Everyday Talk* (Bloomington: Indiana University Press, 1993), pp. 20–42.

Appendix

1. This was published as Paul Lewis, ed., "Humor and Political Correctness," *Humor* 10 (1997): 472.

2. J. Golden Kimball was born in 1853 and was a cowboy before becoming an elder in the Mormon church and one the Seven Presidents of the Seventies. He was known for his directness, wisdom, and profanity. Stories about J. Golden Kimball are a well-known part of Mormon folklore. See Thomas E. Cheney, ed., *The Golden Legacy: A Folk History of J. Golden Kimball* (Santa Barbara, Calif.: Peregrine, 1974).

3. Some of this discussion can be found in a series of articles published in *Journal of American Folklore* 111 (1998): 231–355.

4. The witticism does *not* appear in Freud's work, but Freud does cite a joke about the Athenian statesman Phocion, who after being applauded for a speech said, "What have I said that's stupid, then?" Sigmund Freud, *The Standard Edition of the Complete Psychological Works of Sigmund Freud,* trans. under the general editorship of James Strachey in collaboration with Anna Freud, 24 vols. (London: Hogarth Press and the Institute for Psycho-Analysis, 1953–74), 8:59.

5. Ibid., 12:165.

6. Ibid., 19:45.

7. Ibid., 5:485.

8. Hanns Sachs, *Freud: Master and Friend* (Cambridge, Mass.: Harvard University Press, 1946), pp. 46–47.

9. Ibid., p. 47.
10. Ibid., pp. 63–64.
11. Ibid., pp. 155–56.
12. Ibid., p. 152.
13. Theodor Reik, "Freud and Jewish Wit," *Psychoanalysis* 2 (1954): 17–18.
14. Ibid., p. 18.

Index

ELLIOTT ORING is a professor in the Department of Anthropology at California State University, Los Angeles. He is the author of *Israeli Humor* (1981), *The Jokes of Sigmund Freud* (1984), and *Jokes and Their Relations* (1992) and the editor of *Humor and the Individual* (1984), *Folk Groups and Folklore Genres: An Introduction* (1986), and *Folk Groups and Folklore Genres: A Reader* (1989). He is a member of the Society of Fellows of the American Folklore Society and a folklore fellow in the Finnish Academy of Science and Letters.

The University of Illinois Press
is a founding member of the
Association of American University Presses.

Composed in 10.5/13 Minion
with Minion display
by Celia Shapland
for the University of Illinois Press
Manufactured by Thomson-Shore, Inc.

University of Illinois Press
1325 South Oak Street
Champaign, IL 61820-6903
www.press.uillinois.edu